THE COMPLETE BOOK OF
BASS

DICK STERNBERG, a nationally known multispecies angler and fishing writer, has fished largemouth and smallmouth bass from the shield lakes of southern Ontario to the flatland reservoirs of Mexico. One of his favorite pastimes is light-tackle fishing for smallmouths.

Copyright © 1995 by Cy DeCosse Incorporated

All rights reserved. No part of this work may be reproduced or transmitted in any form or by any means, electronic or mechanical, including photocopying, recording, or any information storage and retrieval system, without permission in writing from the publisher. All requests for permission to reproduce material from this Work should be directed to Cy DeCosse Incorporated, 5900 Green Oak Drive, Minnetonka, Minnesota 55343

Published in 1995 by
Cy DeCosse Incorporated
5900 Green Oak Drive
Minnetonka, Minnesota 55343

Library of Congress
Cataloging-in-Publication Data

Sternberg, Dick
The complete book of bass / by Dick Sternberg
p. cm. – (The Hunting & fishing library)
Includes index.
ISBN 0-86573-050-4 (hardcover)
1. Bass fishing — United States. I. Cy DeCosse Incorporated
SH681.F57 1995
799.1'758 - dc20   95-44656

Printed on American paper by: R. R. Donnelley & Sons Co. (1295)

CREDITS
Editorial Director: Dick Sternberg
Design and Production: Cy DeCosse Creative Department, Inc.

Contents

Introduction 4
Understanding Bass 6
Bassin' in Man-Made Lakes 18
Desert Reservoirs 20
Flatland Reservoirs 36
Swampland Reservoirs 46
Eastern Mountain Reservoirs 56
Bassin' in Rivers 72
Midwest Mainstem Rivers 74
Tidewater Rivers 86
Southern Largemouth Rivers 98
Northern Smallmouth Streams 110
Bassin' in Natural Lakes 118
Two-Story Lakes 120
Bass-Walleye Lakes 128
Bass-Panfish Lakes 140
Florida Bass Lakes 150
Oxbow Lakes 162
Advanced Bassin' Techniques 172
Sight Fishing Secrets 174
Draggin' 180
Soft Stickbaits 186
Yo-Yoing in Milfoil 192
Football Jigs 200
Topwater Tricks 206
Weighted Stickbaits 216
Calling Up Smallmouth 222
Tournament Fishing 230

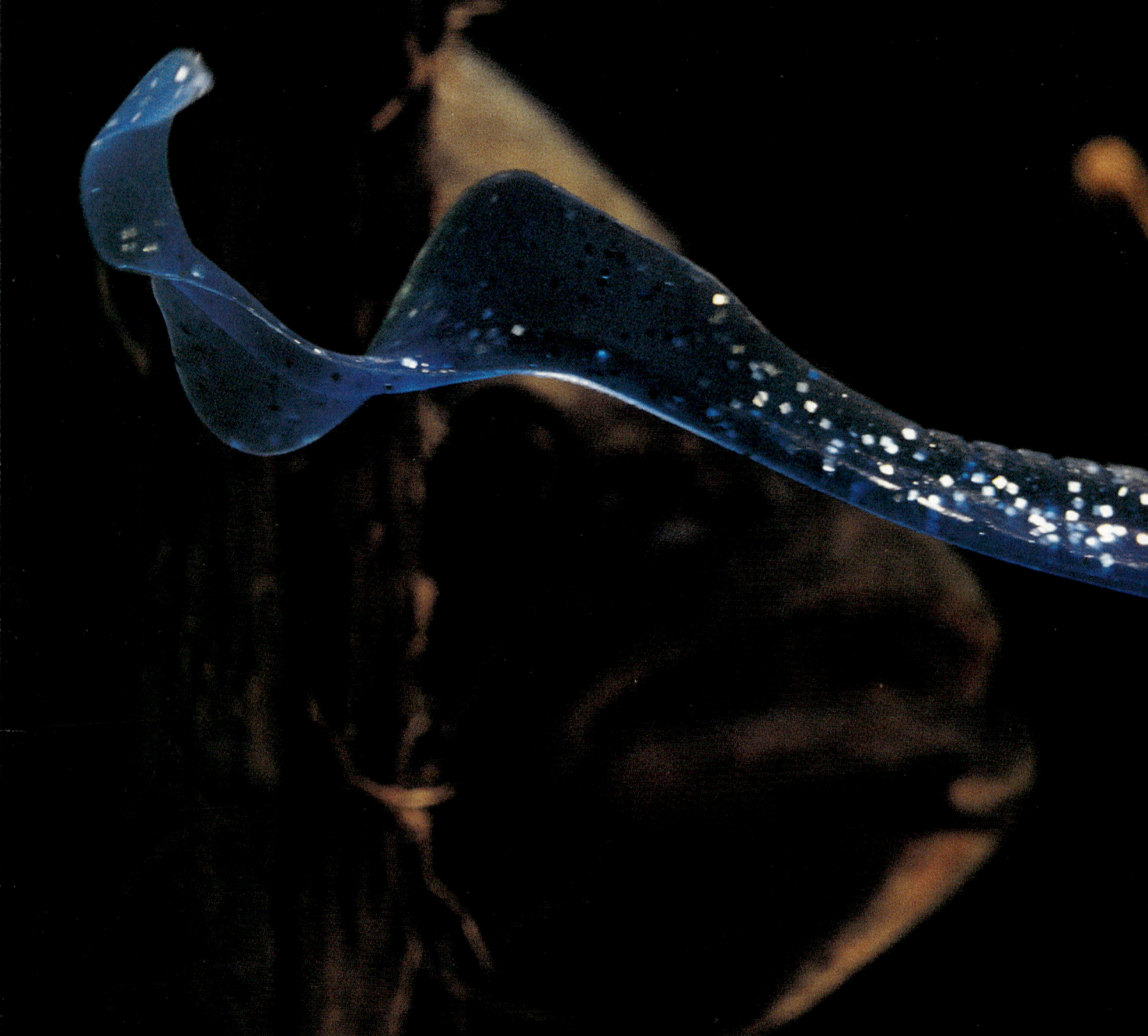

Introduction

Every experienced bass angler knows that bass behave differently in different habitats. *The Complete Book of Bass* was written to help you tailor a strategy for catching bass in practically every type of water in which they are found.

Before getting into strategies, however, you'll need a basic understanding of bass biology. The first chapter, "Understanding Bass," details the differences between all the important bass species and lays the foundation you'll need for consistent fishing success. Then, when the fish refuse to cooperate, you'll have a better idea of what they're doing and how to reformulate your strategy.

The following chapters, "Bassin' in Man-Made Lakes," "Bassin' in Rivers," and Bassin' in Natural Lakes," show you how to catch every kind of bass each class of water has to offer.

Within each of these classes, we identify the most important water types and explain how they differ from other waters in the class. An eastern mountain reservoir, for instance, differs greatly from a swampland reservoir, because it is much deeper and has well-oxygenated water in the depths. We also explain what implications these differences have for fish and fishermen.

Each type of water is represented by a *case study*. For desert reservoirs, for instance, we chose Elephant Butte Lake, New Mexico, as a representative of that water class. The techniques we show you for catching largemouth, smallmouth and striped bass in Elephant Butte can be applied to any water of the same type.

Rounding out this section is the chapter, "Advanced Bassin' Techniques," in which experts from around the country share the secrets that have accounted for their success. We'll also show you how to become a better tournament angler.

This book has something to offer every bass angler, whether you're a beginner or a top tournament pro. The "water type" approach will put you on bass much more quickly than the "generic technique" approach used in most other bass-fishing books.

Understanding Bass

Bass have long been the favorite target of North American anglers. The term "bass" encompasses two major types of gamefish – black bass and temperate bass.

Black bass, including largemouth, smallmouth, spotted and redeye bass, are actually members of the sunfish family (*Centrarchidae*). Black bass get their name from the black coloration of smallmouth bass fry.

The tremendous popularity of black bass results from their willingness to strike a variety of surface and subsurface lures, and their habit of jumping or tailwalking when hooked.

Largemouth and smallmouth bass have been widely stocked throughout the U.S. and southern Canada. When introduced to new waters, they generally reproduce successfully and no further stocking is necessary.

Temperate bass, or *true* bass, belong to the family *Percichthyidae*. Besides striped bass, the family includes many smaller fish, such as white and yellow bass, but only stripers are included in this book.

Unlike black bass, temperate bass are random spawners, not nest builders. They thrive in big rivers or in lakes connected to or fed by big rivers. They require flowing water for successful spawning.

Stripers and other temperate bass are known for their strong schooling tendencies. They feed in packs, surrounding schools of baitfish, herding them to the surface and then attacking them. The desperate baitfish leap out of the water as the bass slash at them, and hungry gulls swoop down to grab the injured baitfish. The frenzied feeding may last only minutes; then the bass sound. But they soon appear in another location.

Striped bass differ from other temperate bass in that they are *anadromous*, meaning they spend most of their life at sea but spawn in fresh water. For decades, however, they have been stocked in man-made lakes throughout the southern half of the country. Because they can reach weights in excess of 50 pounds, they furnish an exciting "big-game" fishery.

On the following pages are biological profiles of each important bass species.

Largemouth Bass
(Micropterus salmoides)

Northern largemouth bass

Common Names — Black bass, green bass, bigmouth and linesides.

Description — Light greenish to brownish sides with a dark lateral band that may come and go. The jaw extends well beyond the rear of the eye. Unlike spotted bass, there is no patch of teeth on the tongue.

Subspecies — Two are recognized: the northern largemouth *(Micropterus salmoides salmoides)*, and the Florida largemouth *(Micropterus salmoides floridanus)*. The two look much the same, but the Florida largemouth has slightly smaller scales in relation to the size of its body. It has 69 to 73 scales along the lateral line, compared to 59 to 65 on the northern largemouth. Originally, Florida largemouth were found only in peninsular Florida, but they have been stocked in several other states including Texas and California.

Table Quality — The meat is white, flaky and low in oil content. Largemouth taken from lakes where the predominant cover is weeds often have a grassy taste; those taken from clean water with woody cover usually have a mild flavor.

Sporting Qualities — The largemouth's liking for heavy cover makes it a challenge to land. A hooked largemouth usually heads for the surface, then opens its mouth wide, shaking its head or jumping in an attempt to throw the hook. Then it dives for cover and often wraps the line around logs, weeds or brush.

Largemouth will strike almost any kind of artificial lure or live bait, but most are taken on plastic worms, surface plugs, spinnerbaits, crankbaits, bass bugs and shiner minnows. The value of the largemouth as a sport fish has prompted a movement toward catch-and-release fishing.

Habitat — Largemouth thrive in eutrophic and mesotrophic natural lakes, especially those with plenty of submerged vegetation; reservoirs with an abundance of flooded timber and brush; ponds; pits; and slow-moving rivers and streams. They can tolerate a wide range of clarities and bottom types, and can even live in brackish water. They prefer water temperatures from 68° to 78°F, and are usually found at depths less than 20 feet.

Food Habits — Largemouth will eat whatever is available, including small fish, crayfish, larval and adult insects, mice, salamanders, leeches, frogs, snakes, and even turtles.

Spawning Habits — Spawn in spring at water temperatures from 63° to 68°F. The male sweeps away the silt to reach a firm sand or gravel bottom, usually along a shallow shoreline protected from the wind. Nests are often near weeds or logs. After spawning is completed, the male guards the eggs and later the fry, attacking anything that approaches the nest including crayfish, minnows, sunfish and fishermen's lures. Female Florida bass briefly share the nest-guarding duties with the male.

Age and Growth — In the North, largemouth may live as long as 16 years, but in the South they seldom exceed 10 years. Female largemouth live longer than males and are much more likely to reach trophy size. The northern subspecies grows only slightly faster in the South than in the North; the Florida subspecies grows considerably faster than the northern.

Typical Length (inches) at Various Ages

Age	1	2	3	4	5	6	8	10
Northern	4.7	8.5	11.3	13.4	15.3	17.1	19.5	20.8
Florida	7.5	12.0	15.5	18.2	20.3	22.1	24.9	—

Typical Weight (pounds) at Various Lengths (inches)

Length	12	14	16	18	20	22	24	26
Weight	1.0	1.9	2.7	3.5	5.4	7.2	8.6	9.5

World Record — 22 pounds, 4 ounces, caught in Montgomery Lake, Georgia, in 1932. This fish is thought to have been an intergrade between the two subspecies.

7-pound northern largemouth — Lake Hamilton, Arkansas

Smallmouth Bass *(Micropterus dolomieui)*

NORTHERN SMALLMOUTH — Jaw extends to about middle of eye. No black spot at rear of gill cover (see Neosho smallmouth, opposite). Found in southern Canada, and in every state except Florida, Louisiana and Alaska.

Common Names — Bronzeback, brown bass, black bass, Oswego bass, green trout and redeye.

Description — Greenish to brownish sides with dark vertical bars that come and go. Three dark bars radiate from the eye. Smallmouth have a chameleonlike ability to change color. See subspecies descriptions.

Subspecies — Two are recognized: the northern smallmouth bass *(Micropterus dolomieui dolomieui)*,

3-pound northern smallmouth — Grindstone Lake, Wisconsin

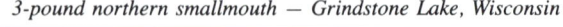

and the Neosho smallmouth bass (*Micropterus dolomieui velox*). The latter is now rare because much of its native habitat was inundated after dams were constructed.

NEOSHO SMALLMOUTH — Prominent dark spot on rear of gill cover. Jaw extends slightly farther back than that of northern smallmouth, almost reaching rear of eye. Found mainly in tributaries of the Arkansas River in Oklahoma, Arkansas and Missouri.

Hybrids — Known to hybridize with spotted bass.

Table Quality — The white, flaky flesh has an excellent flavor; it does not have the grassy taste that largemouth sometimes have.

Sporting Qualities — Considered by many to be the sportiest freshwater fish. Smallmouth are known for their fighting stamina and astounding leaping ability. Like largemouth, they will take almost any kind of lure or bait, but they generally prefer smaller sizes. Favorites include jigs, crankbaits, spinners, streamer flies, shiner minnows, crayfish, hellgrammites, leeches and nightcrawlers.

Habitat — Smallmouth like clean, clear water. They are found in all types of natural and manmade lakes, but are most common in mesotrophic lakes and mid-depth reservoirs. Smallmouth also thrive in rivers and streams with moderate current. Seldom are they found in small ponds, lakes shallower than 25 feet, or any water that is continuously murky or polluted. Smallmouth prefer water from 67° to 71°F. They do not compete well with other predatory fish.

Food Habits — Crayfish are the favored food, but smallmouth also eat larval and adult insects, frogs and tadpoles, and a variety of small fish.

Spawning Habits — Smallmouth spawn in spring, usually at water temperatures from 60° to 65°F. They can spawn successfully in streams or lakes. The male builds a nest by sweeping silt off a bottom of sand, gravel or rock. Usually the nest is protected by a boulder or log, and is not exposed to the wind. After spawning, the male guards the eggs. He continues to guard the fry for a week or two after they leave the nest.

Age and Growth — Smallmouth live up to 18 years in the North, seldom longer than 7 years in the South. But southern smallmouth grow much faster.

Typical Length (inches) at Various Ages

Age	1	2	3	4	5	6	7	8
North	4.2	6.7	8.6	10.9	13.0	14.6	15.8	16.9
South	5.9	10.7	13.5	16.6	18.5	20.4	21.0	21.6

Typical Weight (pounds) at Various Lengths (inches)

Length	12	14	16	18	20	22
Weight	1.0	1.5	2.6	3.9	5.0	6.2

World Record — 11 pounds, 15 ounces, caught in Dale Hollow Lake, Kentucky, in 1955.

Spotted Bass *(Micropterus punctulatus)*

Northern spotted bass

Common Names — Kentucky bass, spot.

Description — Light green to light brown sides with a lateral band consisting of dark blotches, usually diamond-shaped. The jaw extends to the rear portion of the eye. Spotted bass have a distinct patch of teeth on the tongue (photo at right); largemouth do not.

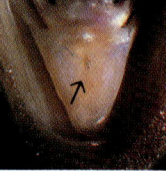

Subspecies — Two are recognized: the northern spotted bass *(Micropterus punctulatus punctulatus)*, and the Alabama spotted bass *(Micropterus punctulatus henshalli)*. The Wichita spotted bass *(Micropterus punctulatus wichitae)* is thought to be extinct.

The Alabama subspecies has a dark spot at the base of the tail and on the rear of the gill cover, and 68 to 75 scales along the lateral line. This subspecies is found only in Alabama, Mississippi and Georgia.

The northern subspecies also has a spot on the tail, but the spot on the gill cover is not as distinct, and there are only 60 to 68 scales along the lateral line. This is the subspecies found throughout most of the spotted bass range.

Hybrids — Spotted bass sometimes hybridize with smallmouth.

Table Quality — White, flaky meat with a good flavor. Generally considered better eating than largemouth.

Sporting Qualities — Although smaller and less acrobatic than smallmouth, spotted bass are strong fighters when caught on light tackle. Popular lures and baits include nymphs, jigs, crankbaits, spinners, small plastic worms, crayfish, spring lizards and hellgrammites.

Habitat — Spotted bass prefer small to medium-sized streams with clear, slow-moving water, and deep reservoirs. They are seldom found in natural lakes. In reservoirs, they inhabit deeper water than largemouth or smallmouth bass, sometimes retreating to depths of 100 feet. They prefer water temperatures in the mid-70s.

Food Habits — Crayfish are usually the most important item in the diet, followed by small fish, and larval and adult insects.

Spawning Habits — Spotted bass spawn in spring at water temperatures of about 63° to 68°F. Males sweep away silt from a gravel or rock bottom to make the nest, generally near brush, logs or other heavy cover. The males guard the eggs, and then guard the fry for up to a month after they leave the nest.

Age and Growth — The maximum life span, about 7 years, is much shorter than that of the smallmouth or largemouth, and the growth rate is slower.

Typical Length (inches) at Various Ages

Age	1	2	3	4	5	6	7
North	4.8	6.8	8.0	9.4	10.4	10.9	—
South	7.4	11.0	12.3	13.8	15.0	17.9	18.1

Typical Weight (pounds) at Various Lengths (inches)

Length	9	11	13	15	17	19
Weight	.33	.69	1.0	1.6	2.3	3.2

World Record — 9 pounds, 4 ounces, caught in Lake Perris, California, in 1987.

3-pound northern spotted bass — Lake Lanier, Georgia

Redeye Bass (Micropterus coosae)

ALABAMA REDEYE — Reddish dorsal, anal and caudal fins; upper sides often have blue spots, and the belly a bluish tinge. No dark spot at base of tail. Found in Alabama, Tennessee, Georgia and North Carolina.

Common Names — Coosa bass, shoal bass, Flint River smallmouth.

Description — The eyes are red, and the sides brownish to greenish, usually with vertical bars. There is a prominent dark spot on the gill cover. The jaw extends to the rear portion of the eye. Redeyes do not have a lateral band and resemble smallmouth more than largemouth. See descriptions of forms.

Forms — Although the taxonomy of the redeye-bass group is uncertain, there are two widely recog-

14 SUNFISH FAMILY

Alabama redeyes — Amacalola Creek, Georgia

nized forms: the Apalachicola form, or shoal bass, and the Alabama form.

APALACHICOLA REDEYE (shoal bass) — Dark spot at base of tail, no blue spots on upper sides, fins not as intensely colored as in Alabama form. Found in the Apalachicola River system in Georgia, Alabama and Florida.

Table Quality — Good; the white, flaky meat is similar to that of smallmouth bass and somewhat drier than that of largemouth.

Sporting Qualities — Scrappy fighters, redeyes often jump when hooked. They can be caught on worms, minnows, hellgrammites and crayfish, as well as small spinners, nymphs, and a wide variety of small surface lures.

Habitat — Alabama redeyes are normally found in the headwaters of small streams, where the water may be too cold for other black bass. Shoal bass are more likely to be found in main-channel habitat.

Redeyes are seldom found in natural lakes, ponds or reservoirs. They prefer a water temperature of about 65°F.

Food Habits — Redeyes feed heavily on terrestrial insects on the surface. They also eat larval insects, crayfish and small fish.

Spawning Habits — Spawn in spring on coarse gravel at the head of a pool. Usual spawning temperature is 62° to 69°F. Males prepare the nest and guard the eggs and fry.

Age and Growth — Redeyes live as long as 10 years. The Alabama form grows very slowly; shoal bass grow much faster.

Typical Length (inches) at Various Ages

Age	1	2	3	4	5	6	7	8
Alabama	3.9	4.9	6.2	6.7	7.2	8.0	8.7	8.9
Shoal	3.8	8.1	11.4	13.9	15.3	18.9	20.7	21.5

Typical Weight (pounds) at Various Lengths (inches)

Length	8	10	12	14	16	18	20
Weight	.25	.47	.79	1.2	2.1	3.7	5.5

World Record — 8 pounds, 3 ounces, caught in the Flint River, Georgia, in 1977. This fish was a shoal bass.

Striped Bass *(Morone saxatilis)*

Common Names — Striper, rockfish, linesides.

Description — The silvery sides have 7 or 8 unbroken horizontal stripes that are darker and more prominent than on a white bass. The body is more elongate, and there are two patches of teeth on the tongue, rather than one. A white bass has a single spine on the rear of the gill cover; a striper has two.

Hybrids — Known to hybridize naturally with white perch. Female striped bass are commonly bred with male white bass to produce a cross called a wiper, whiterock, sunshine bass, or simply hybrid.

WIPER — Body depth intermediate between that of the white bass and striped bass; stripes broken both above and below lateral line. Stocked widely throughout striped bass range.

Table Quality — Excellent eating; the meat is white, firm and flaky.

Sporting Qualities — Its speed, power, and frenzied surface-feeding habits make the striped bass one of the most exciting freshwater sport fish. Stripers are usually caught by deep trolling with large plugs or jigs, or by drifting with live baitfish or cut bait. When "on the jumps," they can easily be caught by casting any type of artificial that resembles the baitfish they are chasing.

Habitat — Stripers are anadromous, entering freshwater streams to spawn. But many have been stocked in fresh water, mainly in large southern reservoirs. They prefer relatively clear water with a good supply of open-water baitfish such as threadfin or gizzard shad. Their preferred water temperature range is 65° to 75°F.

Food Habits — Fish are the primary food, but stripers also eat crustaceans and a wide variety of insects and bottom organisms. Like other temperate bass, they move in packs, and all members of the pack tend to feed at the same time. Heaviest feeding is in early morning and in evening, but they feed sporadically throughout the day, especially when skies are overcast. Feeding slows when the water temperature drops below 50°F, but does not stop completely.

Spawning Habits — Spawn in spring, normally at water temperatures from 55° to 60°F. Stripers in reservoirs swim up tributary streams and often spawn below large dams. As many as fifty fish may spawn together, rolling and splashing in the shallows. The semi-buoyant eggs are deposited in light to moderate current. Moving water is needed to keep the eggs afloat until they hatch.

Age and Growth — Striped bass are fast-growing and long-lived. A 125-pounder caught by commercial netters off the Atlantic coast was estimated to be 29 to 31 years old.

Typical Length (inches) at Various Ages

Age	1	2	3	4	5	6	7	8	9
Length	9.3	16.7	21.1	24.4	27.5	29.8	31.9	33.7	34.9

Typical Weight (pounds) at Various Lengths (inches)

Length	18	21	24	27	30	33	36	39	42
Weight	2.8	4.3	6.3	9.1	12.3	15.9	20.2	26.4	36.8

World Record — Freshwater: 59 pounds, 12 ounces, caught in the Colorado River, Arizona, in 1977. Saltwater: 78 pounds, 8 ounces, caught off Atlantic City, New Jersey, in 1982.

Striped bass taking jig on casting float — Lake Lanier, Georgia

Bassin' in Man-Made Lakes

In the last half century, tens of thousands of small streams in North America have been dammed to create reservoirs.

The dam-building era really began with creation of the Tennessee Valley Authority (TVA) in 1933 and passage of the Flood Control Act of 1936. The TVA, along with the U.S. Army Corps of Engineers and the Bureau of Reclamation, have built the majority of large reservoirs in this country.

When streams are dammed, anglers are forced to learn new fishing techniques. The impounded water may hold new fish species, and even the same species behave differently in the stillwater environment.

This chapter will aquaint you with the most important types of man-made lakes suitable for bass and show you exactly where to find and how to catch every type of bass that swims in these waters.

Specifics on each type of man-made lake are presented through a case study. Each case study shows you how that type of man-made lake differs from other important types. A desert reservoir, for instance, has considerably different fish habitat than a swampland reservoir, and undergoes much greater water-level fluctuation. Consequently, strategies for finding and catching bass are completely different.

Desert Reservoirs

Gamefish now abound where cactuses once grew

Found mainly in the southwestern United States, desert reservoirs provide a reliable supply of water to cities and agricultural areas. Huge irrigation systems have made it possible to grow crops on millions of acres of land that previously were too dry during the growing season.

Most of these reservoirs are at least 100 feet deep, so they can store large volumes of water. But during a long-term drought, much of the water may drain off or evaporate, leaving barely enough to support fish life. Gamefish populations suffer when shallow food-production areas go dry.

When the reservoir refills, however, there is a boom in fish production, similar to what happens when a new reservoir fills. Brush that develops on exposed shorelines during drought periods is flooded

when the water level rises, resulting in an abundance of food and cover for gamefish. Flooded trees and brush are especially important in lakes of this type, because the fluctuating water level limits growth of most aquatic plants.

Desert soils are typically rich in nutrients, so these reservoirs are usually quite fertile and productive. Because of their large watershed, they receive a heavy inflow of nutrients from surrounding lands.

The majority of desert lakes hold only warmwater fish species, primarily largemouth bass. Secondary species include white bass, crappies, catfish, smallmouth bass and sometimes striped bass or walleyes.

Deep desert reservoirs may have enough cold, well-oxygenated water to support trout.

The next world-record largemouth could easily come from a desert lake stocked with a combination of Florida bass and trout. The bass grow rapidly on a trout diet, and several 20-plus-pounders have already been taken from desert lakes in southern California.

Because desert reservoirs are usually found in regions with few other lakes, fishing pressure and other forms of water-based recreational usage are very high. Consequently, the fish tend to be finicky and difficult to catch, especially in lakes that have extremely clear water.

UPPER LAKE. The upper basin is shallower and has much more timber and brush than the lower basin. The timber has a chance to replenish itself when the basin goes dry for extended periods.

Case Study:
Elephant Butte Lake, New Mexico

Imaginative folks say the butte jutting from the water near the dam resembles the profile of an elephant's head – thus the lake's unusual name.

Elephant Butte

Construction of the Elephant Butte Dam across the Rio Grande River was completed in 1916. The lake is part of the Rio Grande Project, a water-control system intended to provide a reliable supply of irrigation water to parts of New Mexico and Texas. Mexico is also guaranteed a portion of the Rio Grande's flow.

A power plant at the foot of the dam was added in 1940. Although the generators operate intermittently, depending on the amount of water being discharged, they are capable of producing enough hydroelectric power to supply a city of about 80,000.

Located between Albuquerque, New Mexico and El Paso, Texas, the lake is surrounded by mountainous, *semidesert* terrain dotted with creosote bushes, mesquite and prickly pear cactus.

Elephant Butte Lake consists of two main basins separated by a 4-mile-long narrows. There is a considerable difference in the character of the basins, as the photos above show.

The reservoir receives most of its water from snowmelt in the mountains. And like most desert lakes, it undergoes extreme water-level fluctuations, sometimes as much as 80 feet over the course of the year.

Long-term fluctuations resulting from drought conditions can be much greater. In the period from 1942 to 1951, the water level dropped about 145 feet, leaving the entire basin, with the exception of the main-river channel, dry. A drop of 60 feet below full-pool level is enough to drain the upper lake.

Besides flooded brush and timber, the lake contains little aquatic vegetation for gamefish cover, with the exception of milfoil and scattered beds of pondweeds. Local anglers sink Christmas trees in some of the coves, and rock outcrops on points and humps also provide cover.

Rated among the top fishing lakes in the Southwest, Elephant Butte is also a mecca for boaters and swimmers.

LOWER LAKE. The lower basin is deeper, wider, clearer and less fertile than the upper basin, with more rocky points and humps. The lower lake comprises 60 percent of the total acreage at full pool.

And the clear waters of the lower lake attract scuba divers.

The lake is best known for its plentiful crop of largemouth bass, which were native to the Rio Grande. White bass, catfish and crappies also occur naturally, and the lake has been stocked with smallmouth bass, walleyes and stripers, with the latter growing to spectacular size. In fact, the lake produced a 54-pound, 8-ounce striper, the current New Mexico record, in 1992.

Gamefish grow rapidly in the lake because the growing season is fairly long and food is plentiful. The surface temperature generally reaches 70°F in early June, and stays above 70 until late October. Shad, both gizzard and threadfin, are the major forage species, but gamefish also feed on yellow perch, sunfish, bullheads and a wide variety of minnows.

The fishing season for all species is continuous on Elephant Butte, and the bag limits are quite liberal. As in other regions where year-round bass fishing is allowed, the practice is controversial. We encourage anglers to gently release any bass caught around their spawning beds. This way, they will usually return to their nests and protect their young.

Elephant Butte Lake Physical Data

Year completed	1916
Dam type	gravity
Draw type	multi-level
Acreage	36,600
Average depth:	
upper lake	20 ft
lower lake	85 ft
Maximum depth:	
upper lake	62 ft
lower lake	197 ft
Water-level fluctuation:	
annual	20 ft
long term	149 ft
Water clarity:	
upper lake	6 in
lower lake	25 ft
Limits of thermocline:	highly variable
Trophic state:	
upper lake	eutrophic
lower lake	meso. to oligo.

Elephant Butte Reservoir

23

Elephant Butte Lake Habitat

THE DEEP POOL above the dam produces stripers in winter and early spring, and a few largemouths and smallmouths from summer through winter.

SECONDARY POINTS in the canyons are good spawning areas for smallmouths and hold largemouths in spring and fall.

BACK ENDS of canyons are spawning areas for largemouths, catfish and white bass. Largemouths move back to milfoil flats in canyons in fall.

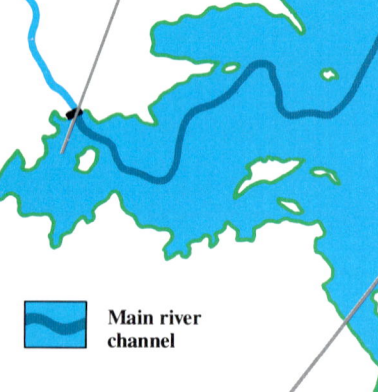

Main river channel

MOUTHS of canyons are prime white bass areas in summer and fall. The fish roam a large area around the mouths and are often suspended.

LOWER-LAKE POINTS with rocky or gravelly bottoms and brush hold all species of gamefish from late spring through winter.

THE NARROWS between the upper and lower lake is the major striper-fishing area in fall. Stripers are drawn by shad moving out of the upper lake.

BRUSHY FLATS in the upper lake, especially where there is a rise, depression or tree clump, hold largemouths and catfish in summer and fall.

ARROYOS (dotted line) are small creek beds that run through the canyons. Largemouth bass use arroyos in early spring and fall; white bass and catfish, most of the year.

UPPER-LAKE POINTS with trees and brush, a hard bottom and deep water nearby are ideal for largemouths and catfish in summer and fall.

Elephant Butte Lake:
Largemouth Bass

The drastic difference in habitat between the upper and lower basins of Elephant Butte Lake means you'll have to tailor your largemouth-fishing strategy accordingly.

In early spring, for instance, the shallow upper lake warms much sooner, triggering spawning activity. Bass in the upper lake start to bite in mid-March, when the water reaches about 50°F. Spawning generally peaks around the full moon in April. In the deeper lower lake, the water doesn't warm enough for good fishing until mid-April, and spawning activity is heaviest around the full moon in May.

A few weeks before spawning, bass feed heavily on points at the mouths of or just inside the canyons where they will eventually spawn. Some fish hold in the arroyos leading into the canyons. Using a surface-temperature gauge, search for the warmest water to locate the active bass.

In shallow, brushy cover, try flippin' a jig-and-pig (p. 29). Be sure to use one with a stout hook that won't bend when you horse the fish out of the cover. On cleaner, deeper structure, slow-hop a jig-and-pig, one with a thinner wire hook for better penetration. Slow-rolling (p. 45) a tandem-blade spinnerbait works well in either shallow or deep water.

For flippin' in heavy cover, use a 7½-foot, heavy-power, fast-action flippin' stick and a baitcasting reel spooled with 25-pound mono. A 6-foot, medium-heavy baitcasting outfit with 17-pound mono is adequate for spinnerbait fishing or working a jig-and-pig in deeper water.

Shallow, protected canyons warm earliest and draw the bulk of the spawners, although a few fish spawn on main-lake reefs and points.

The secret to catching spawning bass is to find their beds. Look for beds at the back ends of the canyons, usually near some type of cover, such as mesquite, rocks or stumps.

Move slowly with your trolling motor, wearing polarized sunglasses to help spot fish on the beds. When you see a fish, hold still and slowly back your boat

Important Types of Timber and Brush for Largemouths

SALT CEDAR. This is the most common type of flooded brush in Elephant Butte and the primary cover for largemouth bass. It holds fish throughout the year. The branches are much straighter than those of mesquite (right).

MESQUITE. These bushes, which have knobby branches with many sharp bends, are found on a gravel bottom, so they draw bass around spawning time. In late summer and early fall, bass hold in mesquite clumps among the salt cedar.

COTTONWOOD. These tall, thick-trunked trees are easy to identify because of their large size. Bass may build spawning beds on roots of trees in water less than 5 feet deep. In fall, bass may suspend in trees in deeper water.

LURES for largemouth bass include: (1) Poe's Super Cedar, series 400, a deep-diving crankbait; (2) Smithwick Devil's Horse, a propbait; (3) Bomber Popper, a chugger; (4) Hopkins Smoothie, a jigging spoon; (5) Bulldog Hawg Dog, a tandem-blade spinnerbait; (6) Ditto Baby Fat Grub, Texas-rigged with a size 1/0 offset hook and a split shot; (7) Stanley Jig with pork trailer; (8) Hale's Craw Worm, Texas-rigged; (9) Fatzee tube bait, Texas-rigged with hook point exposed.

away. Cast a "finesse bait" (p. 31), such as a weenie worm, so it settles into the nest and let it rest motionless for a minute or two. Twitch it occasionally until it pulls away from the nest, then reel in and cast again. Tempting the fish to bite may be difficult.

The difference in spawning times at opposite ends of the lake means you should never have to fish for post-spawn bass, those that are recuperating from the rigors of spawning and very difficult to catch. When bass at the upper end have finished spawning, those at the lower end are just starting. When those at the lower end have finished, those at the upper end have recuperated and started to feed.

Once the fish regain their strength and leave the spawning areas, they begin feeding heavily on shad, so angling success picks up. The shallow, brushy cover in the upper lake produces plenty of good-sized largemouths in summer. Flippin' is the best way to reach bass in the brushy tangle. You'll probably have better success using a jig with a soft-plastic lizard or crawworm, or a Texas-rigged plastic worm, than a jig-and-pig. Spinnerbaits also produce, but you should retrieve them faster than in spring.

The best summertime spots in the lower lake are rocky points and humps with brushy cover, but you can find fish on most any brushy structure from 5 to 15 feet deep. Bass in the lower lake don't run quite as large, and they tend to roam about more in search of shad. Your odds are best early (before 9) and late (after 7) in the day. Then, topwaters worked rapidly across the surface and crankbaits are good choices.

In midday, try jig fishing or split-shotting with a finesse bait. In cloudy or windy weather, the fish bite all day.

You can use the same baitcasting outfit for topwaters and crankbaits as you do for spinnerbaits, but some experts advocate a softer fiberglass rod. This way, you'll lose fewer fish because the rod will bend before the hooks tear out. To cast lightweight split-shot rigs with finesse baits, use a $6\frac{1}{2}$-foot, medium-power spinning outfit with 8-pound mono.

By mid-August, cooling water draws largemouths onto milfoil flats at the back ends of lower-lake canyons. The action is usually fastest in midday.

Propbaits worked with a twitch-and-pause retrieve are excellent fall producers. Let the lure rest for up to 10 seconds when it reaches a stick-up or any object that could hold a bass. Another proven method is split-shotting with finesse baits along edges and openings in the milfoil beds.

Largemouths start moving deeper around mid-November as the water continues to cool. They're much less active, but still catchable. Look for them on any deep structure in the lower lake, usually at depths of 20 to 45 feet.

The best way to catch bass once they go deep is slow-dragging a finesse bait or a live crayfish or shad on a split-shot rig. Or try jigging vertically with a jigging spoon, using a stiff $5\frac{1}{2}$-foot baitcasting outfit and 17-pound mono. This winter pattern holds until the water begins to warm in early March.

Flippin' into Heavy Cover

1. CAST your lure out about the same distance you will be flippin'. You must start with the lure well out in front of you to get the pendulum motion started.

2. PULL the lure out of the water and draw it back toward the boat by lifting your rod tip while pulling on the line with your other hand. Be sure the reel spool is engaged.

3. LOWER your rod tip as the lure begins to swing past you. Continue to hold the line with your other hand so the lure can reach the back of its arc without touching the water.

4. RAISE your rod tip and, at the same time, tug the line slightly with your other hand to propel the lure toward the target. Keep it just high enough so the lure clears the water.

5. BRING the hand holding the line back toward the rod, allowing the weight of the lure to pull the line through the guides. Stop feeding line when the lure reaches the precise target.

6. SET the lure into the water with minimal splash. Lower the rod as the lure sinks so it doesn't swing toward the boat.

Elephant Butte Lake:
Smallmouth Bass

With so much attention focused on largemouths, many anglers do not realize that Elephant Butte sports an excellent population of smallmouths, with plenty of fish in the 3- to 4½-pound class.

You'll find the majority of smallmouths in the lower 10 miles of the lake, where the water is clearest and coolest in summer. As a rule, they'll be near some type of rocky structure.

When the water temperature approaches 60°F, which is usually in mid- to late April, smallmouths move into their spawning areas. Rocky shorelines in the canyons warm first and draw early spawners, but many fish spawn later on rocky shores of the main lake. The best spawning areas are no more than 6 feet deep, with scattered boulders to protect the nests from wind and predators.

Smallmouths spawn at water temperatures in the mid 60s. Total time between the first spawning activity in the creek arms and the last activity in the main lake ranges from 3 to 5 weeks.

When smallmouths concentrate around their spawning areas, you can easily catch them by fan-casting small topwaters and retrieving with a twitch-and-pause motion. Or use a finesse bait (opposite page) on a split-shot rig and work it with a very slow lift-and-drop retrieve over visible beds or through the areas around them. Some anglers let the lure rest right on a bed for several minutes, giving it only an occasional wiggle. When fishing topwaters or finesse baits, use the same outfits as you would when fishing largemouths with these lures (p. 28).

Springtime fishing is best when the water is warming. The action is fastest early and late in the day, especially when using topwaters.

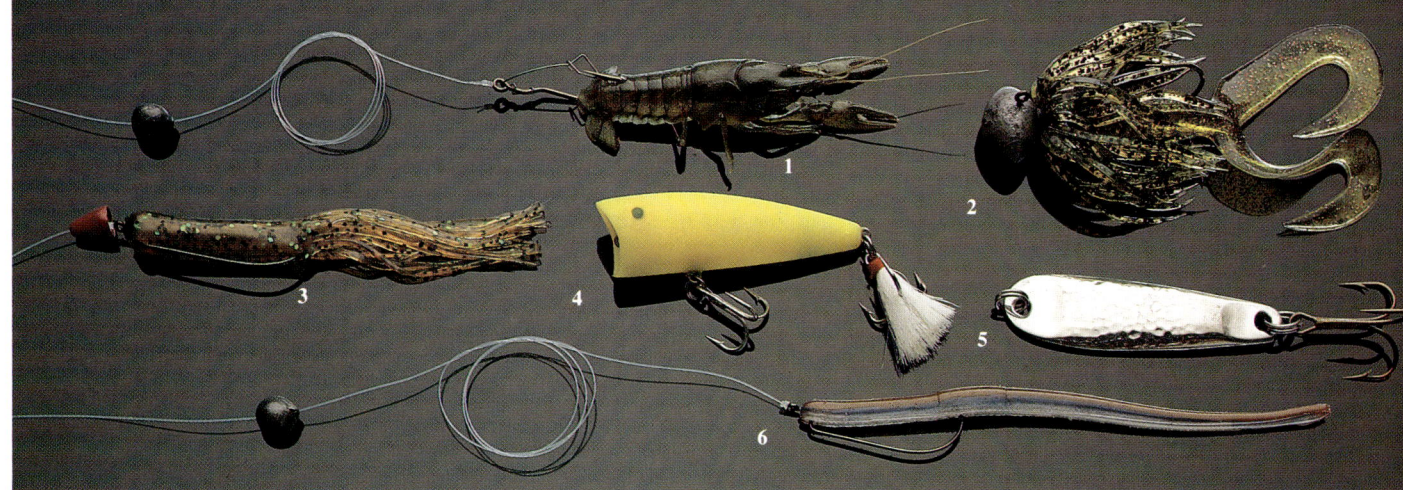

LURES AND BAITS for smallmouths include: (1) crayfish on split-shot rig with weedless hook; (2) Yamamoto Spider Jig; (3) Fatzee tube bait on offset hook with exposed point and bullet sinker; (4) Rebel Pop-R, a chugger; (5) Hopkins Spoon, a jigging spoon; (6) Roboworm, a weenie worm, Texas-rigged on offset hook with split shot.

Finesse Baits and How to Fish Them

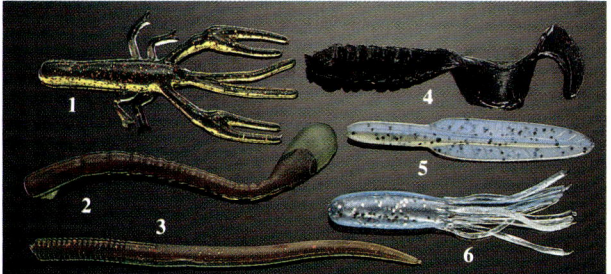

POPULAR FINESSE BAITS include: (1) small crawworm, (2) paddletail worm, (3) weenie worm, (4) curly-tail grub, (5) eel-tail grub, (6) small tube bait.

INCH the lure along slowly with a twitch-and-pause retrieve. On the twitch, the lure rises; on the pause, it sinks slowly since there is no weight on the lure itself.

Once spawning has been completed, you can easily catch nest-guarding males, which are very aggressive. Catching females, however, is next to impossible for a week or two after they spawn. But since they don't all spawn at once, you should be able to find some catchable females through the entire spawning period.

After smallmouths leave their spawning areas, they move to rocky points and isolated rocky humps that top out at about 5 feet and have scattered bushes. In low-light periods, especially in early morning, the fish often feed right on top of the structure. Under bright conditions, they retreat to depths of 10 to 15 feet and do less feeding. Split-shotting with finesse baits is the most productive summertime technique.

As the water cools in fall, the fish spend less and less time in the shallows. By early October, a few smallmouths remain on tops of the points and humps where they were in summer, but most of them have moved to depths of 15 to 25 feet. By mid-November, however, smallmouths spend practically all their time in deeper water. Finesse baits work equally well in fall.

Fall smallmouth fishing is best during periods of stable weather. You can catch fish any time of day, but cloudy weather or a slight chop seems to improve the action.

The water temperature normally drops below 50°F by the middle of January, slowing smallmouth activity to the lowest level of the year. Most of the fish hold at depths of 20 to 30 feet on rocky points and humps that break very sharply into deep water. Often smallmouths suspend just off the structure, where they're difficult to find and catch.

Although fishing is usually tough during the winter, slow-dragging finesse baits or vertically jigging with spoons may take a few smallmouths. Use the same outfit for vertically jigging as you would for largemouths (p. 28).

But if spoons or finesse baits don't produce, try a split-shot rig with a live shad or crayfish. Hook a 2- to 3-inch crayfish through the tail with a size 1/0 weedless hook and retrieve it very slowly. Shad from 3 to 5 inches long are about right for smallmouths; fish them as you would for stripers (p. 35). For live-bait fishing, use a 6-foot, medium-power spinning outfit with 8- to 12-pound mono. These live-bait techniques will take either smallmouths or largemouths year-round.

Elephant Butte Lake:
Striped Bass

The huge stripers in Elephant Butte draw fishermen from all over the Southwest. Each year, anglers do battle with dozens of fish in the 35- to 50-pound class. In 1992, the lake yielded the state-record striper, weighing 54 pounds, 8 ounces.

Although the striper population is not large, you have a reasonable chance of connecting if you fish in known concentration areas at the right time of year.

You can catch a few stripers through the coldest part of the winter, but the action really picks up in mid-March, when the fish begin to congregate above the dam to spawn. Small groups consisting of a female and one or two males cruise the shorelines or roam expanses of open water at depths of 20 to 25 feet.

When the water temperature reaches 55°F, usually in late March, stripers begin to spawn along rocky

LURES for striped bass include: (1) Cordell Pencil Popper, a chugger; (2) Cordell Redfin, a floating minnow plug; (3) horsehead jig tipped with a soft-plastic curlytail; (4) live shad, rigged on a size 2/0 hook.

33

THREADFIN VS. GIZZARD SHAD. Threadfin shad (top) do not work as well for bait as gizzard shad (bottom). Gizzard shad are hardier, and grow to a larger size. You can distinguish between the two by differences in coloration. The gizzard shad has a blackish margin on the tail; the threadfin, yellowish.

shorelines in the vicinity of the dam. Spawning activity continues into early May. But striper eggs require moving water to hatch, so no young are produced in the lake environment. Consequently, the fishery depends entirely on stocking.

Once stripers leave their spawning areas, they begin to appear on large lower-lake flats that top out at 40 to 60 feet adjacent to water at least 80 feet deep. These areas hold fish from the middle of May through early September.

By far the most effective striper technique – one that works any time of year – is slow-trolling, either with live shad or horsehead jigs with 4- to 5-inch curlytails. Most anglers opt for the latter because live shad are not available at bait shops; you have to net your own. But shad are tough to match as bait. In winter and spring, use shad from 4 to 6 inches long; in summer and fall, 7 to 11 inches.

In spring and fall, when stripers are found from the surface to a depth of 25 feet, you can rig the shad on balloon lines, down lines, or unweighted "flat lines" (opposite page). In summer, stripers hold just beneath the thermocline, usually at depths of 40 to 60 feet, so you'll have to rely mainly on down lines. Fishing can be tough in winter, but you may be able to catch a few fish near the bottom on balloon lines and down lines at depths of 25 to 40 feet.

Another good summertime technique, especially in early morning and in cloudy weather, is surface fishing with big minnow plugs and pencil poppers on main-lake points and shallow humps adjacent to deep water. Fish a minnow plug with a slow, steady retrieve so it creates a prominent wake; a pencil popper, with continuous twitches.

Fishing peaks in late November, when stripers are drawn to the narrows by schools of shad forced out of the upper lake by the cooling water. Look for shad schools with a graph; the stripers won't be far away.

Huge shad schools appear as dense clouds on a graph

The most popular way to fish the narrows is casting or slow-trolling with horsehead jigs. When casting, count the jig down to the depth of the fish before beginning your retrieve. Live shad and surface lures also work well in fall. When the water temperature in the narrows drops below 50°F, usually in mid-January, the shad move into the main lake and the stripers follow.

A 7-foot, heavy-power, fiberglass baitcasting outfit works well for all types of striper fishing mentioned. A fiberglass rod will take more punishment than a graphite, and sensitivity is not important in these fishing methods. Spool your reel with 14- to 30-pound mono, depending on the thickness of the cover.

As a rule, stripers bite best early and late in the day. In fall, however, they feed all day long, and in winter, they sometimes bite at night. Stable weather with a light breeze is generally better than stormy or calm conditions.

Multi-line Trolling for Stripers

This technique enables you to cover a range of depths while keeping some of your lines far enough behind the boat that you won't spook the stripers.

If desired, you can attach side planers (p. 65) to some of your lines so they run as much as 50 feet to the side of the boat, further reducing spooking.

PUSH the hook through a shad's nostrils. Use a 1/0 or 2/0 hook for 4- to 6-inchers; a 3/0 or 4/0 for 7- to 11-inchers. This hooking method keeps the shad lively.

PEG a 2- to 3-ounce egg sinker onto each down line, about 4 feet above the hook. Pegging the sinker, rather than tying in a swivel, eliminates knots and reduces line breakage.

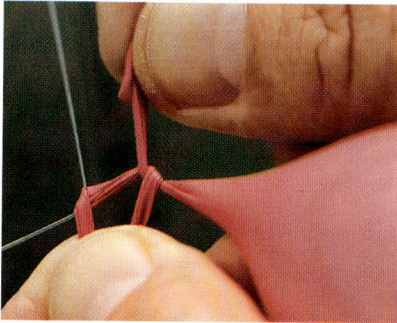

RIG balloon lines using an overhand knot to tie the balloon at the proper depth. Add a large split shot 4 feet above the hook. To change depth, slide the balloon up or down the line.

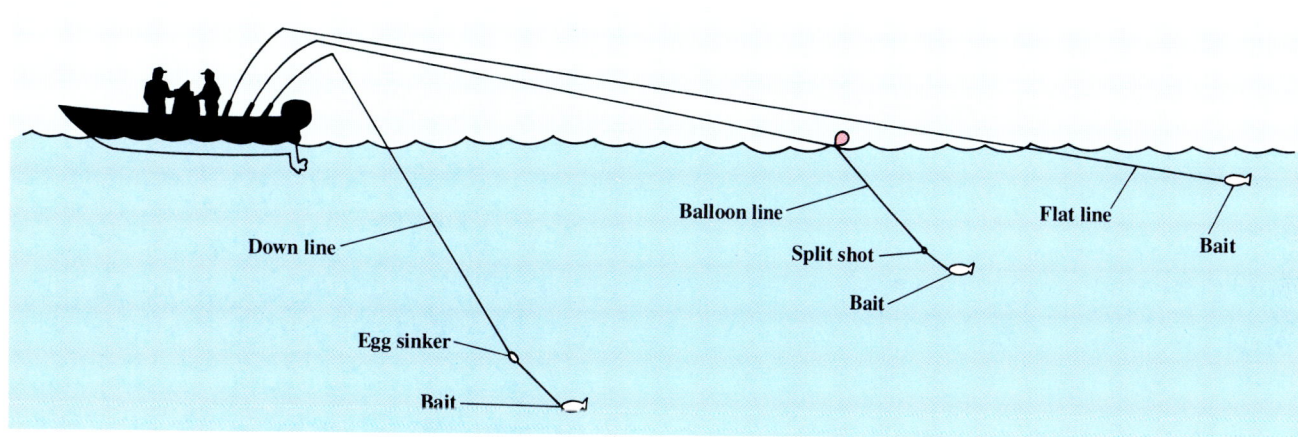

COVER a wide depth range and reduce spooking by using a combination of down lines, balloon lines and flat lines. Down lines run deepest; flat lines, which are not weighted, run shallowest. Down lines trail just behind the boat; balloon lines, about 50 feet back; and flat lines, at least 75 feet back. Stagger the distances to avoid tangling.

Tips for Multi-line Trolling

USE a bow-mounted electric motor so you can troll quietly and avoid spooking the fish. Trolling in an S-pattern also helps; this way, the trailing lines do not follow directly in the boat's wake.

CAST a large floating minnow plug or horsehead jig toward shore as you troll. Angle your casts ahead of the boat and retrieve the plug so it makes a noticeable wake. This technique increases your zone of coverage even more.

Flatland Reservoirs

These shallow, fertile reservoirs rank among the country's top trophy bass waters

The flat to gently rolling terrain around these lakes means the water is relatively shallow, the main basin wide and the creek arms short.

Some flatland reservoirs are more than 100 feet deep near the dam, but the major part of their basins have depths of only 30 to 60 feet. As a result, they're best suited to warmwater fish species, mainly largemouth bass, crappies, sunfish, catfish and white bass. Many deeper lakes of this type have been stocked with striped bass or hybrids.

Because the surrounding land is mainly agricultural, these lakes receive large quantities of nutrients, meaning abundant crops of baitfish (primarily shad) and fast-growing gamefish. But the high fertility also means a lack of coldwater fish, because oxygen levels in the depths fall too low in summer.

Plankton blooms resulting from the fertile water, combined with silt kept in suspension by the mixing effect of the wind, usually keep the water murky.

Timber and brush provide the main cover for fish, especially in the early stages of the reservoir's life. The shallow creek arms are often heavily timbered, as are shoreline points and flats, unless the basin has been clear-cut. But as these lakes age and the woody cover disappears, weeds become more important as cover.

Flatland reservoirs generally undergo less severe water-level fluctuations than most other types of reservoirs. Consequently, aquatic plants become established more easily than in lakes that undergo greater fluctuations.

Case Study:
Richland-Chambers Reservoir, Texas

Impounded by a 6-mile earthen dam in 1987, Richland-Chambers is one of the country's youngest man-made lakes. And, as happens in most youthful reservoirs, the fish population is booming – a phenomenon that will probably continue for at least a decade.

Although the lake was created primarily to supply water to the Fort Worth area, it also reduces flooding of downstream areas. In addition, planners took fishing into consideration during the design phases, leaving a great deal of timber and brush in the shallows to provide spawning cover for adult fish and hiding cover for juveniles. There is also a large expanse of open water that is ideal for sailing and waterskiing.

A typical "flatland" reservoir, Richland-Chambers is surrounded by fertile farm fields and pastureland. The water is shallow and high in nutrients, meaning rapid fish growth. But the high fertility also means low oxygen levels in the depths. In midsummer, the oxygen level in the upper lake is too low to support fish life below 20 feet; in the lower lake, below 40 feet.

Because the surrounding land is so flat, the lake frequently gets buffeted by high winds, stirring up silt and keeping the water clarity low.

The lake produced a surprising number of large fish immediately after impoundment. Richland and

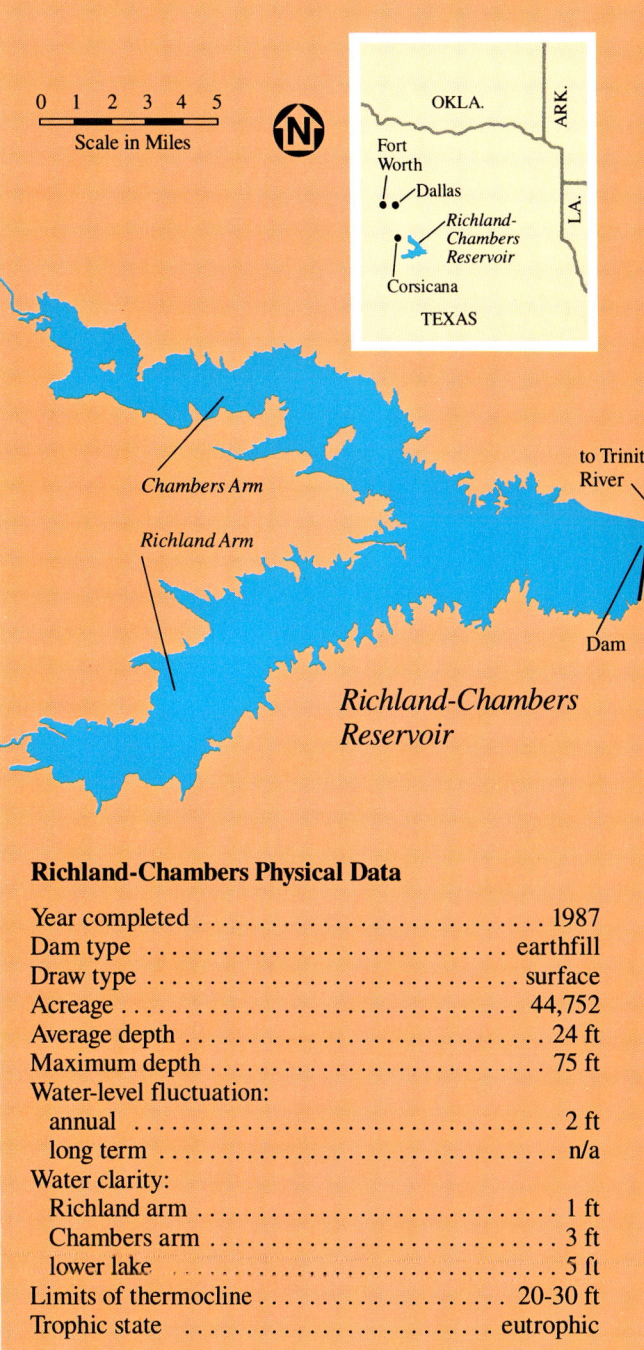

Richland-Chambers Physical Data

Year completed	1987
Dam type	earthfill
Draw type	surface
Acreage	44,752
Average depth	24 ft
Maximum depth	75 ft
Water-level fluctuation:	
annual	2 ft
long term	n/a
Water clarity:	
Richland arm	1 ft
Chambers arm	3 ft
lower lake	5 ft
Limits of thermocline	20-30 ft
Trophic state	eutrophic

Chambers creeks had significant populations of catfish and white bass before the lake filled, good-sized bass came from the many farm ponds that were flooded, and crappies migrated downstream from other impoundments.

Besides the native fish, the lake has been stocked with Florida bass and additional channel and blue catfish. Florida or "coppernose" bluegills (named for the copper-colored patch on the forehead) have also been stocked, but few are caught by anglers, probably because they're heavily preyed upon by catfish and largemouths. The primary forage fish are threadfin and gizzard shad.

Largemouths are the target of most Richland-Chambers fishermen, with crappies running a close second. Catfish are caught primarily on multiple-hook trotlines, although there is some angling.

At present, there are more than a dozen boat landings on the lake, but no resort facilities. A large marina complex is being planned, however.

Richland-Chambers Habitat

BRUSHY CREEK ARMS with flowing water are the major spawning areas for crappies and white bass. They also hold bass in spring and fall.

ROADBEDS offer a hard bottom and deep water in the adjacent ditches. They attract largemouths, and sometimes white bass and crappies, in summer.

WOODED COVES are the main spawning areas for largemouth bass and catfish. They also draw some crappies in spring. Bass return to these areas in fall.

WOODED POINTS make prime cover for largemouths, crappies, white bass and catfish. They hold some fish most of the year.

BRIDGES provide shade, and the piers give white bass and crappies objects to which they can relate. They're most productive from summer through fall.

TREE ROWS along old fencelines make excellent cover for largemouth bass and crappies in summer. Often, the fish suspend among branches far off the bottom.

THE TAILWATERS draw white bass, white bass-striped bass hybrids and crappies, mainly in spring. Catfish move in during the summer.

HUMPS, especially those near deep water with some standing timber, attract most types of gamefish in summer and winter.

THE DAM FACE has shelves where white bass are found in spring. Nearby deep water holds whites, crappies, largemouths and catfish in summer and winter.

Richland-Chambers Reservoir:
Largemouth Bass

Trophy largemouth are becoming routine on Richland-Chambers. And they'll surely be even more common in years to come. With the lake still in its "boom" cycle and well stocked with Florida bass, it's only a matter of time before anglers begin weighing in "teen" fish.

In late February, bass begin moving into creek arms off the upper ends of the main creek channels. A few warm days raise the water temperature into the mid-50s and draw the fish onto 5- to 10-foot timbered flats. The lower end of the lake warms more slowly, so bass move into those creek arms 2 to 3 weeks later.

Spawning begins when the water temperature reaches the low 60s. Look for spawners in 1 to 5 feet of water on a firm, sandy bottom with brushy cover. By late April, all bass throughout the lake have spawned.

During the pre-spawn and spawning period, cast spinnerbaits into the shallows and use a slow-roll retrieve (p. 45), pausing to let them helicopter alongside brush piles and logs. Another good technique is twitching a floating minnow plug through the heavy cover.

Bass stay in the creek arms for 10 days to 2 weeks after spawning, but the females are tough to catch.

You can take a few fish by casting a crankbait, vibrating plug or Texas-rigged worm, lizard or crawworm onto timbered flats from 5 to 15 feet deep.

By early June, most of the bass have moved back to the main lake. You'll find them at depths of 12 to 20 feet on timbered flats and humps along the main creek channels, along fencerows and submerged road ditches and around points. They also move into the many flooded stock tanks (man-made ponds for watering cattle, p. 44). The fish are never far from timber or brush.

The surface temperature reaches the 80s by mid-July, forcing bass to retreat to depths of 15 to 25 feet. But they won't be far from their early summer locations. They stay in these spots until early October.

Texas-rigged worms, lizards and crawworms continue to produce through the summer and into fall. If the bottom is clean enough, try a Carolina rig instead. The lure will drop more slowly, often triggering inactive fish. Another good summertime technique is fishing the brushy cover on deep stock tanks by vertically jigging with a spoon or tailspin, or casting with a jig-and-pig or Texas-rigged worm (p. 44).

By mid-October, most bass have moved into secondary creek arms. You'll catch them at depths of 15 feet or less using crankbaits, spinnerbaits and topwaters such as propbaits, buzzbaits and chuggers. By early November, fish begin moving into the main creek arms. They often suspend 15 to 20 feet down on heavily timbered flats adjacent to the main creek

LURES for largemouths include: (1) A. C. Shiner, a floating minnow plug; (2) Bulldog Buzzbait; (3) Stanley Thumper, a single-spin spinnerbait; (4) 6-inch Mann's Auger Lizard, rigged Texas-style; (5) Storm Rattlin' Flat Wart, a deep-diving crankbait; (6) Penetrator Jig, a rubber-legged brushguard jig, with Guido Bug trailer; (7) Stanley Hale's Craw Worm, rigged Carolina-style; (8) Mann's Mann-O-Lure, a jigging spoon.

channels, but you can draw them up with the topwaters just mentioned, or go down to them with jigs, crankbaits or spinnerbaits retrieved slowly.

When the water temperature drops to the low 50s, usually in late December, bass descend into depths of 25 to 40 feet in the main creek channels. Fishing is slow in winter, but you can catch a few fish by vertically jigging a spoon or tailspin to catch bass suspended 10 to 20 feet deep around flooded trees along the channel edges.

A 6- to 7-foot, medium to medium-heavy baitcasting outfit works well for all the techniques mentioned above. Because of the heavy timber and brush, most anglers use 17- to 20-pound (or heavier) line. Use lighter line, about 14-pound test, only when casting crankbaits and minnow plugs in lighter cover.

Shallow-water bass tend to bite best on overcast days with a light breeze. In this kind of weather, fishing is usually good all day long. On calm, sunny days, you'll catch more fish early and late in the day.

Deep-water bass are most active on sunny, breezy days, except in summer, when cloudy weather is best. You'll normally catch more fish in the afternoon than in the morning.

How to Find and Fish Stock Tanks

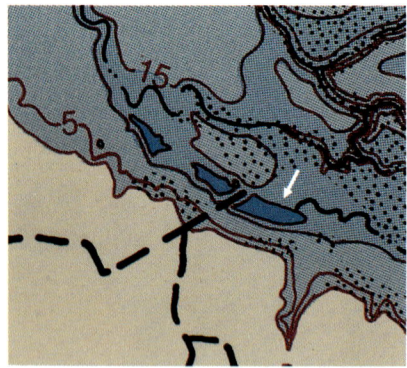

LOCATE flooded stock tanks (arrow) on a detailed reservoir map. Richland-Chambers has hundreds of these tanks.

STOCK TANKS are often surrounded by trees (left) because of the availability of water. After the reservoir fills, the row of trees outlining a stock tank (right) can help you find it in a hurry.

POSITION your boat outside the dam to fish shallow stock tanks. Cast over the dam and work your lure across the top and down the outside edge, the places where bass normally lie. On deeper tanks, vertically jig over heavy timber.

Tips for Finding and Catching Bass

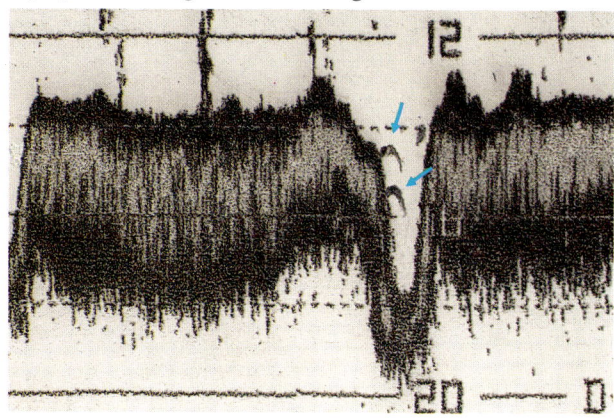

LOOK for ditches alongside submerged roadbeds. Bass (arrows) usually lie along the slopes of the ditches, as shown on this graph tape, but they may feed right on the roadbed early and late in the day or in cloudy weather.

BUCKBRUSH provides excellent pre- and post-spawn bass cover. It grows in shallow creek arms with firm bottoms, near the places where bass spawn. Bass usually hold in the thickest part of the clump.

CEDAR TREES have dense branches that offer perfect cover for bass, especially in spring and fall. Individual cedars commonly grow among stands of hardwoods. The best cedars are found in water at least 5 feet deep.

USE an old spark plug to free lures snagged in timber. With your line near vertical, pinch the electrode over the line, then drop the spark plug. If the lure doesn't come loose right away, twitch your rod tip a few times.

SLOW-ROLL a spinnerbait over brushy cover in early season. Reel just fast enough to make the blades turn, and let the lure actually bump the brush. When the lure reaches the near side of the brush, let it helicopter down.

Swampland Reservoirs

Despite their shallow depth, these reservoirs support a tremendous diversity of fish life

Before these reservoirs were filled, their basins were mainly swampland. And in many cases, the water level was raised less than 20 feet, so they retain their swamplike appearance.

The low-lying terrain surrounding these lakes is quite flat, with only a few subtle hills and ridges. Although a swampland reservoir's maximum depth may be 50 feet, most of the water is no deeper than 25.

As a rule, the main basins of swampland reservoirs are wide and the creek arms short – in some cases barely distinguishable from the rest of the lake.

Because the basins of these lakes contain large amounts of decaying vegetation, the water fertility is high, meaning the depths are low in oxygen in summer. Often, the water is tea-colored, the result of tannic acid produced by the decaying plants.

The warm, shallow, highly vegetated water characteristic of these lakes is ideal for largemouth bass, sunfish and crappies. In fact, the world-record white crappie (5 pounds, 3 ounces) was caught in Enid Reservoir, a swampland reservoir in Mississippi. In addition, many swampland reservoirs have good populations of chain pickerel, catfish and white bass. Some have serious roughfish problems, with an abundance of carp, which root up the bottom, and gar, which feed on young gamefish and compete with adult gamefish for food.

The low oxygen level, combined with the stained water, means that the fish live in shallow water most of the time, with the exception of late fall and winter. Then, the water mixes thoroughly, oxygenating the depths and allowing fish to go deeper.

Case Study:
Lake Bistineau, Louisiana

When you're fishing in a jungle of flooded cypress trees overgrown with Spanish moss, it's easy to see why many consider Lake Bistineau one of the most scenic bodies of water in the country.

Nearly 200 years ago, a massive logjam on the Red River flooded upstream tributaries, including Loggy Bayou, forming Lake Bistineau. Over time, however, the lake slowly drained. In 1938, the State of Louisiana built a permanent dam to preserve the water level, and in 1951, the dam was raised another 4 feet, creating the lake that exists today.

At first glance, many anglers are intimidated by the lake. It appears that navigation would be almost impossible without getting lost or hitting a submerged stump. But with a good lake map, navigation isn't too much of a problem. The main river channel and the adjoining sloughs and bayous are well marked. Take it easy whenever you get off of a marked channel, however.

Even with a good map, it pays to carry a compass; it's easy to get disoriented in the maze of flooded cypress trees.

Lake Bistineau is unusual compared to most other man-made lakes, because its sole purpose is recreation. Besides fishing and duck hunting, the lake is used for pleasure boating and waterskiing. Bistineau has 2 public boat ramps, 2 resorts, 16 marinas and an excellent state park with rental cabins and a campground.

Channel markers show you which direction you're heading, and the numbers provide a locational reference

Best known for its largemouth bass fishing, Bistineau also produces good catches of black crappies (specks), white crappies (white perch), redear sunfish (chinquapins), yellow bass (barfish) and bluegills.

The lake also abounds with catfish, but most of them are caught on limb lines and yo-yo rigs (opposite page). Few anglers fish them with sportfishing gear.

Striped bass and hybrid stripers (wipers) have been stocked in large numbers, but the survival rate is low

Spring-loaded yo-yo rigs hook fish and pull them up

and they don't grow as large as they often do in deeper reservoirs. At present, anglers show little interest in them.

Many other species are found in the lake, but not in fishable numbers. You'll catch a few spotted bass when fishing largemouths, and warmouths and longear sunfish sometimes turn up when you're after bluegills or chinquapins.

The lake has an excellent population of good-sized chain pickerel (jackfish), but most local anglers consider them trash fish. Freshwater drum (goo), while regarded as trash fish in other regions, are a favorite of some anglers on Bistineau.

Seasonal warming and cooling patterns in Bistineau are the opposite of those in deeper reservoirs. Anglers should become familiar with these patterns because they have a dramatic effect on fishing.

The reason for the difference relates to the shallow depth of the entire lakebed. With a wide, flat basin and no deep pool at the lower end, this zone warms and cools more rapidly than the upper end, where the channel is much more confined. As a result, the lower end warms about two weeks earlier than the upper end in spring, and cools about two weeks earlier in fall.

Another important difference: fishing in Lake Bistineau is affected by weather to a greater degree than in most other lakes. On a very cold night, for instance, the water temperature may drop 10 degrees, shutting down the action for most gamefish.

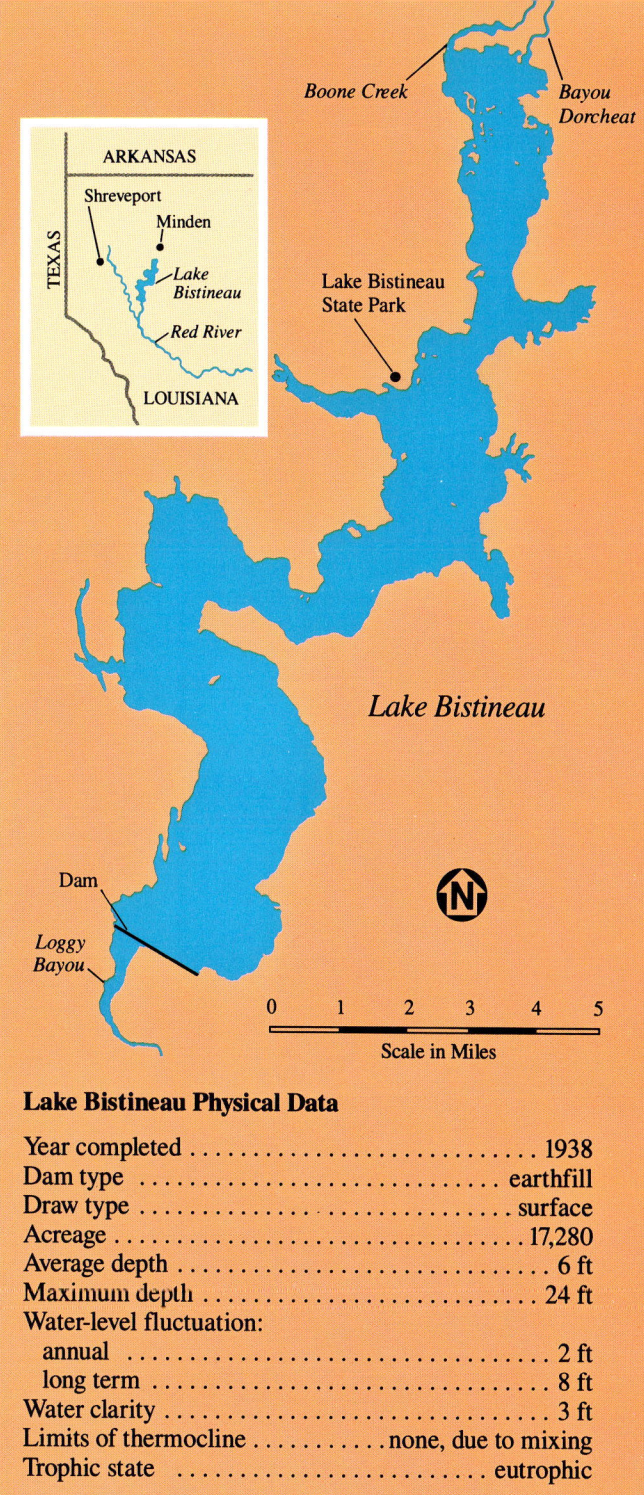

Lake Bistineau Physical Data

Year completed	1938
Dam type	earthfill
Draw type	surface
Acreage	17,280
Average depth	6 ft
Maximum depth	24 ft
Water-level fluctuation:	
annual	2 ft
long term	8 ft
Water clarity	3 ft
Limits of thermocline	none, due to mixing
Trophic state	eutrophic

Lake Bistineau Habitat

CYPRESS FLATS, especially those with deeper creek beds, are good summertime catfish spots. Deeper flats hold largemouths from spring through fall.

MAIN-LAKE POINTS near the old river channel, particularly those with cypress trees, hold largemouths, crappies and sunfish in summer.

ISLANDS generally have a fringe of firm bottom that makes ideal spawning habitat, especially for largemouth bass and sunfish.

THE TAILWATERS is an excellent catfishing spot and attracts most species of gamefish, particularly in spring and fall.

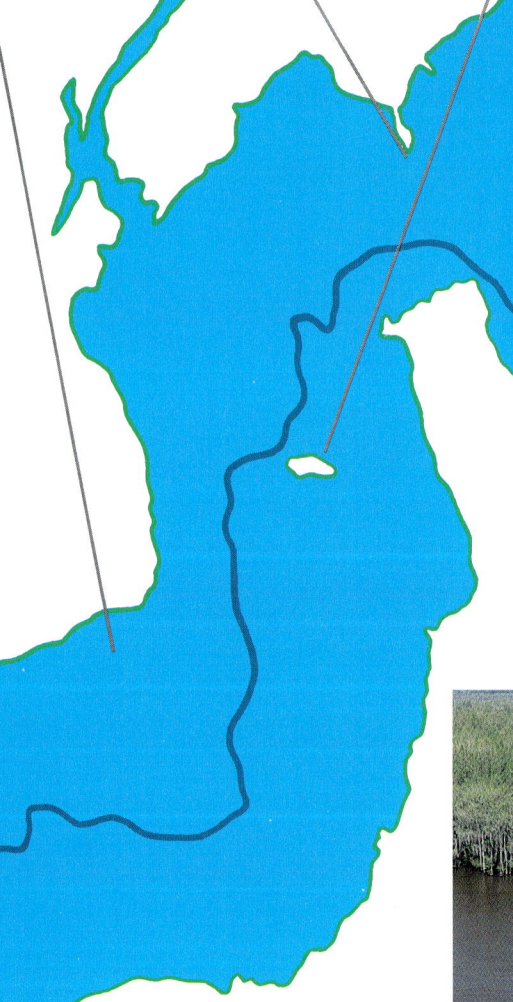

JUNCTIONS of sloughs and the main river channel are important wintering areas for largemouth bass, and sometimes hold a few spotted bass.

Main river channel

OLD CREEK BEDS (dotted line) and ditches wind through cypress flats, offering a deeper refuge for bass, crappies and sunfish from spring through fall.

THE OLD RIVER CHANNEL has the reservoir's deepest water and is the main wintering area for most gamefish. The edges of the channel also hold fish in summer.

THICKETS are excellent crappie, sunfish and largemouth spots in spring. They hold sunfish and largemouths through the summer.

WEEDY SHORELINES draw largemouth bass and chain pickerel early in the year. Most of the weeds die by midsummer, and the fish move to deeper water.

SLOUGHS, which held water before the lake filled, are deeper than the surrounding water. They have dense cypress stands and hold all types of gamefish from spring through fall.

Lake Bistineau:
Largemouth Bass

Tournament fishermen on Lake Bistineau know that it usually takes at least a 4-pound average to be in contention. The bass average about 3, and 7- to 8-pounders are not uncommon.

Although the bass in Bistineau move very little from season to season, they can be difficult to find in the cypress jungle. Unless you know what to look for, the trees all seem to look alike.

As a rule, trees in the vicinity of creek channels, ditches or any type of deeper channel running through the cypress flats will hold more fish than trees far up on the flats. The channels serve as migration routes and provide a deep-water refuge for fish that have been pushed out of the shallows by cold fronts or hot, still weather. Not all of these channels are obvious, so you must pay close attention to your depth finder. A break of even a foot can make a big difference.

In early March, the fish move into shallow water, usually hard-bottomed areas from 3 to 5 feet deep near shorelines or islands. But the fish are reluctant to stray far from the deeper channels.

Spawning begins in mid-March and continues into early April. Prime spawning areas include weedy flats; clean, sandy banks at depths of 2 feet or less; and cypress roots from 6 inches to 2 feet beneath the surface. Often, the fish are so shallow, you'll see their fins sticking out of the water.

To catch spawners in shallow water, try casting with a floating lizard, soft stickbait or 1/4- to 3/8-ounce tandem-blade spinnerbait. Or, twitch a floating minnow plug over the beds.

After spawning, the fish slide out slightly deeper, setting up on cypress flats or in sloughs with 7- to 10-foot-deep channels. They stay in these areas until mid-November, when the water cools enough for them to move back to the same areas they used prior to spawning. They feed heavily in these areas until late December.

Once you find a cypress flat or slough, you must learn to spot the right kind of cypress trees (p. 54). If you catch a fish on a certain type of tree or tree cluster, chances are, similar trees or clusters will also produce.

The major technique for fishing the cypress is *pitchin'* (p. 55). The fish almost always hold right up against the tree, so it's extremely important to get your lure in tight. Pitchin' enables you to get your lure under the branches and set it gently in the water precisely where you want it.

A 6½- to 7-foot, medium-heavy baitcasting rod and a narrow-spool reel filled with 14- to 17-pound mono are ideal for pitchin' 3/8- to 1/2-ounce jigs with pork or crawworm trailers, and Texas-rigged worms, lizards, and crawworms. Pitch the lure right up to the tree or just past it, hop it 2 or 3 times, then reel in and pitch to the next target. Bistineau's cypress trees have a comparatively small root system, so you'll seldom catch a fish more than 4 feet from the tree.

LURES for largemouth bass include: (1) Lunker City Slug-Go, a soft stickbait; (2) Bill Lewis Slap-Stick, a floating minnow plug; (3) Blue Fox Roland Martin Original Tandem Spinnerbait; (4) Toledo Tackle Lizard, Texas-rigged; (5) Sylo's Pro Lures Divin' Ace, a medium-running crankbait; (6) Stanley Hale's Craw Worm, Carolina-rigged; (7) bucktail jig; (8) Bulldog Flippin' Jig, a rubber-legged brushguard jig, with a pork trailer.

By early January, water temperatures in the low 50s drive shad and bluegills out to the main river channel, and the bass follow. You'll find them in deep, outside bends in the channel, especially around submerged brush piles. Another good wintertime spot is the junction of a slough and the main river channel.

The fish are sluggish in winter, but you can often catch them on a Carolina-rigged lizard. Rigged this way, the lizard sinks slowly, tempting the fish to bite.

Another good wintertime lure is a $\frac{3}{8}$- to $\frac{1}{2}$-ounce jig with a large pork trailer. As a rule, a jig will catch fewer, but larger, fish.

Late-winter and early-spring rains increase the river's flow, often causing it to rise 3 or 4 feet. You'll find bass along the downstream edges of sandbars in the main channel.

Where the current flows over the adjacent flats, look for the fish in channels running perpendicular to the current or in eddies that form behind large trees.

Anchor downstream of the spot you want to fish, cast upstream with a $\frac{1}{4}$-ounce bucktail jig and work it back slowly. This unusual technique produces some impressive catches under what most anglers consider to be adverse conditions.

How to Spot Productive Cypress Trees

POINT TREES. Active bass usually hold on the outside edge of the outermost trees in a cluster. When the fish are not active, they're usually found in pockets between the trees (below).

THICKETS. Dense clusters of trees in shallow water hold lots of minnows and sunfish, so they attract pre-spawn bass. Deeper thickets provide food and shade for bass during the summer.

EXPOSED ROOTS. Visible roots alongside cypress trees indicate mats of submerged roots. Bass are more likely to hold around trees with heavy root growth than around slick trees.

POCKETS. Trees growing in a ring form a pocket that often holds bass. If a pocket has submerged roots extending across it, like the exposed roots in the inset, it makes a good nesting site.

"GRANDDADDY" CYPRESS TREES. Huge trees in deep sloughs often hold bass in summer because the massive root systems offer more shade than those of smaller trees.

How to Pitch in the Cypress

PULL out enough line so the lure reaches back to the reel. Start the pitchin' motion with the reel at chest level and hold the rod at the 4 o'clock position. Keep the reel in free-spool and the spool tension loose.

SWEEP the rod forward, pulling the lure out of your hand. Stop the sweep at 2 o'clock so the lure maintains a low trajectory. If you bring the rod up too much, the lure will travel in a high arc and catch limbs.

STOP the lure in the precise spot by thumbing it *before* it touches down. The lure should enter the water with practically no splash. With the spool tension loose, the reel will backlash if you don't thumb it.

Tips for Catching Largemouths

TIP your jig with a larger pork chunk to slow the sink rate. Largemouths often hang beneath shallow cypress limbs. If the jig sinks too fast, they may ignore it or miss it.

LOOK for schools of bass around cypress tree points along the main river channel in summer. Sometimes these spots hold a dozen or more 2- to 5-pound bass.

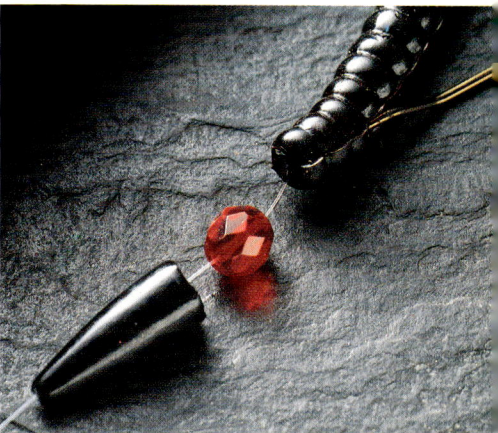

ADD a glass bead between your worm sinker and hook. The noise made by the sinker clicking against the bead helps attract largemouth bass in the dark-colored water.

Eastern Mountain Reservoirs

These deep, clear lakes offer superb multispecies fishing

Sometimes called *hill-land*, *highland* or *cove reservoirs*, these deep, steep-sided lakes are found in hilly or mountainous terrain, mainly in the eastern half of the country. The long, narrow basins exceed 100 feet in depth, and the creek arms (coves) may be several miles long.

Most of these lakes were made for the main purposes of power generation, flood control and navigation, so water levels vary greatly throughout the year. The level is gradually drawn down over the summer, sometimes by 50 feet or more, providing water to generate power and maintain downstream flows and, at the same time, making room for spring runoff.

These drastic water-level fluctuations limit growth of aquatic vegetation. Plants that took root at high water are exposed when the water drops, and those that took root at low water do not get enough sunlight when the water rises. Besides rocks, the main

types of cover are flooded timber and brush, which may also be in short supply because many of these basins were clear-cut before being filled.

Water fluctuations may also inhibit fish spawning. Any change in water level around spawning time reduces hatching success.

Although these lakes are normally very clear, spring runoff may color the water, especially in the upper end of the lake and in arms fed by good-sized creeks. Fertility levels in most mountain lakes are quite low, so the depths stay well-oxygenated throughout the year.

White bass and black bass, including largemouth, smallmouth and sometimes spotted, are native to most of these lakes. Striped bass or hybrids (white x striped bass) have been stocked in many mountain reservoirs. These species thrive because of the plentiful supply of shad. Crappies and sunfish inhabit secondary and tertiary creek arms, but the scarcity of woody cover limits their numbers.

Walleyes inhabited many mountain rivers and streams before they were dammed, but the native fish have now disappeared from most of the lakes and stocking is necessary to maintain walleye populations.

Mountain reservoirs with enough cold, well-oxygenated water in the depths are sometimes stocked with trout, primarily rainbows and browns.

The world's biggest walleyes and smallmouth bass are caught in mountain reservoirs. Greer's Ferry Lake, Arkansas, for instance, has produced several walleyes over 20 pounds. And the world-record smallmouth, 11 pounds, 15 ounces, was taken in Dale Hollow Reservoir, on the Kentucky-Tennessee border, in 1955.

Case Study:

Lake Cumberland, Kentucky

Sprawling through the Cumberland foothills of the Appalachians, this deep, cold mountain lake was created in 1950, when the U.S. Army Corps of Engineers completed the Wolf Creek Dam across the Cumberland River. The reservoir reduces flooding and the discharge generates enough power for a city of 375,000.

Like most mountain lakes, Cumberland has a deep, steep-sided basin and clear, infertile water. The depths stay cold and well-oxygenated all year. The main lake, which is 101 miles long, is only one mile across at its widest point. The main creek arms are 10 to 15 miles long, with many secondary and tertiary arms.

Although the lake has plenty of rocky points, bluff faces, humps and ledges, other types of natural fish cover are scarce. The entire lake basin was cleared of timber before the lake was flooded, and because the water level fluctuates as much as 50 feet over the year, there is little aquatic vegetation. However, the Kentucky Department of Fish and Wildlife Resources has placed hundreds of brush piles throughout the lake, and trees slide into the water as the bluffs erode or are cut intentionally by anglers.

As in most deep, cold reservoirs, the upper end of Lake Cumberland warms up earlier than the lower end. In most years, the difference is a week to 10 days. The upper end also tends to be murkier.

Although Lake Cumberland now boasts one of the country's premier striper fisheries, an equally good walleye fishery vanished when the Cumberland River was impounded.

In years past, the Cumberland River system was famous for its giant walleyes. Besides the 25-pound world record caught in Old Hickory Lake in 1960, the Kentucky record, a 21-pound, 8-ouncer, was taken in Lake Cumberland in 1958.

But the native Cumberland River walleyes were a river-spawning strain and, after the river was impounded, they gradually disappeared. Lake Cumberland was then restocked with the Lake Erie strain of walleyes, which are lake spawners, but do not grow as large.

Cumberland also has excellent fisheries for largemouth, smallmouth and spotted bass. Because the Wolf Creek Dam has a coldwater discharge, the river downstream of the reservoir stays cold enough for trout for a distance of 85 miles. Browns and rainbows are stocked annually, with many of the browns reaching trophy size.

Crappies (black and white) and sunfish (bluegill and longear) abound in Lake Cumberland, but they're on the small side. Other common species of gamefish include channel and flathead catfish, white bass and sauger.

Special regulations have been established to promote quality fishing in Lake Cumberland. The current limit on stripers is 3 per day, and there is a 15-inch minimum size limit on largemouths, smallmouths and walleyes.

Like most southern reservoirs, Cumberland has a healthy forage crop consisting mainly of threadfin and gizzard shad, in addition to plenty of crayfish and small sunfish. There's also a booming population of skipjack herring, an open-water forage fish that makes excellent striper food.

Besides fishing, the reservoir also supplies other forms of water-based recreation, such as swimming, waterskiing, pleasure boating and scuba diving. There are 11 privately owned marinas, 11 public boat ramps, 3 state parks with campgrounds and 16 private campgrounds.

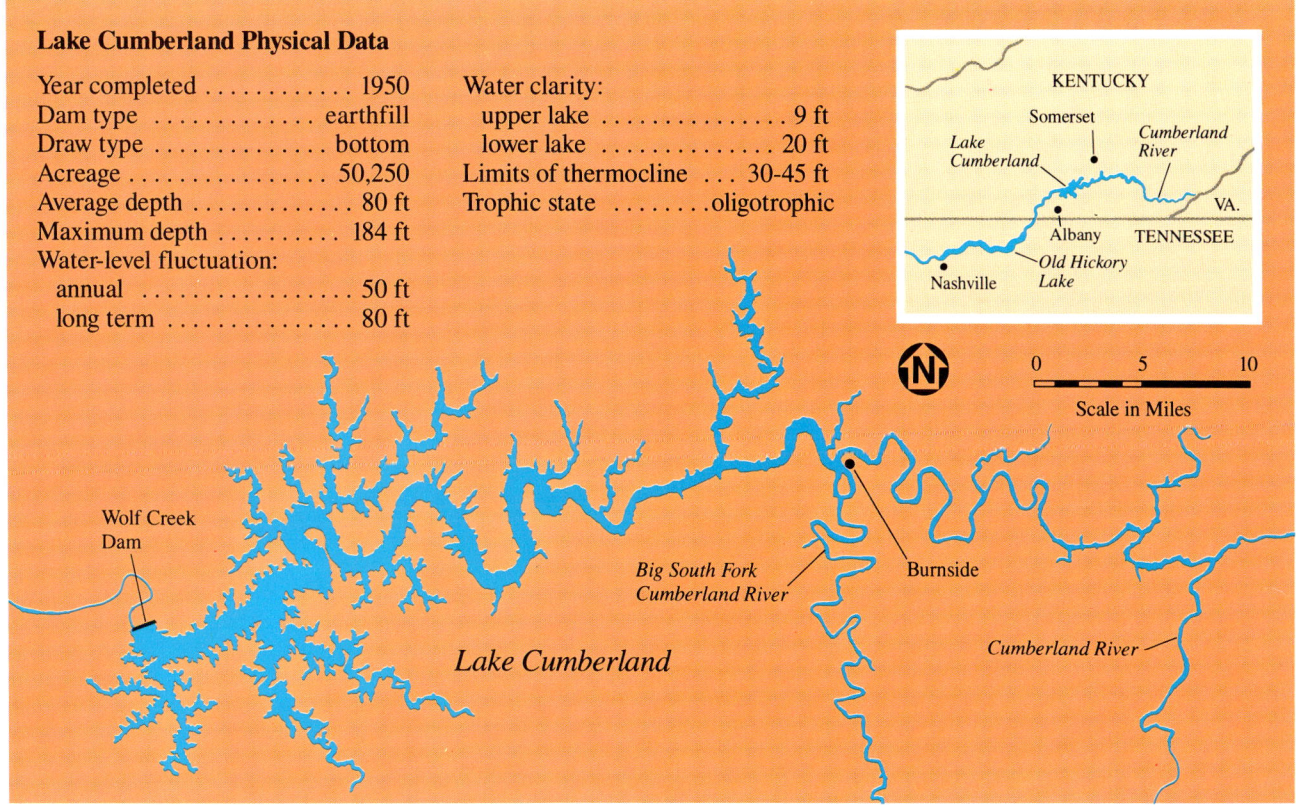

Lake Cumberland Physical Data

Year completed	1950
Dam type	earthfill
Draw type	bottom
Acreage	50,250
Average depth	80 ft
Maximum depth	184 ft
Water-level fluctuation:	
annual	50 ft
long term	80 ft
Water clarity:	
upper lake	9 ft
lower lake	20 ft
Limits of thermocline	30-45 ft
Trophic state	oligotrophic

Lake Cumberland Habitat

STEEP ROCKY BLUFFS make good year-round habitat for spotted bass and hold smallmouths in summer. The best bluffs have fallen trees for cover.

ROCKY POINTS with a gradual taper are top smallmouth areas from summer through winter. They're also good for summertime spots and largemouths.

SECONDARY CREEK ARMS are prime spawning areas for all black bass. Smaller tertiary arms also draw bass and sunfish at spawning time.

THE POOL AREA above the dam holds stripers all year. The riprapped shorelines draw smallmouths in summer and fall and walleyes year-round.

ROCK SLIDES may provide the only cover along steep bluffs. They hold walleyes, smallmouths, spots and stripers from summer through winter.

BRUSHY FLATS in shallow creek arms are excellent early-season largemouth spots. They also attract bluegills from spring through fall.

FALLEN TREES, intentionally cut for fish cover, draw largemouths and sunfish from spring through fall. They're best when the leaves are still green.

Main river channel

MAIN CREEK ARMS draw spawning stripers in spring. Largemouth, smallmouth and spotted bass can be found around points in the arms in summer.

MAIN-LAKE POINTS, especially those with timbered lips, hold largemouth, smallmouth and spotted bass from spring through fall and stripers in early spring.

BROKEN-ROCK BANKS with soft clay produce a mudline when the wind blows in, attracting walleyes and smallmouths from spring through fall.

Lake Cumberland:
Striped Bass

Veteran Lake Cumberland guides believe the next world-record striper may well be lurking in the lake's chilly depths. Cumberland has everything a striper needs to reach trophy size: cool, well-oxygenated water and an ample supply of food in the abundant shad and skipjack herring crop.

Twenty- to 30-pounders are routine during the peak fishing months and several 40-pounders are taken each season. The lake has even produced a few 50s, including the current Kentucky record, a 58-pound, 4-ouncer.

In January, stripers begin working their way up creek arms. Biologists call this migration a mock spawning run, because the fish cannot spawn successfully in the lake environment. The main wintertime technique is multi-line trolling with live baitfish, mainly shad and suckers, at depths of 30 to 60 feet. Cumberland trollers use the same technique as trollers on Elephant Butte (p. 35). But on Cumberland, side planers (p. 65) are often added to cover a wider swath of water.

You can also catch stripers in winter by vertically jigging with spoons or bucktail jigs. Make long upward sweeps of your rod to lift the lure 5 or 6 feet, then quickly lower the rod. The fish usually strike when the lure is sinking.

By early April, most stripers have reached the upper ends of the creek arms, where they will attempt to spawn. You can find some fish throughout the arms, but the heaviest striper concentrations will be around points in the upper halves, generally at depths of 20 feet or less.

The most effective springtime technique is casting a floating minnow plug or large chugger on a calm day. Work minnow plugs slowly enough so they stay near the surface and make a heavy wake; jerk chuggers hard, for maximum splash (p. 64-65). Spoons, spinners and bucktail jigs tipped with plastic curlytails also work well, as does slow-trolling with live baitfish. These techniques will take fish in the upper parts of the creek arms through May.

LURES for stripers include: (1) Cordell Pencil Popper, a chugger; (2) Blue Fox Super Vibrax spinner; (3) Cordell Redfin, a floating minnow plug; (4) Luhr-Jensen Crippled Herring, a jigging spoon; (5) live shad on trailer-hook rig with size 2/0 chemically sharpened hooks; (6) bucktail jig tipped with curlytail.

Jump-fishing for Stripers

LOOK for schools of stripers chasing shad on the surface. When you spot fish in the "jumps," motor to within 100 yards or so, then put down your trolling motor and sneak quietly to within casting distance.

CAST well past the surfacing fish, using a large floating minnow plug. If possible, position your boat so it is upwind of the school. This way, you can use the wind to your advantage for longer casts.

RETRIEVE the minnow plug just fast enough so its back is barely out of the water, creating a noticeable wake. If you reel too fast, the plug will dive beneath the surface, and the fish will usually ignore it.

In spring, you'll often see schools of stripers busting shad on the surface in morning and evening. But if you run your outboard up to the school and start casting, you'll spook them. Instead, sneak up with your trolling motor.

Although April and May are prime striper months, June and July are even better. The fish have completed their mock spawn and are gorging themselves on shad as they gradually work their way back down the creek arms. You'll still catch surface-feeding stripers by casting minnow plugs or chuggers in morning and evening. But the fish go as deep as 35 feet in midday, so you'll have to slow-troll with live bait or vertically jig with a jigging spoon or bucktail jig.

By early August, you'll find most of the stripers in the main lake, usually at depths of 35 to 60 feet, although a few remain in the mouths of major creek arms. Use a graph to scout for stripers or schools of shad along deep ledges or sharp drops near the old river channel. If you find shad, the stripers will usually be 5 to 20 feet beneath them. Slow-trolling with live bait and vertical jigging continue to produce, but the fish may be scattered. Some anglers prefer to troll jigs and minnow plugs on downriggers so they can cover more water.

Beginning in early November, stripers return to the mouths of creek arms, where they'll stay until January, when they begin to feel the spawning urge.

Wintertime fishing may be slow, especially when the water temperature dips below 50°F, but you can catch some fish by slow-trolling live baitfish or still-fishing cutbait on a gravel bottom at depths of 20 to 25 feet. Rig the bait as shown on the opposite page, cast it out, put your rod in a rod holder and wait for a bite.

Stripers roam open water in pursuit of food; the spot where you find them one day may be devoid of fish the next. If you're not sure where to look, start near the dam. The deep water above the dam is a prime wintertime striper area, but it holds some fish all year.

As a rule, stripers bite best very early or very late in the day. The bite extends later into the day in overcast weather than in calm, sunny weather. Prior to spawning, stripers feed heavily after dark, and sometimes through the night. Night fishing is usually best 2 or 3 days either side of the full moon.

A good all-purpose striper outfit consists of a 7-foot, medium-heavy baitcasting rod or flippin' stick and a heavy-duty reel with 17- to 20-pound mono. With a quality graph, you can see stripers or schools of shad, which indicate that you're in the right area and help you find the best depth. You'll need a large, aerated and insulated bait tank to keep baitfish alive, particularly in hot weather.

How to Use a Side-planer for Multi-line Trolling

ATTACH a rubber-jawed alligator clip with a split ring to replace the plastic clip, which could damage your line.

REPLACE the snap at the rear of the planer with a snap-swivel so the fish can't twist your line should it roll.

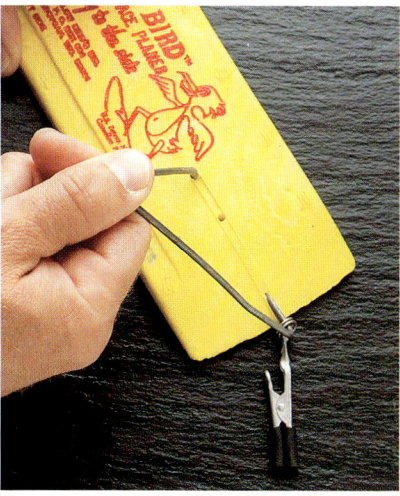

CAREFULLY BEND the metal bar on the planer slightly downward. This way, it will plane farther to the side.

SPLICE in a size 3/0 barrel swivel, and add a ½- to 1-ounce sinker and size 2/0 hook with a 2/0 trailer. Let out the desired amount of line, then attach the snap and clip.

FEED line as the planer pulls to the side; it will go out as far as 50 feet. When a fish strikes, the alligator clip will detach, and the planer will slide down to the sinker.

Striper-fishing Tips

MAKE a cutbait rig by slicing just behind the gill of a shad, sucker or bluegill, and rigging it on a size 3/0 to 5/0 hook with a 2-foot leader and a ½- to 1-ounce egg sinker.

JERK a large chugger hard enough to produce violent splashes. The surface commotion attracts stripers; they probably mistake the splashing for other stripers busting shad.

Lake Cumberland:
Largemouth Bass

A look at the old "braggin' boards" around Lake Cumberland shows that largemouth fishing during the lake's boom cycle in the 50s and 60s was incredible by today's standards. Stringers of 5- to 8-pounders were commonplace, with some as large as 11. You can still catch trophy bass, but the percentage of big ones is much lower.

Largemouths turn on in March, as warming water draws them into the upper ends of creek arms. As a rule, you'll find them farther up the arms than spotted or smallmouth bass.

Most tertiary and some secondary creek arms with shallow, discolored water and brushy cover will attract largemouths after a few warm spring days in a row. You'll find them at depths of 5 to 15 feet, often around submerged treetops. On sunny days, they often hold on steep shale banks, where the water is slightly warmer. Don't hesitate to fish under mats of floating debris and pollen, which provide good overhead cover.

The best way to fish tight pockets in the brush and to penetrate the mats of debris is flippin' (p. 29) with a 3/8-ounce jig-and-pig. Other good pre-spawn patterns are twitching floating minnow plugs on the surface, or bulging spinnerbaits along creek arm banks leading into spawning areas.

The fish normally start bedding in mid-April, when the water temperature reaches the mid-60s. They build their nests at depths of 1 to 4 feet, usually on gradually sloping banks with a gravel bottom, and often beneath overhanging tree limbs. Seldom do they spawn where a creek flows in.

LURES include: (1) Hart Beater, a buzzbait; (2) Bulldog Hawg Dawg Spinnerbait with craw-frog trailer; (3) Smithwick Rogue, a floating minnow plug; (4) Rebel Pop-R, a chugger; (5) Hopkin's Smoothie, a jigging spoon; (6) Poe's Super Cedar series 400, a deep-diving crankbait; (7) Penetrator Jig, a rubber-legged brushguard jig with pork trailer; (8) Lunker City Slug-Go, a soft stickbait; (9) Johnson Super Floater Worm; (10) Original Culprit, a Texas-rigged ribbontail worm.

If you can see largemouths on the beds, try twitching a floating worm or minnow plug right over them. You may have to skip the worm under limbs to reach the fish (below).

Bass throughout most of the lake complete spawning by mid-May. As the water warms into the 70s, they move farther down the creek arms, holding at depths of 8 to 20 feet on shoreline points and sharp breaks along the creek channels, especially where you find brush or stumps. Or, they may suspend just off these areas. Work the heavy cover and open water adjacent to it with soft stickbaits or topwaters, using medium-power spinning or baitcasting gear and 10-pound mono.

In early July, largemouths start moving deeper. Look for them on major points in the creek arms or the main lake, generally at depths of 25 to 45 feet. Rounded points with stumps generally hold the most fish. At times, you'll find largemouths suspended off points or bluffs. Summertime fishing can be tough because of heavy boat traffic, especially on weekends, so many anglers prefer night fishing. After dark, the fish move up to depths of 15 to 20 feet on the points. Work these areas with a plastic worm, Texas-rigged with a ¼- to ⅜-ounce bullet sinker, a jig-and-pig or a ⅜-ounce single-blade spinnerbait. To slow the sink rate and interest bigger bass, try tipping your spinnerbait with a pork chunk.

The summer pattern usually holds until mid-September. Then, largemouths move back up the creek arms and begin feeding more heavily. By early October, you'll find them at the upper ends of major creek arms, especially around downed trees, brush, broken ledge rock, boulders or indentations in the bank. Work water less than 15 feet deep with topwaters, such as buzzbaits and chuggers, or try bulging spinnerbaits on the surface. Morning and evening surface action continues until the water temperature drops to 55°F, normally in late November.

When the fish aren't feeding on the surface, try crankbaiting 15- to 25-foot flats adjacent to the creek channels with a deep-diving shad imitation.

As the water continues to cool, bass suspend at depths of 15 to 25 feet over creek channels from 30 to 60 feet deep, or they move into the main lake and suspend off major points. These suspended fish are tough to catch, but you can take a few by working the edges of the structure with a ¼- to ⅜-ounce jig-and-pig or by jigging a ¼- to ⅜-ounce spoon just off the breakline.

The best time to catch wintertime bass is a day or two after a heavy rain. Warmer, darker water flowing into the head of a creek arm draws bass into 5 to 15 feet of water and turns them on. As long as the water stays warmer than normal, a crankbait or spinnerbait retrieved along the mudline is an effective presentation.

Because the trees were cleared before the lake filled, there's usually no need for heavy tackle. Most anglers prefer spinning gear with 8- to 10-pound mono or a baitcasting outfit with 10- to 14-pound mono, all medium power. For flippin' in heavy brush, however, use a stiff flippin' stick with 25-pound mono.

In Cumberland's clear water, largemouths generally bite best early and late in the day, or whenever the light is low. But from late fall through early spring, the action is fastest on sunny afternoons, when the water is warmest.

How to Fish a Floating Worm

SKIP an unweighted, Texas-rigged worm under the cover, using a 6½-foot, fast-tip spinning outfit and 10-pound mono. Use a bulky worm because it has more surface area, making it easier to skip than a thin-bodied worm.

TWITCH the worm on a slack line, making it dart sideways while moving only slightly forward. Continue to twitch and hesitate, trying to keep the worm under the cover. If you jerk the worm on a taut line, it will just move forward.

WATCH closely when a fish bites; often it will grab the worm by the tail. Wait until the fish has the head of the worm in its mouth before attempting to set the hook. This strategy will greatly improve your hooking percentage.

Lake Cumberland:

Spotted Bass

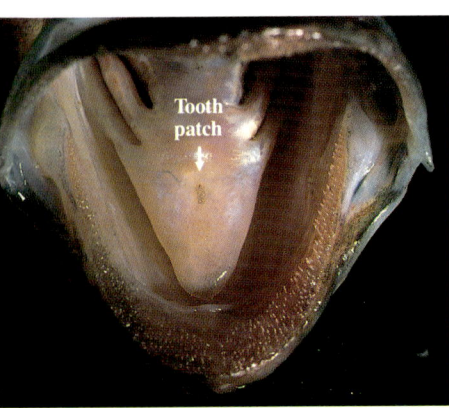

Tooth patch on tongue of spotted bass

What Cumberland's spots lack in size, they make up for in numbers. Although most of them run less than a pound, there's a chance to catch one over 5.

At first glance, spots look like largemouths, but they have wider blotches on the side and a small patch of teeth on their tongue (left). Their lower jaw does not extend past the eye, as it does on the largemouth.

As the water starts to warm in spring, spots move into coves off the main creek arms, especially those with plenty of brush and fallen trees. Toss a $\frac{1}{4}$-ounce willowleaf spinnerbait past the cover and retrieve right through it, keeping your rod tip high so the lure bulges the surface.

This technique produces until the fish start to spawn, which is normally about early to mid-April, a little before largemouths. They also build their nests in slightly deeper water, usually from 2 to 5 feet. and not as far back in the creeks. Often, they nest on shale ledges in pockets off the creek arms. Some fish spawn on points in the creek arms and main lake.

When you see spotted bass nesting, toss a small stickbait or floating minnow plug past the bed and retrieve so it runs directly over the fish. Work a stickbait with a slow, walk-the-dog retrieve; a minnow plug, with a twitch-and-pause retrieve. Another good

Tips for Finding Spotted Bass

STEEP ROCK LEDGES hold spots all year. They spend much of their time suspended in open water off the ledges, moving onto the ledges to feed on crayfish and baitfish.

OVERHEAD COVER, such as branches or horizontal rock overhangs along an otherwise clean ledge, is a magnet for spotted bass. Such cover will almost always hold a fish or two.

LURES include: (1) Mann's Classic Buzz Bait; (2) Stanley Vibra-Shaft Spinnerbait; (3) Mann's Little George, a tailspin; (4) Heddon Zara Puppy, a stickbait; (5) Storm Jr. Thunderstick, a floating minnow plug; (6) ball-head jig with soft-plastic ringworm; (7) Lunker City Slug-Go, a soft stickbait; (8) Stanley Jig, a rubber-legged brushguard jig with pork trailer; (9) Ditto Baby Fat Grub on split-shot rig.

technique for enticing spawners is twitching soft stickbaits (p. 71). Spotted bass continue spawning through late May.

Many fish that spawned in the creek arms return to the main lake after spawning, but some stay in the creek arms all year, dropping a little farther down toward the mouth. Use the same methods as in the pre-spawn and spawning periods, or try working a ¼-ounce jig-and-pig along steep shale banks and off rocky main-lake points.

Spotted bass can be difficult to catch in summer, because of their tendency to go very deep and suspend. By mid-June, it's not unusual to find them at depths of 45 to 60 feet, particularly off steep rocky points in the creek arms and on long main-lake points and deep reefs. Large spots are usually found in deeper water than small ones.

When spots are suspended, try fishing them at night or on cloudy days. Then, they move up to depths of 15 to 25 feet and hold tighter to structure, so they're easier to find and more aggressive.

The trick to finding summertime spots is to look for schools of shad; spots will probably be at the same depth. Productive techniques include counting down ¼- to ⅜-ounce tailspins and jigs tipped with soft-plastic grubs, and finesse fishing (p. 31) weenie worms and grubs.

In September, spots that were suspended in deep water begin to suspend closer to the surface, often only 20 feet down. They'll come up to strike a ¼- to ⅜-ounce spinnerbait bulged on the surface, or a ¼-ounce single-blade buzzbait. This pattern holds up through November.

Like largemouths, spots move into the warmer, darker water at the back ends of active creek arms following a heavy winter rain. A ¼-ounce tandem-blade willowleaf spinnerbait retrieved along the mudline is an excellent lure choice.

Because Lake Cumberland has very little submerged timber or brush, you can use the same lighter-than-normal tackle for spotted bass as you would for smallmouths (p. 71).

Lake Cumberland: Smallmouth Bass

Lake Cumberland's nearby sister lake, Dale Hollow Reservoir, is arguably the top trophy smallmouth lake in the country. Besides the current world record, just an ounce short of 12 pounds, the lake has produced at least five others over 10. Cumberland is not far behind, with several smallmouths around the 9-pound mark.

Surprisingly, the biggest smallmouths are taken in winter, from mid-November to mid-March. Look for them on rocky main-lake points at the junction of creek arms, usually at depths of 25 to 35 feet. Live 4- to 6-inch creek chubs or suckers, lip-hooked on a split-shot rig, account for most of the big ones. Simply cast the bait out, wait for it to reach bottom, then inch it in ever so slowly.

When the water begins to warm in spring, most smallmouths abandon the points and begin working their way up the creek arms. But they don't go as far up as largemouths or spots, and they stay in deeper water, usually 15 to 25 feet, until spawning time. The most effective pre-spawn technique is casting deep-diving crankbaits over points and along steep banks.

Spawning begins in mid-April. The fish nest over a bottom of broken shale, pea gravel or small rock, usually at depths of 6 to 10 feet, considerably deeper than largemouths or spots. A few fish spawn on main-lake points with a gravel bottom and scattered boulders. Spawning activity continues through mid-May.

Smallmouths are more aggressive than largemouths or spots at spawning time; catch them by twitching a floating minnow plug or soft stickbait (opposite page) over their beds.

LURES AND BAITS for smallmouths include: (1) Stanley Vibra-Shaft Spinnerbait; (2) Mister Twister Meeny jig; (3) Original Floating Rapala minnow plug; (4) Culprit Wienee Worm; (5) Culprit Jerk Worm, a soft stickbait; (6) Yakima Hawg Boss Super Toad, a deep-diving crankbait; (7) live sucker on a split-shot rig.

How to Work a Soft Stickbait

RETRIEVE a soft stickbait with 12- to 18-inch twitches, starting with your rod at 7 o'clock and moving it to 6 o'clock (right). Pause briefly between twitches. This motion gives the worm an enticing side-to-side gliding action (left).

Tips for Finding Smallmouth

CHUNK ROCK holds lots of smallmouths in summer, when they're feeding heavily on crayfish. The broken rock provides ideal crayfish cover.

LIVE TREES, especially willows, growing on rocky points draw summertime smallmouths early and late in the day. In midday, the fish slide into deeper water off the points.

After spawning, smallmouths concentrate on points in the main creek arms. You can catch some fish at depths of 10 to 15 feet during the day, but they usually bite better at night. Cast a ¼-ounce single-blade spinnerbait up to the bank; the fish generally hold at depths of 1 to 5 feet.

By early June, most smallmouths have worked their way to outer creek-arm points or to long main-lake points and reefs that top out at 20 to 30 feet. The fish gradually slide deeper as the water warms, and some of them suspend. By early July, most of them are at depths of 20 to 30 feet; by mid-August, 30 to 60 feet. As a rule, big smallmouths hang much deeper than small ones.

Like spotted bass, smallmouths are easiest to catch at night in summer. Using the same type of spinnerbait as in the post-spawn period, cast over a point or reef and allow the lure to helicopter down 15 to 25 feet before starting your retrieve.

In September, cooling water begins to draw smallmouths shallower, and some of them move back into the creek arms. The smaller fish move in first and the big ones follow a few weeks later.

Using ¼-ounce curlytail jigs or weenie worms on split-shot rigs, work depths of 10 to 15 feet on points and flats adjacent to the creek channel. You can catch fish in these areas through December.

From late fall through the pre-spawn period, smallmouths usually bite best in late afternoon, when the water temperature peaks. Mornings are better from spawning time until early summer, when the fish begin feeding heavily at night. Keep in mind, however, that you can catch some smallmouths at night throughout the year, especially when daytime conditions have been clear and calm.

For live-bait, minnow-plug, weenie-worm or jig fishing, use a 6- to 6½-foot, medium-power spinning outfit and 6- to 8-pound mono. For crankbaiting and spinnerbaiting, a 6- to 6½-foot, medium-power baitcasting outfit with 8- to 10-pound mono is a better choice. The lack of submerged timber in Lake Cumberland makes it possible to get away with light tackle.

Bassin' in Rivers

To anglers who do most of their bass fishing in lakes, fishing in rivers and streams can be frustrating. The bass behave differently in moving water, so you must alter your techniques to fit the situation.

In rivers, conditions are constantly changing. A heavy rain can transform a gently gurgling stream into a raging torrent within hours. You must know how to adjust to changes in water level, clarity and current speed.

But rivers can also be forgiving. When a cold front shuts down bass fishing in lakes, river fish continue to bite. They also seem less affected by changes in air temperature and cloud cover.

This chapter provides the information you need to fish the most important types of moving water that bass inhabit. You'll learn the characteristics of each of these river types and how they differ from other bass rivers.

Case studies show you exactly where to find every kind of bass that rivers of each type hold throughout the year. They also show you the best techniques for catching them, along with many of the tricks that local experts use to give themselves an edge.

You may never fish one of the case-study rivers, but the information presented applies to many other rivers of that type. What you learn in reading about the Cooper River in South Carolina, for instance, will apply to practically any tidewater river along the eastern seaboard.

Midwestern Mainstem Rivers

When fishing a mainstem river, you'll always catch something, but you're never sure what it will be

Because of the tremendous importance of river transportation in the 1800s, most large midwestern cities developed along the banks of major waterways. Today, millions of anglers live within easy driving distance of these rivers.

A *mainstem* river could be defined as the major river into which all other rivers and streams in a given drainage system flow. As a rule, these rivers share the following characteristics:

- large size, usually 10,000 cubic feet per second or more.
- murky water, especially if located in farm country.
- pattern of severe flooding and dramatic changes in water level.
- dams along their course, to control floods and maintain water levels for navigation.
- a diverse fish population; fish can move into the river from a large tributary network.

Many of these rivers are still important navigation routes, accommodating barges carrying commodities such as grain, coal and oil. As such, the rivers are often subject to dredging, channelization and pollution. In some, the gamefish population has dwindled to the point where there is very little sport fishing.

But big rivers are remarkably resilient; despite man's disregard for these mainstem waterways, many still provide excellent multispecies fishing. Some support a dozen or more gamefish species and even more species of roughfish.

Mississippi River, Minnesota and Wisconsin

THE UPPER MISSISSIPPI has a complex network of backwater lakes, sloughs and connecting channels.

Case Study:
Upper Mississippi River, Minnesota & Wisconsin

One of the best examples of a midwestern mainstem river is the Upper Mississippi where it splits the states of Minnesota and Wisconsin. The 118-mile stretch from Lock and Dam No. 3 upstream of Red Wing, Minnesota, to Lock and Dam No. 8 near Genoa, Wisconsin, is regarded as the river's most varied and productive zone.

When the U.S. Army Corps of Engineers built these dams in the 1930s, thousands of acres of marshland adjacent to the river were flooded, creating a maze of backwater lakes connected to the main river by narrow cuts.

"Ol' Man River isn't really a river at all," wrote Mel Ellis in the *Milwaukee Journal* in 1949. "In fact, he's a hundred rivers and a thousand lakes and more sloughs than you could explore in a lifetime."

The navigation channel in this stretch averages 300 feet wide and 12 feet deep, although there are holes more than 30 feet deep. Along the channel is the *main-channel border,* a shallower zone extending from the edge of the channel to shore. In this area are numerous wing dams, structures made of rocks and sticks that deflect the current toward the center of the river. Constructed in the late 1800s and early 1900s, the wing dams help keep the channel from filling in with sand.

Current speed in the main channel measures 1 to 2 mph at normal water stage; up to 6 in high water. Current-tolerant species, such as smallmouth bass, white bass, catfish, walleye, sauger and sturgeon,

Because of the diverse habitat, this portion of the river supports a variety of gamefish and roughfish.

THE LOWER MISSISSIPPI, from Alton, Illinois, downstream, has little habitat diversity because the river is confined between high banks or levees. Roughfish predominate, with few gamefish species present.

spend most of their time in the main channel or along the main-channel border. Man-made cover is very important in this zone. Besides wing dams, man-made cover includes riprapped shorelines, bridge pilings, and the rock piles that support channel markers.

Navigation dams are spaced at 10- to 44-mile intervals along the Upper Mississippi River. Each has a lock to allow passage of boats, including river barges. The dams are not high compared to dams on most other major rivers. They hold back only 6 to 9 feet of water at normal stage. Most of the dams are too low to create a lakelike zone upstream, although the river above a dam is nonetheless called a pool. Each dam has a number, and the pool extending upstream to the next dam has the same number. For example, Pool 5 encompasses all of the water area from Lock and Dam No. 5 upstream to Lock and Dam No. 4.

The dams provide good habitat for many kinds of gamefish, especially the current-tolerant species. The large eddies that form below the gates and along the edges of the fast-water zone provide refuge from the swift current.

Backwaters generally have little or no current, average less than 5 feet deep, and have excellent cover, including flooded trees and stumps, and lush stands of submerged and emergent vegetation. They make ideal habitat for slack-water species such as largemouth bass, northern pike, sunfish and crappies. Other species, such as smallmouth bass and catfish, use the backwaters for spawning.

Although backwaters may be found anywhere in a pool, the most extensive ones are usually at a pool's lower end, where the dam elevates water levels the most.

Some of the backwater areas are vast, covering several thousand acres. In these areas, the river (including the main channel and backwaters) may be more than 3 miles wide.

Another type of habitat found in the Upper Mississippi is a *river lake*. The best example is Lake Pepin,

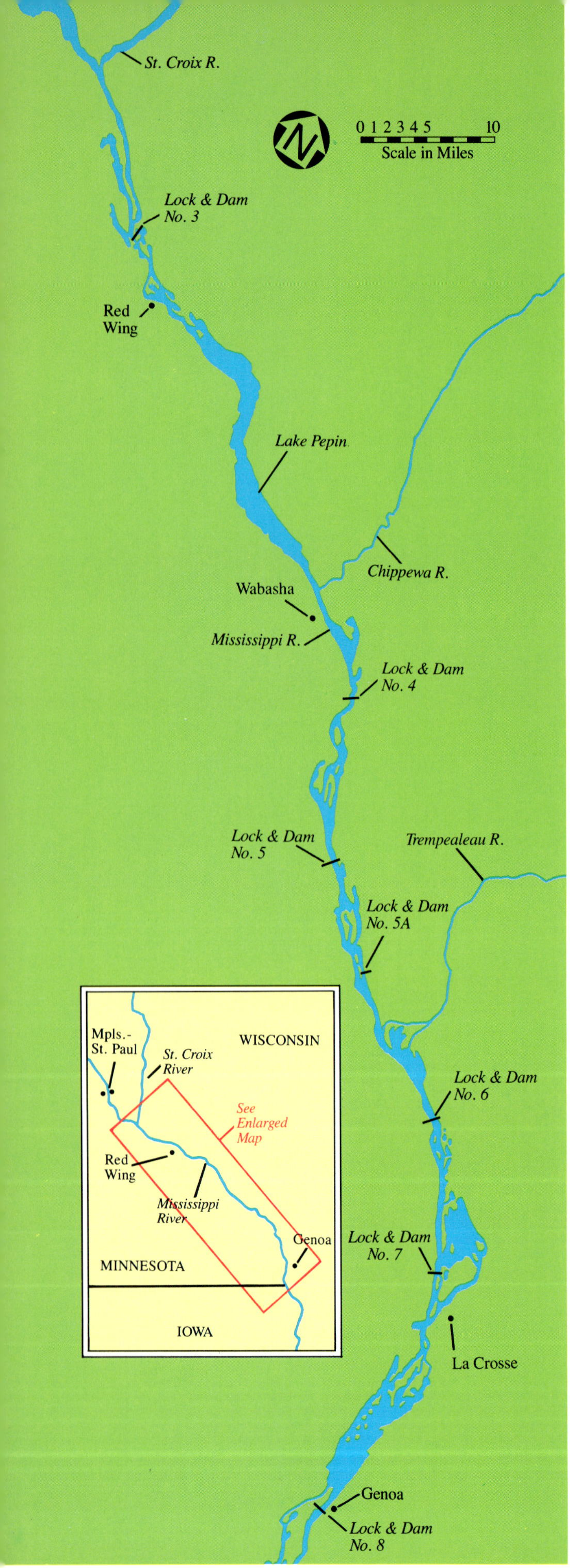

YOUNG-OF-THE-YEAR SHAD (top) are ideal for food. They predominate because of the annual die-off. If not for the die-off, there would be more older shad (bottom), too large for food, and fewer young ones.

a 25,000-acre body of water formed by the delta of the Chippewa River. The delta acts somewhat like a dam, partially blocking the flow of the Mississippi and creating a lakelike environment upstream. The lake has very little current, except at the extreme upper and lower ends. The average depth is about 20 feet; the maximum, 65. Lake Pepin holds good populations of practically all gamefish found in the river.

One of the biggest challenges in fishing a big river, especially one with such diverse habitat, is locating fish at different water stages. Runoff generally peaks in mid- to late April, and the water level may rise as much as 20 feet above normal. As the water rises, fish abandon their normal haunts. They continue moving until the water level returns to normal. Rainy weather in summer and fall may cause the river to rise several feet, enough to move gamefish out of their usual habitat. But these movements are seldom as dramatic as those associated with spring runoff.

High-water mark

The primary food for most of the river's gamefish is the gizzard shad, a species found in few other waters in the region. This portion of the river is at the northern edge of the shad's range, so most of the annual crop dies off in winter because of the cold water. But some shad survive the winter by staying in spring holes and warmwater discharges

GAMEFISH in the Upper Mississippi grow rapidly because of the abundant food supply. The highly fertile water teems with plankton that nourishes invertebrates and baitfish. The Mississippi's fast-growing gamefish have smaller heads and fatter bodies than fish from most other waters in the region. Notice the difference in body shape between a Mississippi River bass and a slower-growing bass (inset) from a nearby lake.

from power plants. At first glance, the shad die-off would seem counterproductive to good fish production. But the reverse is actually true (see opposite page).

Most of the fishing on the Upper Mississippi is done from small boats, although there is a great

Fishing barge

deal of bank fishing and some fishing from commercially operated barges moored in the tailwaters of several of the dams. For a small daily fee, barge operators will ferry you out to fish from a floating platform anchored in a prime fishing area.

Jon boats and semi-V aluminum boats from 14 to 16 feet are popular in this area. Because they draw very little water, they can run cuts and sloughs where larger boats would bottom out.

One of the major environmental problems on the river is dredging. The main channel must be dredged frequently by the Corps of Engineers to maintain the minimum 9-foot channel depth necessary for barge traffic. The dredge spoil (10 percent sand,

Spoil from dredging operation

90 percent water) is pumped onto land adjacent to the river, often spilling into backwater lakes and sloughs and channels leading into the backwaters. The sand smothers bottom organisms and plant life, greatly reducing the backwaters' capacity to produce gamefish.

The fishing season for most gamefish is open year around on this part of the Mississippi. Prime fishing times for each species vary considerably, but you can bet that something will be biting every month of the year.

Upper Mississippi River Physical Data (at Wabasha)	
Average width	1,000 ft
Average depth	12 ft
Gradient	low
Clarity	1.5 ft
Color	brown
Discharge (cubic feet per second)	33,300
Winter low temperature	32° F
Summer high temperature	85° F

Mississippi River Habitat

MAIN CHANNEL is home to a variety of gamefish, mainly walleyes, saugers, smallmouths, white bass and catfish.

RIPRAP shorelines provide better cover than sand or muck. They attract practically all species of gamefish.

WING DAMS deflect water toward the center of the river. They're best for smallmouths and walleyes.

CLOSING DAMS were built to restrict the flow into backwaters, keeping more water in the main channel. The rocky structures attract smallmouths and walleyes.

RUNNING SLOUGHS have a major inlet and outlet, so there is a noticeable current. They are well suited to smallmouth bass, catfish and, in spring, walleyes.

SIDE CHANNELS connect backwater lakes and sloughs to the main channel. They make good habitat for largemouth and smallmouth bass, walleyes and catfish.

BACKWATER LAKES are deeper and have less submerged vegetation than dead sloughs, but hold the same fish.

DEAD SLOUGHS have no outlet, so the water is slack. They hold largemouths, panfish and pike.

TAILWATERS are known for spring walleye and sauger fishing, but draw most river gamefish some time of year.

Upper Mississippi River:
Largemouth Bass

The Mississippi's weedy, stump-strewn backwaters are made-to-order for largemouth bass. The fish start to bite in late April, when the water warms to about 55° F. In early season, the warmest water generally holds the most bass.

From late April through May, you'll find bass in beds of green weeds around stumps close to deep water. Work the weeds using spinnerbaits, or run a bright-colored crankbait over the weedtops. For fishing pockets in thick beds of coontail or lily pads, try flippin' with a jig-and-pig. A slower-than-normal retrieve works best in spring.

Weedy backwaters produce bass throughout the summer, but some of the fish move into the main channel and side channels, where there is more current. When changes in weather, such as cold fronts, cause fishing in the backwaters to slow, bass in these channels continue to bite. The fish are not actually in the current but hold in eddies near current.

Prime channel areas include deep eddies near the head of an island, and wing dams with slow-moving water. You'll also find bass on sand flats near deep water, around beaver houses, along riprapped shorelines or islands, and in eddies created by bridge pilings. Few weeds grow in these areas, so most of the bass hang near timber.

Work the timber by flippin' a jig-and-pig or casting a crankbait into an opening, then bumping the wood as you retrieve. Plastic worms and spinnerbaits also account for a lot of bass. When fishing early or late in the day or during a light rain, try retrieving a buzzbait tight to the cover.

In July and August, largemouths may follow schools of surface-feeding shad. You can find the shad by looking for ripples on the surface on a calm day. Select a light-colored lure that you can cast a long way, such as a Sonar, jig or crankbait. Then retrieve it through or just below the shad. Be sure to stay far enough away to avoid spooking the bass.

Bass start to school in September and October. In early fall, you can still catch them in the main channel and side channels, but by mid-September most are moving into the backwaters. Weeds in the backwaters are beginning to die, so bass move into deep holes to find cover and spend the winter. But if you can find green weeds, you'll probably find bass. Another good fall location is a riprapped railroad embankment in the backwaters.

LURES AND RIGS for largemouths include: (1) Bomber Model A, (2) Heddon Sonar, (3) Buzz-ard buzzbait, (4) Lazer Eye spinnerbait, (5) River Rat Ringworm rigged Texas-style using a 2/0 hook and a bullet sinker pegged with a toothpick, (6) Hildebob rubber-skirted jig tipped with a size 11 Uncle Josh pork frog.

When bass are in deep holes or along deep banks, try a crankbait or jig-and-pig. On a warm, sunny day, they may move up on shallow flats next to the deep water, where you can catch them on spinnerbaits. Use larger baits in fall and work them more slowly than in summer. Fishing stays good until the water cools below 50° F.

During the first few weeks after freeze up, ice fishermen catch some largemouths in shallow, weedy backwaters. Most bass are taken by accident by pike anglers using tip-ups baited with big minnows, or panfish anglers jigging teardrops tipped with waxworms.

Largemouths bite best during periods of stable weather, although the action is usually fast just before a front. As a rule, cloudy days are better than sunny ones; mornings and evenings better than midday.

Upper Mississippi largemouths run from 1 to 3 pounds and occasionally reach weights up to 6. They spend a good deal of their time around dense cover, so most anglers use beefy tackle. A medium-heavy 5½- to 6-foot baitcasting outfit with 17-pound mono is a good all-around choice. For pitchin' (below), use a reel with a thumb bar and set the spool tension as loose as possible.

Pitchin' for Largemouths

QUIETLY APPROACH the cover you plan to fish. Stop within 15 to 20 feet of the cover.

POINT the rod tip down so you can cast with an upward motion; hold the lure in your other hand.

PITCH the lure with a low trajectory. To minimize splash, thumb the reel just before the lure hits.

Upper Mississippi River: Smallmouth Bass

In the early 1900s, the Upper Mississippi was renowned for its smallmouth bass fishing. The fish were big and plentiful. Four- to six-pounders were common, and a few exceeded 7.

The river still produces trophy smallmouths, but today you'll have to work a little harder for them. Most of the fish run 1½ to 2½ pounds.

Beginning in early May, smallmouths move into certain backwater areas where they spawn each year. Like largemouths, they start to bite when the water temperature reaches about 55° F. The best areas are less than 5 feet deep, have firm sand or gravel bottoms with rocks, logs, stumps or brush for cover, and are near but not in current.

The most popular springtime lure is a ⅛- to ¼-ounce jig–plastic grub combo. Other good lures include 4-inch plastic worms; small, shallow-running crankbaits and minnow plugs; and ⅛- to ¼-ounce spinnerbaits. With any of these lures, a slow retrieve works best in spring.

The bass finish spawning by late May, then filter out of the backwaters. Smallmouths everywhere love rocks, and the Mississippi River is no exception. Starting in early June, they start to congregate off rocky points, along riprapped banks and along the upstream lips of main-channel wing dams. The best wing dams have little sand or silt and plenty of exposed rock. Rocky areas in side channels also hold

LURES AND RIGS for smallmouths include: (1) Fuzz-E-Grub, (2) Lightning Bug, (3) River Rat Ringworm, Texas-rigged with a bullet sinker, (4) Mepps Bass Killer, (5) Original Floating Rapala, (6) Shad Rap.

How to Fish a Wing Dam with a Popper

ANCHOR upstream of a wing dam, within easy fly-casting distance of the upper lip. Select a spot where the current is moderate. As a rule, the current gets slower as you move toward shore; faster toward the outside end of the wing dam.

CAST downstream; the popper should alight on top of the wing dam. Twitch the popper so it barely disturbs the surface (inset), pause a few seconds, strip in 1 to 2 feet of line, then give it another twitch. When the popper is about 10 feet above the wing dam, pick up and cast again.

smallmouths, as do sand flats along channel edges. Weedy flats hold more fish than those with clean sand bottoms. Another good spot is an eddy around a bridge piling with a rock pile at its base. As a rule, you'll find the fish at depths of 12 feet or less through the summer.

When smallmouths are rooting crayfish from the rocks, they'll hit deep-diving crankbaits; ¼- to ⅜-ounce jig-grub or jig-and-pig combos, or tube jigs; and 6-inch Texas-rigged plastic worms. Fly fishermen enjoy fast surface action early or late in the day on divers, poppers and sliders.

You can catch some smallmouths in these rocky areas through the summer and into fall. Most of the bass move shallower in fall, but the biggest ones hang on the deep ends of the wing dams. Fall fishing peaks in late September or early October as the fish start feeding up for winter. They're more concentrated than in summer, so if you catch one, there's a good chance there will be more. This late-season feeding binge usually starts when the water temperature drops below 60° F. Use the same lures you would in summer. Smallmouths feed very little from late fall through the winter months.

Like largemouths, smallmouths bite best in stable weather, on overcast days, and in morning and evening. But early or late in the season, the action is often fastest in the middle of the day.

Serious smallmouth anglers carry at least two rods: a 5½- to 6-foot medium-power baitcasting outfit with 10- to 14-pound mono for crankbaits, spinnerbaits, plastic worms and jig-and-pig combos; and a 5- to 6-foot medium-light spinning outfit with 4- to 6-pound mono, for light jigs and minnow plugs. For fly-fishing, use a 9-foot, 7-weight rod with a floating, weight-forward line.

Tidewater Rivers

Because of their link to the sea, tidewater rivers produce gamefish in tremendous abundance and variety

At first glance, tidewater rivers resemble other types of warmwater rivers, but the likeness is superficial. The tidal influence causes major differences, not only in the species of fish you can expect to catch, but in when, where and how you fish.

Tidewater rivers usually produce more and bigger fish than similar inland rivers. Most have vast acreages of food-producing flats off the main channel. The marine organisms that inhabit the river also mean a greater variety of food for fish.

To fish these rivers effectively, it helps to understand some basic principles about tides. Tidal fluctuations result mainly from the moon's gravitational pull on the earth's surface (see diagram at right).

This pull creates a bulge of water that stays under the moon as the earth revolves. Centrifugal forces create another bulge of about equal magnitude on the side of the earth opposite the moon. The earth makes one revolution relative to the moon about every 25 hours, and during this time, a given point on the earth experiences a high tide as it passes under the moon, a low tide as it turns away from the moon, another high tide as it passes under the bulge opposite the moon, and another low tide as it turns toward the moon again.

Atlantic coastal waters experience this typical pattern of two highs and lows every 25 hours; a low tide occurs about 6¼ hours after a high. But the angle of the moon, the shape of the ocean's basin and

Cooper River, South Carolina

other geophysical factors may result in a different pattern. Some regions, such as the Gulf coast, experience only one high and one low every 25 hours; the low comes about 12½ hours after the high.

Tides vary considerably in different locations. Some places on earth have tides of 30 feet or more; in others, the tide is only 1 foot. And the amount of tidal fluctuation changes throughout the month. The greatest fluctuation, called a spring tide, takes place during the full moon and new moon; the smallest (neap tide) occurs during the first and last quarter moon.

Weather conditions along the coast also affect water levels in the river. The levels are higher than nor-

How the Zones of Tidal Influence Change Throughout the Day

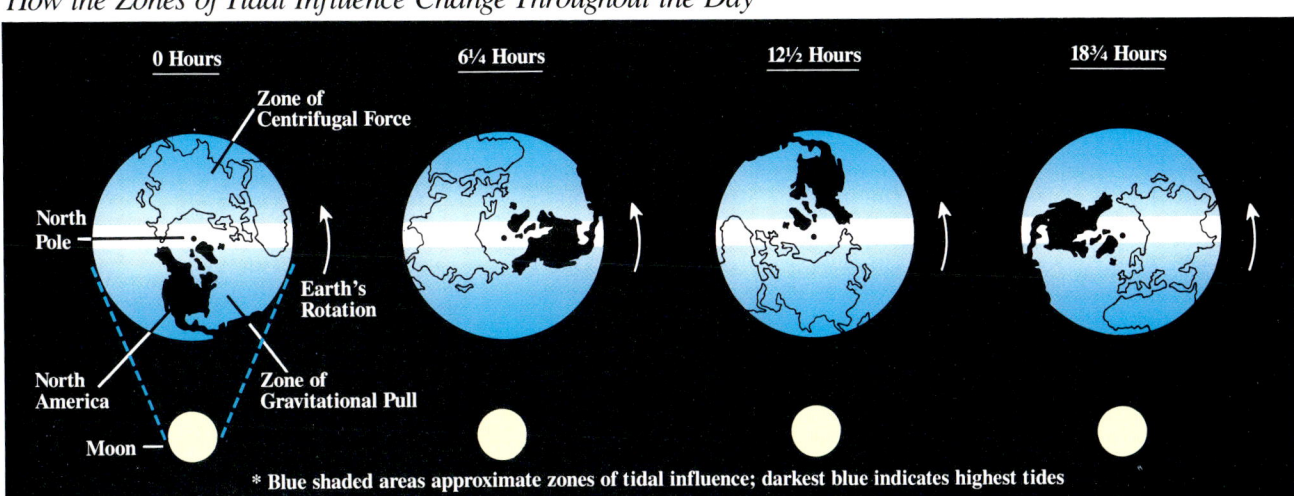

* Blue shaded areas approximate zones of tidal influence; darkest blue indicates highest tides

mal with onshore winds; lower with offshore winds. Water levels are higher than normal with a low barometer; lower with a high barometer.

As the tide rises in coastal areas, salt water flows up coastal rivers. The higher the tide, the farther its effects extend upstream. Tidal peaks occur at different times at different points on the river. How fast the tide moves upstream depends on the configuration of the channel; the straighter and deeper it is, the faster the tide progresses.

The downstream reaches of tidewater rivers are nearly as salty as seawater, the middle reaches are brackish, and the upper reaches are fresh. The extent of tidal influence varies in different rivers, depending on the amount of streamflow, gradient of the river channel, and location of dams or waterfalls.

In a high-gradient river, only the lower portion is affected by tides. In a low-gradient river, tidal influence may extend more than 100 miles upstream. Of course, a dam or waterfall prevents tidal influence above that point, assuming the dam or falls is higher than the tidal rise.

Tide Table: South Carolina Coast

Date		AM	Feet	PM	Feet
Wednesday April 19	Hi	7:43	5.0	8:09	5.7
	Lo	1:39	0.3	1:47	0.3
Thursday April 20	Hi	8:19	5.0	8:45	5.8
	Lo	2:19	0.2	2:23	0.2
Friday April 21	Hi	8:53	4.9	9:19	5.8
	Lo	2:59	0.2	2:57	0.3
Saturday April 22	Hi	9:28	4.7	9:52	5.8
	Lo	3:37	0.3	3:32	0.3
Sunday April 23	Hi	9:59	4.6	10:27	5.7
	Lo	4:16	0.4	4:06	0.4
Monday April 24	Hi	10:33	4.5	11:05	5.7
	Lo	4:55	0.5	4:41	0.5
Tuesday April 25	Hi	11:13	4.5	11:50	5.6
	Lo	5:37	0.7	5:23	0.6

To find times of high and low water add or subtract as indicated.

Sullivan's Island: High, −8 minutes. Low, −12 minutes. Isle of Palms: High, −25 minutes. Low, −28 minutes. Folly Beach: High, −8 minutes. Low, −14 minutes.

Georgetown: High, +1 hour and 34 minutes. Low, +2 hours and 29 minutes. Cape Romain: High, −22 minutes. Low, −17 minutes. McClellanville: High, +27 minutes. Low, +25 minutes. Sewee Bay: High, +13 minutes. Low, +11 minutes. Rockville: High, +19 minutes. Low, +7 minutes.

Beaufort: High, +1 hour and 7 minutes (approximate). Low, +52 minutes (approximate). Edisto Beach: High, −26 minutes (approximate). Low, −35 minutes (approximate).

TIDE TABLES list times of high and low tides and expected tide levels at specific coastal cities or harbors. Tables may also tell you how much time to add for up-river locations or subtract for downriver locations.

Case Study:

Cooper River, South Carolina

INCOMING TIDE means water is flowing into the rice fields. The rising water covers vegetation and old dock posts, and makes it possible to navigate almost anywhere in the field.

The Cooper River in South Carolina's coastal plain is considered one of the top fishing rivers on the Eastern Seaboard. Besides a healthy population of good-sized largemouth bass, the river also supports a tremendous catfish population and plenty of panfish, particularly redears, or shellcrackers. Anglers often catch saltwater species such as redfish, summer flounder, spotted seatrout and striped bass, and there are seasonal runs of American shad and blueback herring.

During the 1700s, giant rice plantations bordered many of the low-country rivers, including the Cooper. Dikes separated the rice paddies from the main channel, and water levels in the paddies were regulated by wooden gates on channels leading to the river. The plantations relied on slave labor to maintain the paddies and harvest the rice.

The Civil War ended the plantation system, and the paddies started to deteriorate. Eventually, the dikes and control gates washed out, leaving a vast network of backwater lakes whose water level changed in concert with the river. Today these backwaters, which are still called "rice fields," attract many species of gamefish.

The cuts, or breaks, leading into the rice fields make excellent feeding areas, as do the ditches across the fields. Dug to allow passage of rice boats, the ditches make ideal havens for bass, especially at low tide. And the extra depth makes it easier to run a motor.

The Cooper River arises from two branches. The West Branch gets most of its flow from Lake Moultrie (one of the Santee-Cooper lakes). The Lake Moultrie discharge flows through a man-made tailrace canal for 4 miles before joining Wadboo Creek to form the West Branch. The West Branch then flows on for 12 miles before joining the East Branch. The junction of the two branches is called the "Tee." The main branch then flows to the south for 33 miles, joining the Ashley and Wando rivers near the lower end before emptying into Charleston Harbor.

The Pinopolis Dam, which forms Lake Moultrie, is a hydroelectric dam. When water is released to gen-

OUTGOING TIDE means water is flowing out of the rice fields. As the water level drops, vegetation and dock posts become exposed, and boat fishermen oblivious to the tides are trapped in water too shallow to navigate.

Cooper River Physical Data (downstream of the Tee)	
Average width	700 ft
Average depth	20 ft
Gradient	low
Clarity	2 ft
Color	brown
Discharge (cubic feet per second)	4,500
Winter low temperature	43° F
Summer high temperature	88° F

erate electricity, the river rises. Both high and low tides are higher when electricity is being generated.

In 1985, the U.S. Army Corps of Engineers completed a canal to divert 70 percent of the Cooper River's flow into the nearby Santee River. The idea was to reduce the rate at which the Cooper deposited silt into Charleston Harbor. The Corps, however, miscalculated the effects of the diversion. The result was greater saltwater intrusion than originally intended. Besides rusting out the equipment of many factories along the river, the salt water changed the mix of fish species. Each year saltwater species move farther and farther upriver. Recently, anglers reported a school of jack crevalle in the tailrace of the Pinopolis Dam.

Although saltwater fish are becoming more common in the upper river, most are still found in the lower 20 miles. Largemouth bass, white perch, channel catfish and occasionally blue catfish are caught below the Tee. But it is unusual to find other freshwater species that far downstream because they are not as salt tolerant.

FRESHWATER SPECIES	SALT TOLERANCE
Largemouth bass	high
Channel catfish	high
White perch	high
Blue catfish	moderate
Redear sunfish	moderate
Flathead catfish	low
Bluegill	low
Redbreast sunfish	low
Black crappie	low
SALTWATER SPECIES	FRESHWATER TOLERANCE
Summer flounder	high
Striped bass	high
Red drum	moderate
Spotted seatrout	moderate

Cooper River Habitat

THE PINOPOLIS DAM tailrace attracts a variety of gamefish, including striped bass, American shad and blue catfish.

BRIDGES, especially those with wood pilings alongside the concrete piers, break the current and provide good cover for gamefish.

RICE FIELDS are ideal spots for largemouth bass and panfish to avoid the current and find cover.

DITCHES in rice fields offer bass and panfish a deepwater refuge when the tide is low.

CUTS into the rice fields are feeding spots for a variety of fish. Many have wooden pilings for cover.

DEEP HOLES, along outside bends or near rice field cuts, hold catfish, stripers and, in winter, largemouths.

VEGETATION along the river's edge makes excellent panfish cover, especially around spawning time.

FEEDER CREEKS and canals draw largemouth bass and panfish, often to the upper ends, at spawning time.

Cooper River:
Largemouth Bass

Everyone in the Southeast has heard about the great bass fishing in the Santee-Cooper lakes, but few know how good Cooper River bass fishing can be.

Most local anglers concentrate on the lakes, where the fishing is not complicated by the influence of the tides. Those who have taken time to learn the river, however, have equally good success. And they can fish the river on many days when high winds keep anglers off the big water.

Like all fish in the Cooper River system, bass grow big. Seven- to nine-pounders are not unusual, and the river has produced fish over 12 pounds. Medium to heavy baitcasting tackle with 14- to 20-pound line is recommended for extracting big bass from the heavy weeds and woody cover common on the river.

You can catch Cooper River bass year around. Most of them winter in deep holes adjacent to the rice fields, but starting in early March, they move into the cuts leading into the fields.

The best rice fields are those with current running in one end and out the other. Depth is also important. If the field becomes nearly dry at low tide, chances are it won't hold many bass at high tide. The cuts, however, may still hold some fish.

On an incoming tide, stay on the inside of the cuts and cast out toward the channel using a crawfish-pattern crankbait. On an outgoing tide, stay on the outside and cast into the cuts. Another good bait for working the cuts is a chartreuse spinnerbait.

As the water warms, bass move farther back in the rice fields, although some can still be found around the cuts. By late March or early April, when the water temperature reaches 65° F, bass begin bedding in ditches in the rice fields or on weedy rice field flats. They also spawn in tributary creeks and man-made canals. Spawning activity peaks in mid- to late April. Bass stay in the vicinity of bedding areas for several weeks after spawning is completed.

One popular springtime technique is casting buzzbaits around bedding areas. Starting about three hours before low tide, work buzzbaits over weed patches on the flats. Then, as low tide approaches, move to the ditches. Good fishing usually continues for about 1½ hours into the rising tide. You can also catch bass in spring on Texas-rigged floating worms, using only a barrel swivel for weight; floating minnow plugs fished on the surface with a twitch-and-wait retrieve; or spinnerbaits, although they tend to foul in the thick weed patches. Another

How to Work the Cuts

POSITION your boat on the river side of the cut and cast from the outside in on the outgoing tide. This way, your lure moves with the current, just like natural food drifting out of the rice fields. On the incoming tide, position your boat on the rice field side, cast out toward the river and work the lure in.

good technique, especially at high tide, is casting over the weedtops with noise-producing vibrating plugs, such as Rat-L-Traps or Rattl'n Raps.

Experts advocate fishing in moving water throughout the year. When the tide goes slack, run up- or downriver to find a spot where the water is flowing.

Fishing can be tough in summer, and the bass usually run smaller. By late May, water temperatures rise into the upper 70s and bass feed more often at night. As the summer progresses and water temperatures approach the 90s, most feeding is at night.

You can catch some bass during the day, however, by fishing the cuts on an outgoing tide. Bass lie along the outside edge of the cut, waiting for food to wash out to them. Cast a Texas-rigged plastic worm into the cut, then drift it slowly along the bottom with the current. Topwater baits, especially floating minnow plugs, may be effective in early morning.

On summer nights, fish the rice fields using noisy surface baits, such as crawlers, chuggers and buzzbaits. Big Texas-rigged worms also work well because they imitate the eels found in the river. Dark colors, especially black, are the best choice. At high tide, work the weedtops; low tide, the ditches.

As the water begins to cool in fall, you'll find bass in rice field ditches, cuts, and outside bends adjacent to rice fields. The best fall spots have hard, sandy bottoms with water 6 to 8 feet deep.

By early October, bass are feeding heavily on shad, so experts rely on crankbaits and jigging spoons. Work them around points that form the cuts leading into the rice fields. At night, you can catch bass in the same cuts, only in shallower water.

By mid-December, the water drops below 55° F, and bass move into deep holes in the main channel adjacent to cuts in the rice fields. The holes vary in depth from 10 to 35 feet. You can catch good numbers of bass by hovering over these holes and jigging vertically with a shad-imitating jig, jig-and-pig, vibrating blade or jigging spoon. On an outgoing tide, you can catch some bass by casting into the cuts with a jig or jigging spoon and letting the current wash it out.

Winter fishing is best when water is being discharged from the Pinopolis Dam. The current draws bass to the holes, where they can easily ambush food that drifts by. Without current, the bass scatter in search of food, making them difficult to find.

Many Cooper River anglers consider winter the peak time for largemouth bass, especially for big ones. The deepwater winter fishing lasts until early March, when bass begin moving into shallow water in preparation for spawning.

How to Fish a Buzzbait

BEGIN your retrieve with your rod tip high after casting to weedy cover in the rice fields.

LOWER your rod tip as the lure nears the boat. Keeping the tip high would pull the blade out of the water.

DELAY setting the hook until you feel extra weight. The tendency is to set the hook at any swirl or splash; if you do, you'll probably pull the lure away from the fish.

LURES AND RIGS include: (1) Lehi worm Texas-rigged, (2) Triple Wing buzzbait, (3) Houston Model spinnerbait, (4) Bang-O-Lure, (5) Ivie's Shad, (6) Deep Wee R, (7) Rattl'n Rap, (8) Stanley Jig and pork frog, (9) Strata Spoon.

NIGHT FISHING is the best way to catch bass in summer. Around high tide, fish weed patches in the rice fields. Use noisy surface lures or plastic worms, all in black or dark colors.

Bass-Fishing Tips

WORK your lure across points that form cuts. Here, bass can get out of the current, yet be in position to grab shad, crayfish or other food passing through the cut.

CAST to dock posts or any kind of stick-ups around the cuts or in the rice fields themselves. The posts may be the only woody cover available to bass.

Cooper River:
Striped Bass

As in most coastal rivers, striped bass runs in the Cooper have declined in recent years. But you can still catch them if you know where to look. Cooper River stripers run 7 to 8 pounds, but there's a chance of catching fish up to 45 pounds.

In late February, stripers begin moving into the tailrace of the Pinopolis Dam, where they will spawn. To protect the spawners, a closed area has been established from the dam to 175 yards downstream. Anglers using jigs catch a few stripers just downstream

LURES for Cooper River striped bass include: (1) Bomber Long A, (2) Bagley Bang-O-B, (3) Mann's 30+, (4) ¾-ounce banana-head bucktail jig tipped with an Ivie's Shad, and (5) Bett's Bucktail Worm.

from the closed area, but fishing is slow because of the reduced numbers of fish.

After spawning, stripers begin working their way downstream. Some, however, stay in the closed area all year. Once the fish leave the dam, they are difficult to find. By October, most have moved downstream to the brackish water. Seldom will you catch one above the Tee.

Fishing peaks in December and January, with the best catches coming at night. The exact tide is not too important, although slack tides are not good. There should be enough current to flush food out of the deep holes.

Look for striped bass in deep eddies that form along outside bends, around docks or bridge piers, and below rock piles. Stripers in deep eddies do not have to fight the current, yet they can easily ambush baitfish hanging along the current margin. Other good spots include shelves downstream from deep holes, and lighted piers adjacent to deep water. All are prime feeding areas.

Two techniques account for most stripers: casting with jigs and trolling with plugs. Jigs are best for working specific objects, such as piers, or where the water is too deep for trolling. With either technique, use a 6- to 7-foot heavy baitcasting outfit with 20- to 25-pound mono.

For jigging, tie on a ½- to ¾-ounce jig, hold the boat just below the spot you want to fish, cast upstream, then bounce the jig slowly with the current. When running the river, be on the lookout for jumping menhaden or shrimp. If you see surface activity, it could mean feeding stripers. Stop and make a few casts with a jig.

Trolling works better than casting when the fish are scattered. Troll slowly against the current using big-lipped crankbaits that will reach bottom at depths of 20 to 30 feet. If you troll with the current, you'll snag up more often, and the plugs won't have as much action. You can also use these deep-diving crankbaits for casting to specific spots, such as eddies and rock piles.

Striper Hotspots

BRIDGES, especially those nearest the Pinopolis Dam, are striper magnets. Baitfish concentrate in the eddies and around the wooden pilings, making a natural feeding area for stripers in the tailrace.

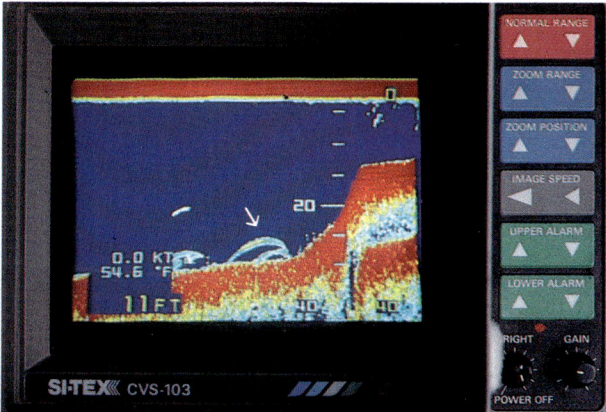

SHELVES downstream from deep holes make ideal feeding areas for stripers. The fish (arrow) rest in the holes during the day and then move up on 10- to 12-foot flats in the evening to feed.

ROCKY AREAS, such as riprap shorelines, submerged rock piles and ruins of old buildings, are good feeding spots for stripers. Baitfish are attracted by the insect larvae that live among the rocks.

Southern Largemouth Rivers

Dams have impounded many southern rivers, but there's still plenty of free-flowing water teeming with bass

Pearl River, Mississippi

When you mention bass fishing in the South, most folks automatically think of the famous southern reservoirs — sprawling man-made lakes, such as Bull Shoals, Percy Priest and Truman. The idea of river fishing is foreign to most.

But many of the rivers feeding the reservoirs had good numbers of gamefish long before the dams were built, and the free-flowing portions of these rivers still hold plenty of fish. And not just bass, but also catfish, crappies, sunfish and introduced species, such as stripers.

Although the dams have destroyed enormous amounts of habitat for stream-dwelling species, fishing has actually improved in much of the free-flowing water that remains. The reservoirs reduce the intensity of flooding in the rivers, minimizing bank erosion and giving weedbeds a better chance to develop. Tailwaters of the dams are concentration points for a variety of gamefish, especially during spring spawning runs. And the reservoirs produce tremendous quantities of fish, some of which migrate upstream into the free-flowing rivers at certain times of the year.

The average southern angler avoids river fishing because he feels he can catch fish more consistently in the lakes. It's true that river fish are more difficult to locate and catch because of constantly changing conditions, but anglers skilled at fishing moving water know there are times when a river is the better choice.

In windy weather, for instance, a good-sized reservoir is tough to fish and may even be treacherous; rivers are fishable even in a high wind. To get out of the wind, simply move around a bend. Also, river fish seem less affected by cold fronts and thunderstorms, conditions that usually cause lake fishing to shut down.

Case Study:
Pearl River, Mississippi

The Pearl River, which splits the southern half of Mississippi before emptying into the Gulf of Mexico, is typical of many southern rivers. Approximately 150 miles below the headwaters, the Ross Barnett Dam backs up water for 36 miles, forming a 33,000-acre reservoir of the same name. Below the dam, the lower river flows on for more than 300 miles, spilling into the Gulf near Port Bienville.

Although the upper and lower river both offer excellent fishing, the emphasis in this book will be on the upper river because it typifies hundreds of small to medium-sized rivers found throughout the South. Also included will be information on fishing the tailrace, below the reservoir.

The upper river, from the town of Philadelphia to the Ross Barnett Reservoir, meanders slowly through mixed hardwood and conifer forest as well as tupelo gum and cypress swamps. The channel, which averages about 120 feet wide and 12 feet deep, is laced with deadfalls, submerged stumps and towering cypress trees. The bottom consists mainly of sand, clay and silt, and the water carries a heavy silt load at all times, even when the river is low. At normal stage, the visibility may be 2 to 3 feet; at high water, only 6 inches. By comparison, the lower river is wider, deeper and somewhat clearer. It meanders much more, and the lower 13 miles are influenced by the tides.

Along the upper river's course are numerous sloughs connected to the main channel by narrow cuts. The sloughs are actually the lower ends of tributary streams, although some are oxbow lakes that have not completely separated from the river.

Most of the upper river is navigable in a fishing boat, although some stretches require a very small boat or a canoe. About 24 miles above the reservoir, a low-head dam restricts boat traffic. The 4-foot-high dam is intended to raise the water level upstream for better navigability.

Important fish in this stretch include largemouth and spotted (Kentucky) bass, white crappies (white perch), black crappies, bluegills (bream), channel catfish, blue catfish, flathead catfish (tabby cats), wipers (striped bass–white bass hybrids), and occasionally striped bass.

Pearl River Physical Data
(at low-head dam)

Average width	120 ft
Average depth	12 ft
Gradient	low
Clarity	2 to 3 ft
Color	brown
Discharge (cubic feet per second)	450
Winter low temperature	45° F
Summer high temperature	90° F

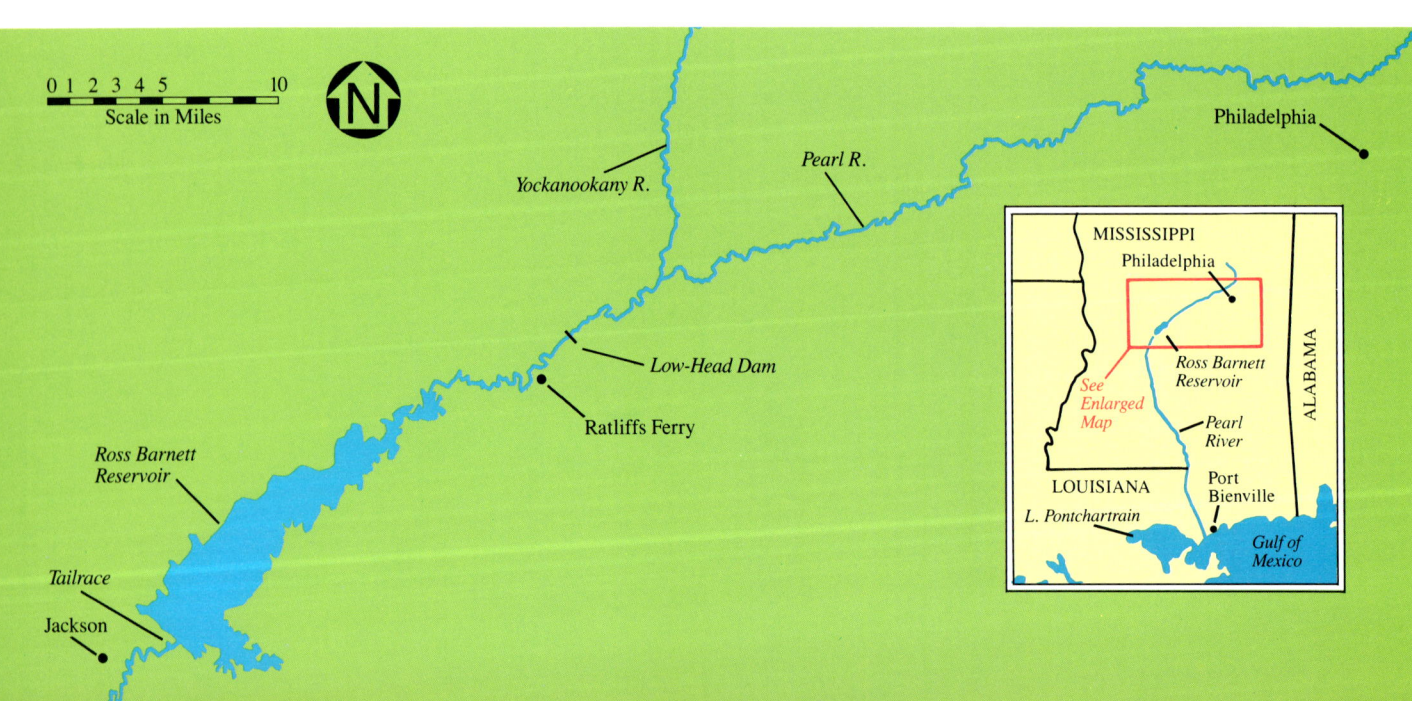

Pearl River Habitat

SANDY POINTS in the main channel make good feeding areas for spotted bass and catfish.

CREEK MOUTH SLOUGHS connected to the river make ideal spawning areas for largemouth bass and crappies.

POINTS at a slough junction attract bass and crappies, especially if there are weeds and stumps.

DEEP CUTS connecting sloughs to the river appeal to crappies, largemouth bass and spotted bass.

OXBOW SLOUGHS remain when the river changes course. They make ideal habitat for bass and panfish.

LOW-HEAD DAM blocks upstream migration, so it concentrates migratory fish, such as wipers.

Pearl River:
Largemouth Bass

Anglers accustomed to catching largemouth bass in clear lakes or reservoirs may have a hard time adjusting to the murky waters of the upper Pearl. Because of the low visibility, the fish spend their entire life in shallow water, seldom venturing below 8 feet.

But it's well worth learning how to catch them since the river receives much less fishing pressure than the reservoir. The bass are good-sized, but not huge, averaging about 2 pounds with an occasional fish up to 7.

Although some local anglers consider the upper portion of the reservoir to be part of the river, the information that follows pertains only to the free-flowing portion upstream from Ratliffs Ferry.

Starting in late March, largemouths move into the sloughs where the warm, slack water and thick beds of lily pads offer good conditions for spawning. Normally, they spawn in water less than a foot deep. The cuts leading into the sloughs also hold bass this time of year; deeper cuts with good cover hold bass all year.

The best lures for this shallow cover include buzzbaits and weedless frogs, but spinnerbaits, plastic lizards and minnow plugs twitched on the surface also produce plenty of bass. When the fish go deeper, try a jig-and-pig. Most local anglers prefer flippin' sticks with 17- to 30-pound mono, but a 5½-foot medium-power baitcasting outfit with 14- to 17-pound mono is better for working minnow plugs.

In early May, bass start moving out to the main river to feed on shad. Look for them around lily pad points at slough mouths, eddies at the edge of the main channel, undercut banks, log and brush piles, and standing cypress trees. To attract fish, any of these spots must adjoin deep water.

Early or late in the day or in overcast weather, you can catch bass on the same shallow-water lures as in spring, but crankbaits or plastic worms work better on sunny days when the bass go deeper.

You'll find bass in these locations through the fall and winter, although they move a little deeper when the water dips into the mid-50s. The fish may move back into the sloughs after a heavy rain if the current in the river becomes too swift. When the water is falling, look for bass where the cuts empty into the main river.

As the water cools in fall, bass will roam farther from cover. Work a larger area around obstructions and retrieve more slowly than you would in summer. Once the water temperature drops into the low 60s, surface lures are no longer effective. A jig-and-pig is the best overall choice, although crankbaits work well in light cover.

The peak times for largemouths on the Pearl are from May through early July, and October through December. Early spring fishing may be tough, because the water is often high and muddy. Fishing is best when the river is within its banks and falling slowly.

How to Work a Weedless Frog

1. CAST a weedless frog into openings in the lily pads; wait for the ripples to subside.

2. SKIP the frog across the lily pads, letting it lie for several seconds in each opening.

3. PAUSE when you see a boil, then set the hook. If you set too soon, the fish may not have the lure.

4. PULL the largemouth's head upward to prevent the fish from diving into the lily pad stems.

LURES AND RIGS include: (1) Spoiler Lizard, Texas-rigged, with 1/8-ounce bullet sinker; (2) Toledo Worm, Texas-rigged, with 1/8-ounce bullet sinker; (3) Toledo Worm, Carolina-rigged, with a 3/4-ounce bullet sinker; (4) Snagproof Frog; (5) Racket Buzz; (6) Bang-O-Lure; (7) Stanley Jig tipped with a pork frog; (8) Bitty B.

Tips for Catching Largemouths

LOOK for stumps among the weeds in sloughs or on points at creek junctions. The stumps provide better cover for bass than the weeds alone.

USE a buzzbait with styrofoam floats (inset) so you can slow your retrieve without the lure sinking.

SPRAY a soft-plastic lizard with oil-based scent to make it slide through the weeds without fouling.

Pearl River: Spotted Bass

When fishing the upper Pearl, you may hook a fish that looks much like a largemouth, but fights with the stamina of a smallmouth. Called "spots" by local anglers, these never-give-up battlers are actually spotted bass. They're also known as "Kentuckies."

Spots are often found in the same places as largemouths, but they will tolerate more current. They don't average quite as big, although the river has produced spots over 6 pounds.

In mid- to late March, when the water temperature hits the mid-60s, spots move into cuts leading into the sloughs or into eddies along the main channel. Most of the fish spawn in pockets in brushy cover, usually at inner ends of the cuts, or in the sloughs.

As a rule, lures for spots should be smaller than those for largemouths. The most effective lures in springtime cover, such as brush or lily pads, are ⅛-ounce spinnerbaits and 4-inch lizards. In lighter cover, you can catch spots on small crankbaits and vibrating plugs.

Some spots hang around the cuts all summer. Others move onto sandy points above outside bends or into deep pools in the bends. Although the fish may go as deep as 20 feet in summer, most are caught at depths of 6 to 8 feet.

Medium-diving crankbaits and plastic worms provide most of the summertime action. In deep pools or cuts with few snags, or on clean sandbars, use a Carolina rig; in brushy cover, a Texas rig.

Beginning in October, shad congregate below the low-head dam and spots are close behind. You'll find them in the turbulent water directly below the dam, or around points, cuts and outside bends in the first mile downstream of the dam. The fish remain in these locations into December. Use crankbaits when fishing below the dam; otherwise, use the same lures as in summer.

Winter is the best time for big spots. Work sharp breaks along outside bends, particularly where there is woody cover on a 6- to 8-foot-deep shelf. One favorite wintertime lure is the Whing Ding, a type of tailspin with a body that can slide up the line, making it more difficult for a bass to throw the hook. Cast it to the bank and retrieve with 3-foot lifts, letting it hit bottom each time. Spots strike as the lure is sinking, so keep your line taut on the drop. This presentation lets you cover a lot of water in a hurry. Once you find the fish, try a slower presentation with a jig-and-pig or plastic worm.

A good all-around outfit for spots is a medium-heavy baitcasting rod and matching reel spooled with 12- to 14-pound mono. This outfit is heavy enough to horse spots from thick cover yet will still cast fairly light lures.

Spots are easiest to find and catch when the water is low because they're concentrated in eddies, and the water is clear enough to see the bait easily.

LURES AND RIGS for spotted bass include: (1) Bitty B; (2) Whing Ding; (3) Rat-L-Trap; (4) Phenom Worm, rigged Carolina-style, weighted with a ¾-ounce bullet sinker; (5) Mepps Bass Killer; (6) Bagley Kil'r B2; (7) Super Lizard, rigged Texas-style, weighted with a ¼-ounce bullet sinker; (8) Stanley Jig tipped with a pork frog; and (9) Phenom Worm, rigged Texas-style, weighted with a ⅜-ounce bullet sinker.

Prime Locations for Spots

DEEP CUTS connecting the river to the sloughs are good spotted-bass producers. With your boat at the mouth of the cut, cast a medium-diving crankbait to the points on either side, then make a few casts down the middle.

SANDY POINTS that have lots of woody cover and drop sharply into the main channel hold spots from late August into December. Work the wood with spinnerbaits, crankbaits, or plastic worms.

SLAB SPOONS (see below) are ideal for catching hybrids in the tailrace. With a 1-ounce spoon and 12-pound mono, you can cast up to 200 feet to reach the fast water in the middle of the river.

LURES AND RIGS for wipers include: (1) Rat-L-Trap; (2) ¼-ounce twister-tail jig; (3) tandem rig, tied with 12-pound mono and a pair of ¼-ounce jigs, one attached to a loop 12 to 18 inches up the line; (4) Glow Top Popping Float with an 18- to 24-inch leader of 14-pound mono and a Buck's Top Striper jig; and (5) Skipper Shad.

Pearl River: Wipers

When the wipers are running in the Ross Barnett tailrace, you're likely to see bank fishermen standing elbow to elbow. Often, several are battling fish at the same time. This hectic scene is repeated each spring, normally from late February to late May.

Wipers are actually striped bass–white bass hybrids or, to many folks, simply "hybrids." These gamy fighters, running from 3 to 14 pounds, prefer the fast water immediately below the dam. The smaller ones can be caught in the margins of the eddies on either side of the fast water, but the bigger fish stay in the swift water in the middle of the river.

When the water warms in summer, wipers leave the tailrace and scatter downstream. But they return again in fall, usually in September, and fishing stays good until late December. Many consider fall the best time for big wipers.

To fish the tailrace effectively, you'll need surf-casting tackle or baitcasting gear suitable for making 150- to 200-foot casts, and 10- to 14-pound mono. Some local anglers modify their baitcasting reels by removing the gear grease and substituting WD-40. Many fishermen use a specially designed, lead-bodied slab spoon. The line threads through the body, and when a fish strikes and shakes its head, the lure slides up the line. This way, the fish cannot use the weight of the lure to throw the hook. Not only is the lure easy to cast, it's shaped like a shad, the hybrids' usual prey.

Weighted popping corks, or "agitators," also add casting distance, and the popping action attracts curious wipers to a slender plastic-bodied fly suspended from the cork.

Another effective technique is to cast with a tandem-jig setup. Tie a ¼-ounce jig in a loop about 2 feet up the line; tie another ¼-ounce jig to the end of the line. When a hybrid grabs one jig, others often give chase in a competitive frenzy. When they see the other jig, they grab it. Use monofilament of at least 12-pound test; otherwise, if you hook two fish, they could pull against each other and snap the line. The tandem-jig technique is not recommended for large hybrids.

With any of these techniques, cast into the swift water, then retrieve fast enough to keep the lure running a few inches below the surface. If this retrieve doesn't work, slow down and let the lure sink deeper.

Wipers are also stocked in Ross Barnett Reservoir. These fish migrate upstream in spring, about the same time wipers are moving into the tailrace. The most productive area of the upper river is from Ratliffs Ferry to the low-head dam. Wipers tend to school immediately below the dam, but you'll also find them below sharp bends in the river, usually around logs or brush.

To locate the fish, cast a Rat-L-Trap or other vibrating plug using a medium-power spinning or baitcasting outfit with 8- to 10-pound mono. Once you find the fish, switch to a lighter outfit with 4- to 8-pound mono and cast with ⅛- to ¼-ounce jigs with soft plastic or bucktail dressings.

Wipers school by size, so if you're catching only small fish, you'll probably have to move to find bigger ones.

Fishing is generally best early or late in the day, in cloudy weather, and at normal water stage. When conditions are right, you can catch more than 50 fish in a day.

How to Catch Wipers on Popping Corks

MAKE a long cast to reach wipers in midriver. Using the weighted cork, you can cast up to 150 feet.

RETRIEVE by snapping your rod, reeling down quickly to take up the slack, then snapping again.

SNAP your rod hard enough to throw water, and reel fast enough to keep the fly near the surface.

Northern Smallmouth Streams

One of the best-kept secrets in the northern states and southern Canada is the prime stream fishing for smallmouth bass

The northcountry is laced by thousands of small to medium-sized smallmouth bass streams that offer anglers an exceptional fishing opportunity. Within easy reach of millions of anglers, these streams receive surprisingly light fishing pressure.

As in most other parts of the country, fishermen in the North are lake-oriented. Because there are so many lakes, and access to them is easy, anglers tend to bypass the streams.

Most northern smallmouth streams have water that is relatively clear and unpolluted, and a fish population that also includes walleyes and northern pike. The majority flow through forested country, so they are immune to most of the problems afflicting streams in agricultural or urban areas. Because the wooded shorelines keep streambank erosion to a minimum, the bottom has plenty of clean sand and gravel for spawning and food production.

The main problem in fishing these streams is access. Most lack well-developed launching sites, so you may have to slide a small boat or canoe in at a road crossing. And once you're on the stream, you'll have to contend with shallow sandbars and riffles.

Another problem is learning which streams have the best fishing potential. Often, these streams are fished only by local anglers who don't divulge much information. But the state or provincial natural-resources agency may have some good recommendations based on current survey information. They may even direct you to the portion of the stream with the highest fish counts.

St. Louis River, Minnesota

Case Study:
St. Louis River, Minnesota

The St. Louis River is a picturesque, mid-sized smallmouth stream in northeastern Minnesota. It originates in Seven Beaver Lake, then flows on for 190 miles to the western tip of Lake Superior, near Duluth, Minnesota.

Used heavily for logging in the 1800s, the St. Louis was an important route for early traders and explorers because it connected the Great Lakes with the Mississippi River. After a trip up the East Savanna River, a tributary of the St. Louis, travelers portaged 7 miles to the headwaters of the Savanna River, which took them into the Mississippi.

Along its course, the St. Louis undergoes dramatic changes. The upper river flows through wild country, with few farms or other developments. Black bears, moose and even timber wolves frequent the area. The upper 40 miles of the river averages only 60 feet in width; the gradient is high and there are many shallow class 1 and 2 rapids that are impassable with a fishing boat. Then, the river flattens into a very slow, meandering stretch extending downstream another 85 miles to Floodwood.

While there is some good fishing in these upper reaches, fishing is best in the 33-mile reach from Floodwood downstream to Cloquet. This zone has several class 1 and 2 rapids, but there are long fishable reaches in between with slow to moderate current and no dams. Despite the easy navigability and good fishing for bass, walleyes and channel catfish, you'll find few anglers.

Below Cloquet, the gradient becomes much steeper. Five dams create a series of small lakes along the river's course. From Cloquet to the Thomson Dam, there is one class 3 and many class 2 rapids, which are impassable in a normal fishing boat. Then, in a mile-long stretch below the Thomson Dam, the river plunges violently through a rocky gorge, dropping more than 200 feet. This is class 6 water. Besides being unnavigable, these lower reaches have little access, so fishing is minimal.

Below the Fond du Lac Dam, the river's character again changes dramatically. Instead of being confined to a definite channel, it winds through an

St. Louis River Habitat

DEEP POOLS are prime catfish haunts, but also hold some walleyes, northern pike and smallmouth bass.

ROCK OUTCROPS along shore attract walleyes and smallmouths if there is deep water nearby.

LILY PAD BAYS are ideal for northern pike, but they also draw good-sized smallmouth bass.

RAPIDS with deep-water pockets below them are choice feeding spots for all gamefish.

ROCKY POINTS adjacent to deep water are sure to hold walleyes and smallmouth bass.

estuary that in some places is 1½ miles wide. The main fishing attraction is a seasonal walleye run from Lake Superior. Fishing is best from the time the season opens around May 1 through mid-July. The estuary also produces big northern pike, crappies, bluegills, channel catfish, smallmouth bass and an occasional muskie. In spring and fall, anglers pick up a few trout and salmon.

Most fishing on the upper and middle reaches of the St. Louis is done from 12- to 14-foot semi-V aluminum boats or jon boats with 5- to 15-hp, short-shaft outboards. However, many anglers prefer canoes and some even use float tubes.

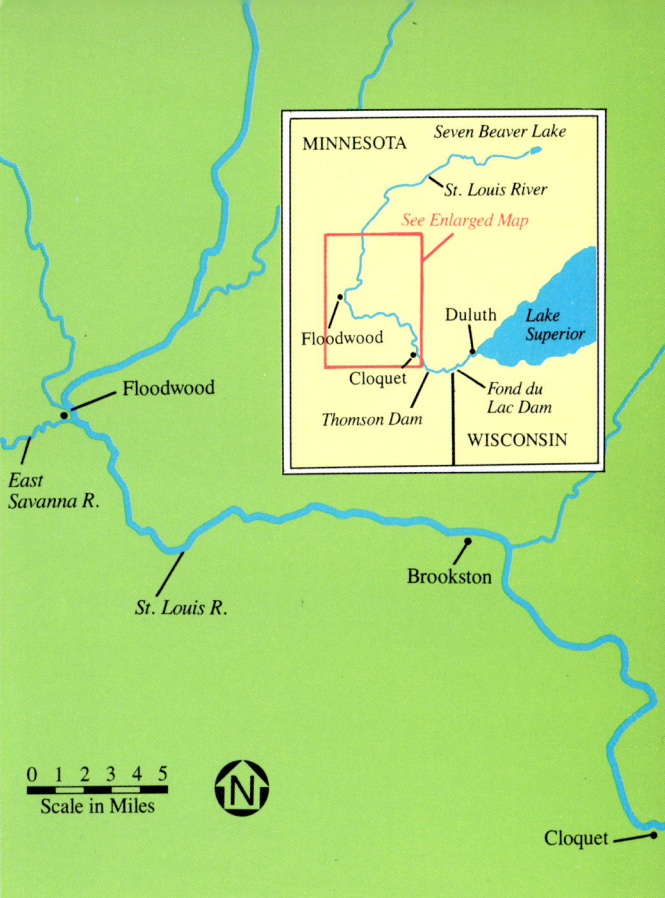

St. Louis River Physical Data (at Brookston)	
Average width	200 ft
Average depth	3.5 ft
Gradient	moderate
Clarity	3 to 4 ft
Color	coffee stained
Discharge (cubic feet per second)	1,850
Winter low temperature	32° F
Summer high temperature	82° F

EDDIES that form below point-bars make good resting spots for walleyes and smallmouths.

WEED EDGES along the main channel may hold smallmouths and walleyes, but the fish are scattered.

LOGJAMS provide good smallmouth cover and, on occasion, produce big northern pike.

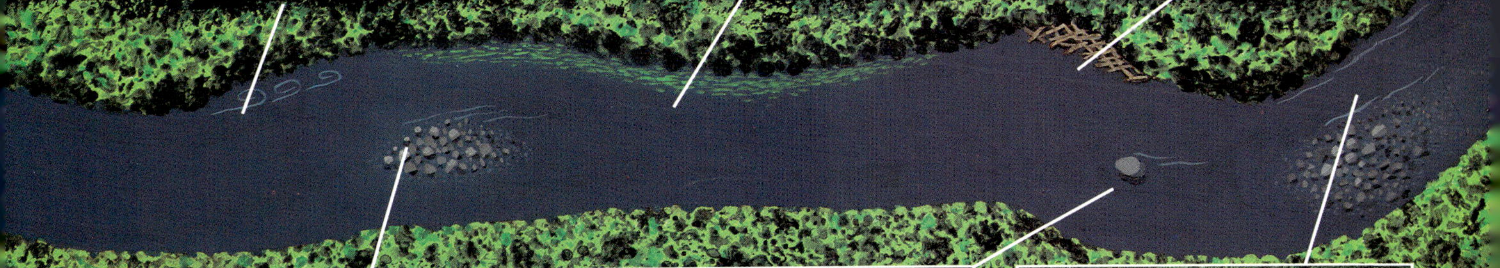

ROCK PILES in midstream, either exposed or submerged, yield walleyes and smallmouth bass.

LARGE BOULDERS with a deep eddy below them often produce one or two big smallmouths.

CHUTES, where water funnels rapidly through a constriction, make good feeding spots for smallmouth bass.

St. Louis River:
Smallmouth Bass

When you walk along the rocky banks of the St. Louis, you'll see crayfish scurrying everywhere. With this much good bass food, it's not surprising that smallmouths are plentiful.

Besides the abundance of natural food, the river also has plenty of natural smallmouth cover in the form of big boulders, rock outcrops along shore, logjams and weedbeds. There's also man-made cover such as bridge pilings and rock piles that were used to tie off rafts of timber during the logging days.

In most years, snowmelt and cool weather keep the river too high and cold for good smallmouth fishing until early June. When the river drops to normal stage, water clarity improves and the fish concentrate in predictable locations. As a rule, fishing is best from late July through October, assuming the water is at low or normal stage. Time of day is not important, but sunny days are usually best.

Most St. Louis River smallmouths run from 1 to 2 pounds, but when conditions are right, it's possible to catch fish over 4. They're found in many different kinds of spots, but all have one thing in common:

an eddy with faster current nearby. Seldom will you find them where the water is uniformly slack.

To fish smallmouths effectively in the St. Louis, you must be able to recognize the types of spots that hold fish and learn the techniques for fishing each of them.

Local experts use the "hit-and-run" approach to smallmouth fishing. As they run the river, they stop to make a few casts at each likely spot they encounter. Often they carry several rods rigged with different lures to avoid having to rerig for different presentations. Smallmouths are usually aggressive biters; it doesn't pay to spend a lot of time in one spot trying to entice them.

Live bait is seldom necessary to catch smallmouths on the St. Louis. The trend is toward catch-and-release, and fish caught on live bait may be hooked too deeply to survive.

When fishing is tough, however, you may do best by fishing with leeches, crawlers or crayfish, either on a jig or split-shot rig.

A good tackle selection includes a medium-power, 5½- to 6-foot baitcasting outfit with 8-pound mono for crankbait fishing; and a medium-light, 7- to 8-foot spinning outfit with 4- to 6-pound mono for jig and spinner fishing. For live-bait fishing, carry a similar spinning outfit rigged with a split-shot and size 4 or 6 hook.

Smallmouth-Fishing Tips

UNSNAG baits and lures more easily by using an extra-long rod. With a longer rod, you can reach out much farther, giving you a better angle of pull to free your hook from the rocks where smallmouths are often found.

CATCH crayfish using a small-mesh dip net (shown) or a minnow seine. Where crayfish are plentiful, simply scrape the net over the bottom. Otherwise, turn over rocks in a riffle and hold a seine just downstream.

HOOK a small crayfish, 1½ to 3 inches long, in the back using a size 4 hook. Push the hook in one side of the shell and out the other. If you hook the crayfish in the tail, you'll miss more fish.

The Hit-and-Run Technique

LURES AND RIGS include: (1) Ugly Bug and leech, (2) Super Vibrax, (3) dropper rig with Phelps Floater and crawler, (4) Shad Rap, (5) Fat Rap.

WORK a logjam with a spinner by keeping your rod tip high and reeling fast enough to keep the lure from sinking and snagging the logs.

CAST a shallow-running crankbait across a chute. Angle casts upstream; reel immediately to reach bottom before the lure washes downstream.

TOSS a spinner past a boulder, then retrieve it through the downstream eddy. After covering the eddy, try a cast upstream of the boulder.

116

POSITION your boat downstream of a point-bar; cast into the eddy using a floater baited with a crawler or leech on a split-shot dropper rig.

WORK a medium-running crankbait over a rock outcrop. Cast to shore; reel rapidly so the lure bumps the rocks, giving it an erratic action.

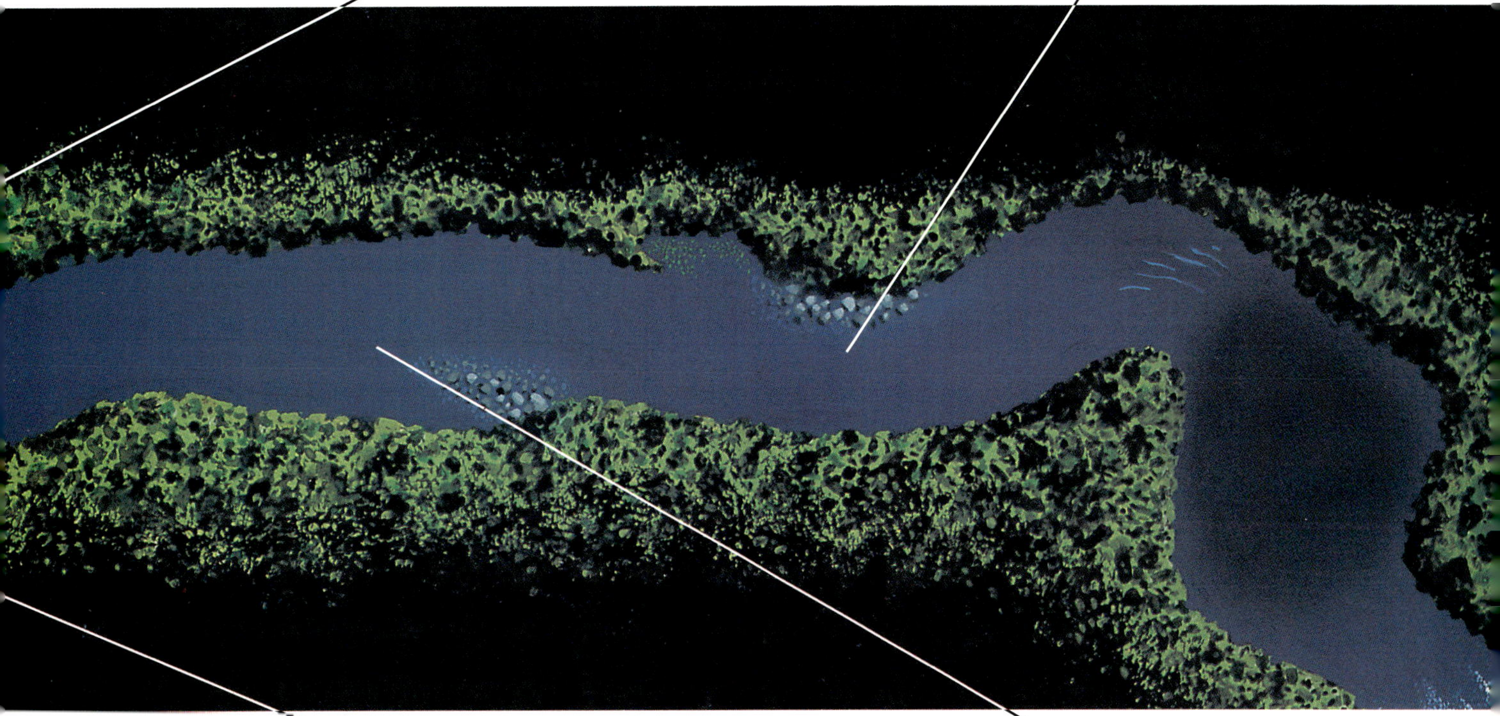

ANCHOR below a rock pile; work both sides and the downstream eddy using a jig-and-leech combo. If snags are a problem, add a slip-bobber.

FAN-CAST a rocky point using a spinner. Retrieve slowly enough so the lure can sink into the crevices between the rocks.

Bassin' in Natural Lakes

Practically any type of natural lake will hold bass, including deep, cold Canadian Shield lakes whose bays commonly teem with smallmouths. But you're more likely to find bass in warm, shallow, weedy lakes where the water is much more fertile.

The way bass behave in natural lakes differs greatly from the way they behave in rivers and reservoirs. Most natural lakes stratify into distinct temperature layers, and the location of these layers, which changes throughout the year, affects the movement pattern of bass.

Another important difference: natural lakes tend to be weedier than rivers or reservoirs. Water levels remain more stable, so weedbeds have a better chance to develop. This explains why bass in most

natural lakes are so strongly oriented toward aquatic vegetation.

Scientists categorize natural lakes into as many as 100 different types representing about 2 million natural lakes in North America alone. This chapter will concentrate only on those types that hold largemouth or smallmouth bass.

You'll learn how bass lakes differ in regard to water temperature and stratification, fertility, clarity, oxygen content, food supply and vegetation type. The lake-type discussions in this chapter will show you how to recognize the important lake classes so you'll be able to categorize the lakes that you commonly fish.

The case studies in this chapter will show you exactly how to find and catch bass in natural lakes of each type. The strategies shown for one type of lake, however, may work equally well on another. It pays to experiment with all the techniques shown and then fine-tune your methods to the conditions.

"Two-Story" Lakes

You've got a choice of warmwater or coldwater fish in these "two-in-one" lakes

Two-story lakes, also called *combination* lakes, are thermally stratified bodies of water that support warmwater fish in the shallows and coldwater fish in the depths. In order for coldwater fish to survive, the lake must have a good supply of oxygen in the depths year round.

The majority of two-story lakes are ice-scour lakes, formed when glaciers scraped away the topsoil overlying a huge area of the northern states and Canada.

As the ice receded 10,000 years ago, gouges in the bedrock filled up with water, creating hundreds of thousands of clear lakes, many very deep. The bedrock area left behind by the glaciers is called the Laurentian Shield, or more commonly, the Canadian Shield, so these lakes are often called *shield* lakes.

Most shield lakes have changed very little since their creation. A sediment layer has covered some of the deeper portions, but the basins still consist primarily

of rock. Because of the low mineral content of the water, most of these lakes are classed as oligotrophic.

On the extreme northern portion of the shield, the climate is so severe that the lakes hold only coldwater fish, primarily lake trout, grayling and Arctic char. Farther south, many lakes have lake trout in the depths and northern pike in the shallows, but they're not true two-story lakes because the water temperature in the upper story never gets high enough for most warmwater fish.

Many lakes on the southern half of the shield, however, support a variety of warmwater fish in addition to the coldwater species. Throughout most of the northern states and Canadian provinces, walleyes and northern pike are the dominant shallow-water species in these lakes. Some two-story lakes also have smallmouth bass and muskies, but these species don't range as far north. Lake trout predominate in the deep water, although other coldwater species, such as whitefish and burbot, are usually present.

Two-story shield lakes in the northeastern states have a different mix of fish species. Smallmouth bass and chain pickerel dominate the upper story while lake trout and landlocked salmon prevail in the lower. Another type of two-story lake is the deep, steep-sided ice-block lake. Because these lakes have basins of earthen material, or till, rather than bedrock, their water is more fertile; most are classed as mesotrophic. Although they don't have a year-round supply of oxygen all the way to the bottom, coldwater fish can find enough cool, oxygenated water in and just below the thermocline during periods when oxygen is too low in the depths.

Because the warmwater and coldwater fish in two-story lakes use separate habitats and consume different foods, there is little competition between them. Smallmouth bass, for instance, seldom go deeper than 30 feet, and lake trout rarely move shallower than 30 feet, except to spawn. Smallmouths feed on crayfish, shiners and other warmwater baitfish, while lake trout eat coldwater baitfish, such as ciscoes and smelt.

Case Study:
Cliff Lake, Ontario

When you're fishing in the shadow of a towering rock wall, it's easy to understand where Cliff Lake got its name.

A classic two-story shield lake with a deep, rocky basin, Cliff Lake has an appealing list of gamefish. You'll find smallmouth bass, walleyes, northern pike and muskies in the warmwater zone, along with yellow perch and shiners for forage. Lake trout swim in the deeper, colder water, where they feed on ciscoes. Good numbers of whitefish occupy the depths.

This surprising assortment of fish results from the variety of habitat. Besides the deep, cold lake trout haunts, the lake's irregular basin has plenty of shallow-water habitat, such as weedy bays for pike and muskies, and rocky reefs and points for smallmouth bass and walleyes.

There are no smelt in Cliff Lake, and their use as bait has recently been banned in northwestern Ontario for fear they will become established and endanger gamefish populations.

Although the surface temperature on Cliff Lake may rise into the 70s in summer, the depths remain frigid, about 43 degrees. Below 70 feet, the temperature changes very little throughout the year. A thermocline generally forms between 25 and 40 feet.

The lake is fed by two small inlets, but most of its water comes from springs. This may explain the higher-than-normal clarity, approximately 15 feet. The clear water can make fishing tough, especially on a calm, clear day.

Even though Cliff Lake is easily accessible by road, fishing pressure is moderate. There are three resorts and one public boat access on the lake, but few private cabins. Most anglers who come to the lake fish for lake trout.

Moose are common visitors to the bogs around Cliff Lake

Cliff Lake's reputation for tough fishing probably keeps some anglers away, but those who have taken time to learn the lake enjoy some of the best mixed-bag fishing Canada has to offer.

Other attractions include blueberry picking in August and ruffed grouse hunting in September and October. There's excellent moose hunting, and some hunting for black bear.

Cliff Lake Physical Data	
Acreage	5,739
Average depth	35 ft
Maximum depth	112 ft
Clarity	15 ft
Color	clear
Limits of thermocline	25 to 40 ft
Total phosphorus (parts per billion)	8
Average date of freeze-up	December 1
Average date of ice-out	April 28

LUND

ONTARIO
MANITOBA
Cliff Lake
Dryden
MINNESOTA
Northwest Bay
Cliff Lake
N
0
1
2
3
Scale in Miles

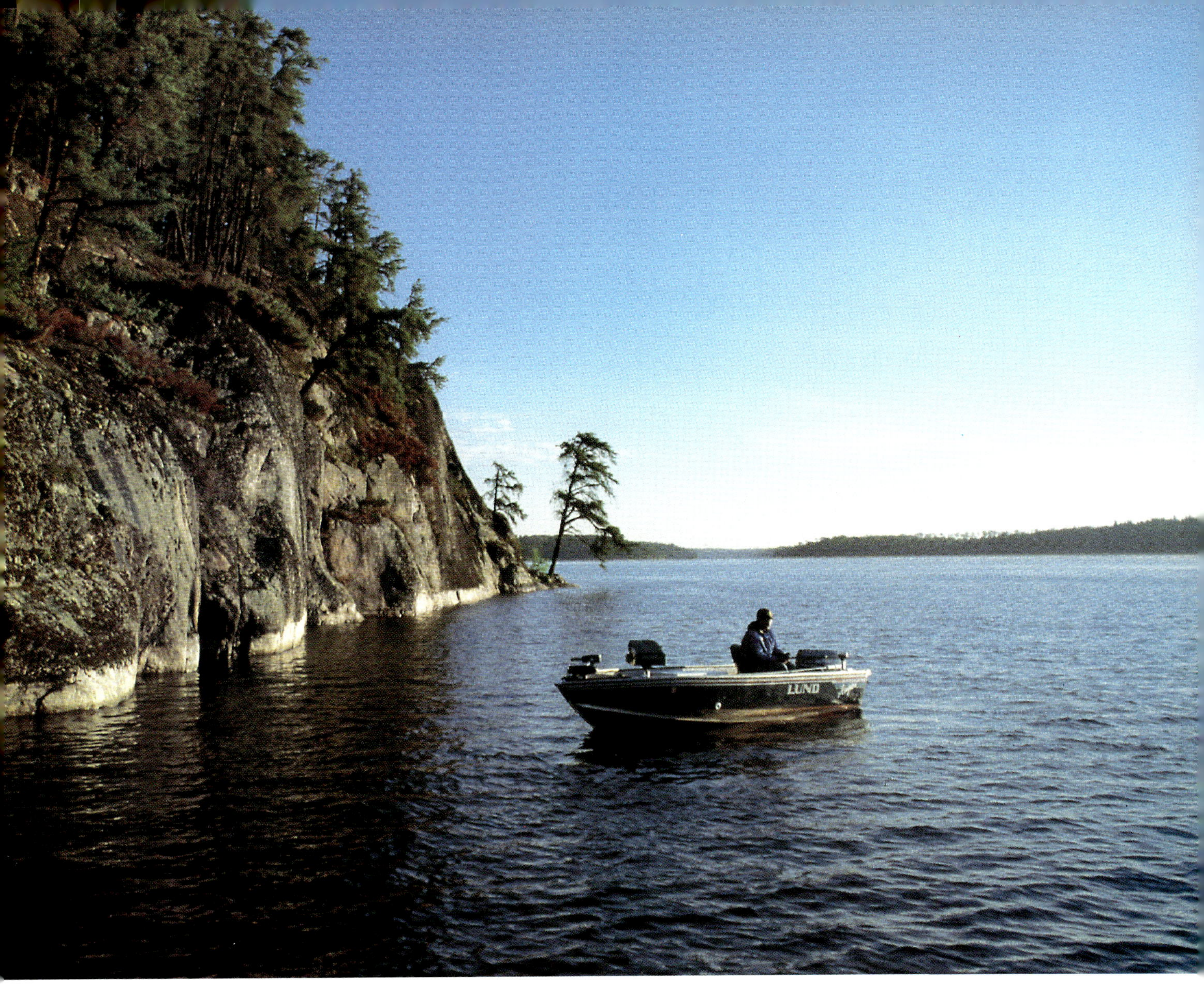

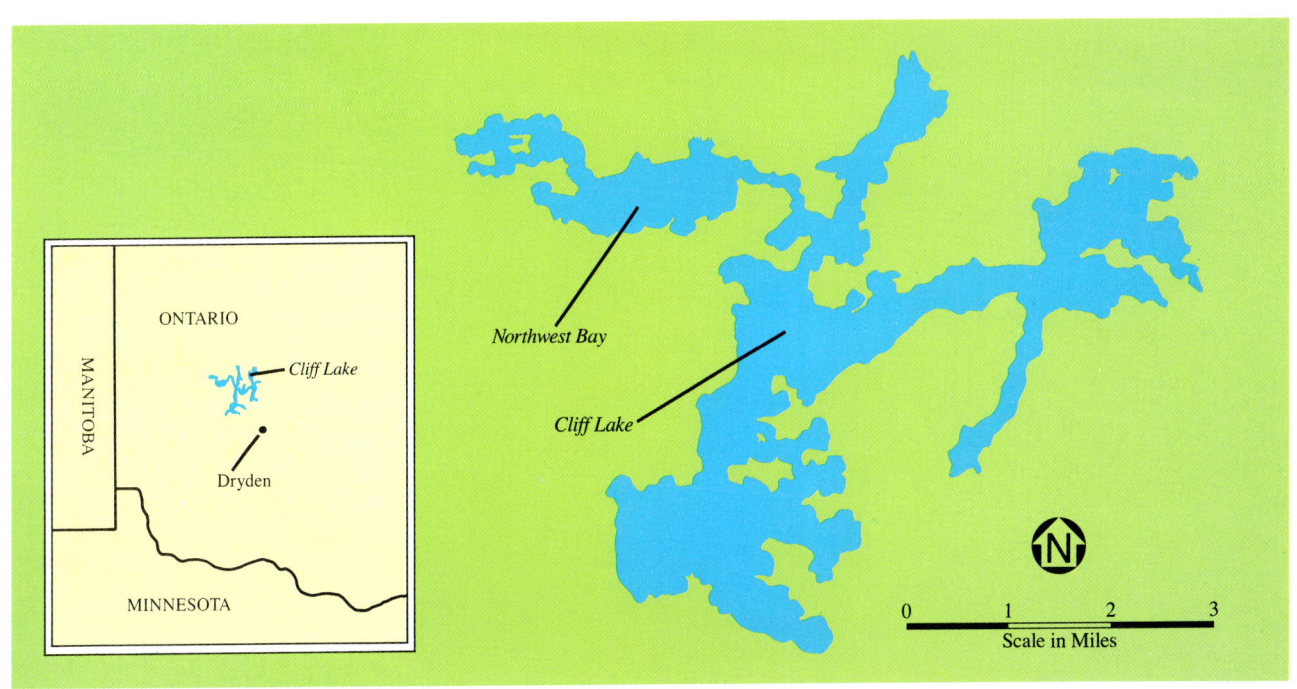

Cliff Lake Habitat (sample locations of habitats are numbered on aerial photo)

1. SHALLOW BAYS, 4 feet or less, are good spawning areas for muskies and northerns. On hot summer days, muskies sun themselves in the bays.

2. DEEP BAYS, those with at least 6 feet of water, are prime muskie producers. The best bays have a good growth of cabbage.

3. UNDERWATER EXTENSIONS off points hold smallmouth bass, walleyes and sometimes muskies from late spring through fall.

4. ROCKY REEFS are good spots for walleyes, smallmouths and muskies from late spring through fall. Look for reefs that top off at 10 feet or less.

5. POINTS with a moderate slope draw walleyes, smallmouth bass and a few pike in summer. Walleyes also use these points in spring.

6. STEEP-SLOPING POINTS attract walleyes and smallmouths in fall. The fish change depth more then, and a steeper slope makes it easier to do.

7. ISLANDS that slope gently into deep water are excellent springtime lake trout spots. You'll find the fish at depths of 10 to 40 feet.

124

Cliff Lake:
Smallmouth Bass

With so many big fish such as muskies and lakers in Cliff Lake, smallmouths get little attention. But there are plenty of them, and they provide a lot more action than the "glamour" fish.

In June, when smallmouths concentrate in bays and along shallow, rocky shorelines to spawn, you can catch them by the dozens. They're not big, averaging a little more than a pound, but there's a chance of connecting with a 4- to 6-pounder.

For excitement, try catching them on propbaits. Using a light spinning outfit with 6-pound mono, cast the lure right up to shore and retrieve it with short twitches followed by long pauses. Sometimes the water explodes when a smallmouth takes the lure, but other times, you'll see only a dimple on the surface. Stay alert and set the hook at any hint of a strike.

LURES AND RIGS: (1) Floating Rapala, (2) ¼-ounce Northland Fireball Jig and minnow, (3) Gaines Crippled Killer, (4) Rebel Deep Wee R, (5) single-spin spinnerbait, (6) ¼-ounce Gapen Ugly-Bug tipped with a piece of crawler, (7) slip-bobber rig with a size 4 hook and leech.

Another good lure around spawning time is a small floating minnow plug. Cast toward shore and retrieve with sharper, faster twitches so the lure "walks" on the surface.

You can also catch early-season smallmouths on small crankbaits, preferably crayfish or shad patterns, and on ⅛- to ¼-ounce jigs in dark or neutral colors.

Smallmouths are harder to find in summer because they spread out over a wide depth range. Some stay in the shallows; others drop into water more than 25 feet deep. You'll find the largest concentrations on rocky points and on humps that top off at 10 feet or less, but smallmouths will scatter along the entire shoreline. It's not unusual to catch them along with walleyes, although smallmouths tend to be a little shallower.

Jigs and crankbaits produce smallmouths through the summer. When the fish are finicky, tip your jig with either a leech or half a nightcrawler. Or fish the bait on a slip-bobber rig.

You can catch smallmouths well into the fall, but few fishermen go after them. When the fish move out of their summertime spots in mid- to late September, try fishing deep points or humps with a jig and minnow. Don't be afraid to go as deep as 35 feet.

Time of day is not critical, but afternoon fishing is usually best in spring; morning fishing in summer. As in walleye fishing, however, the wind is all-important. If it's buffeting a rocky point or shoreline, you might catch smallmouths in water less than 5 feet deep, even on a hot summer day.

You can catch little smallmouths almost anyplace where the depth is 25 feet or less. But where you find a school of small ones, you probably won't find big ones. Don't waste your time and bait; keep moving until you find an area with fewer but larger fish.

Tips for Finding Smallmouths

LOOK for small rocks, no bigger than a basketball. They hold more crayfish, the smallmouth's favorite food, than do large boulders or slab rock.

WATCH for a mudline or clayline along the bank. Wave action discolors the water and carries in plankton, drawing baitfish and smallmouths.

CHECK any downed trees whose tops are submerged. The branches offer shade, attract baitfish and provide a substrate for insect larvae. Cast into pockets between the branches using a crankbait or spinnerbait.

DETERMINE the right depth using the "high-low" method. While one angler casts a crankbait into shore, the other jigs in deeper water.

TROLL with a deep-diving crankbait along the base of a cliff wall. Smallmouths hold tight to the wall or lie along a projecting lip.

Bass-Walleye Lakes

These big, windswept lakes offer a potpourri of gamefish.

Scattered throughout the northern states and southern Canada are tens of thousands of sandy, windswept, moderately fertile lakes that are known mainly for their walleye fisheries, but also have excellent populations of largemouth, and sometimes smallmouth, bass.

Most are ice-block lakes or lakes formed in depressions on the glacial moraine so they have basins of glacial till consisting mainly of sand and gravel, often with boulders.

The water clarity in lakes of this type typically ranges from 5 to 10 feet. But the clarity in some lakes toward the shallow, fertile end of the spectrum may be less than three feet; in lakes toward the deeper, less-fertile end, 15 feet or more.

Besides bass and walleyes, these lakes may contain northern pike, sunfish, crappies and even muskies. The major forage fish is usually the yellow perch, but bass also feed heavily on crayfish, sunfish and a wide variety of invertebrates.

Because of the popularity of walleye, pike and muskie fishing throughout the northcountry, the largemouth bass fishery in many of these lakes is virtually untapped. Consequently, the fish run good size and are often less "educated" than those in waters that see more fishing pressure.

Most anglers on these lakes simply don't fish the back channels, slop bays, docks or bulrush beds where largemouths hang out.

Smallmouth bass, however, get more attention in lakes of this type, because they inhabit much the same kind of water as the walleyes, and they're susceptible to the same presentations, namely jigging and live bait fishing with leeches, nightcrawlers and minnows.

Case Study:

Woman Lake, Minnesota

Versatility pays when fishing Woman Lake. With most anglers concentrating on walleyes, there are excellent opportunities for catching largemouth and smallmouth bass, not to speak of northern pike, crappies, bluegills, jumbo perch and trophy-caliber muskies.

Classified as mesotrophic, Woman Lake shares the qualities of many other first-rate walleye-bass lakes.

It has a broad, shallow basin and a bottom consisting mainly of sand and rubble. The water clarity, however, is much greater than that of a typical lake of this type, measuring 10 to 14 feet most of the year.

Like many other shallow, windswept lakes, Woman Lake does not stratify into distinct temperature layers. During the hottest part of the summer, the surface is only a few degrees warmer than the bottom.

Fed mainly by the Boy River, Woman Lake's water level remains quite stable. Long-term fluctuations are seldom more than a foot from the normal level. The lake drains into a series of other small lakes, into Leech Lake, and then into the Mississippi River.

Woman Lake was formed when a huge ice block buried in the Glacial moraine slowly melted. Like the hilly terrain surrounding the lake, the bottom is a maze of structure. Spanning the center of the lake is a huge, sand-gravel flat with many points and inside turns along its perimeter. Dozens of gravel and rock bars dot the western half of the lake. There are several holes at least 40 feet deep, with the deepest measuring 60 feet.

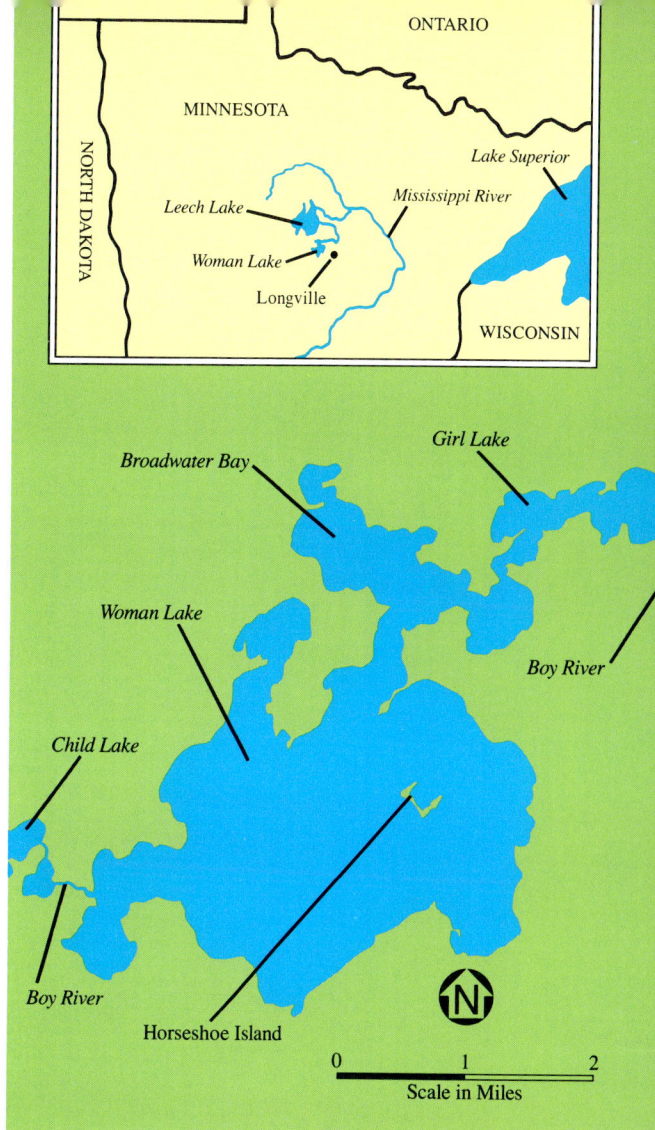

Joining the main lake are several large bays, two of which in turn connect to smaller lakes, Girl Lake and Child Lake. The bays and smaller lakes differ greatly from the main lake. They have a softer bottom and considerably more vegetation.

The wide variety of fish species in Woman Lake is a direct result of the diverse habitat. The bays and smaller lakes are best suited to largemouth bass, bluegills and crappies. The main body of the lake is better for walleyes, smallmouth bass and perch.

As in most lakes of this type, perch are the primary forage fish. But Woman Lake also supports healthy populations of shiners, bullheads, small panfish and even ciscoes.

Private cabins and homes ring Woman Lake's shoreline, and 12 fishing resorts offer cabins, boats, motors and bait. There are two public access sites on Woman Lake itself. Access is also possible through Girl Lake. Despite the development and heavy use, pollution is not a problem.

Because of its large size (over 3 miles across), rounded shape and expanses of shallow water, Woman Lake gets rough on windy days. Most anglers use deep, 16- to 18-foot semi-V aluminum boats powered by 25- to 50-hp motors, although bass boats work better for plying the slop bays. A depth finder is a must for following the irregular breaklines.

Although most of the fishing on Woman Lake takes place from mid-May through August, there is quite a bit of fall fishing. Smallmouth and largemouth continue to bite well into October.

Woman Lake Physical Data	
Acreage	4,782
Average depth	25 ft
Maximum depth	60 ft
Clarity	4 to 12 ft
Color	light green
Total phosphorus (parts per billion)	20
Thermocline	none
Average date of freeze-up	November 25
Average date of ice-out	April 24

Woman Lake Habitat (sample locations of habitats are numbered on NASA photo)

1. DOCKS, especially those near the inside weedline, draw largemouths and bluegills in summer and fall. Look for the fish on the shady side.

2. OLD BULRUSHES hold spawning crappies, bluegills and largemouth bass. Some bass stay in the rushes until early to mid-fall.

3. SLOP provides heavy shade, so it makes excellent bass cover from late spring through fall. It consists of lily pads, wild rice and submerged weeds.

4. RICE BEDS offer overhead cover for largemouths and bluegills. The rice lies flat on the water in early summer; later, it stands upright.

5. CABBAGE BEDS with deep water nearby serve as ambush points for predator fish. They produce until the weeds turn brown in fall.

6. EXTENDED LIPS off main-lake points are excellent summertime spots for smallmouth bass and walleyes.

7. MIDLAKE HUMPS and flats draw walleyes, smallmouth bass, muskies and northern pike in summer and fall. Look for points or dips in the breakline.

8. ROCKY REEFS that top off at 8 feet or less hold walleyes and smallmouths early in the season; smallmouths use the reefs through the summer.

9. BOAT CANALS in shallow bays provide access for property owners. Bluegills and largemouth bass spawn in the openings.

Woman Lake: Smallmouth Bass

While not considered a "numbers" lake, Woman Lake produces some of the region's biggest smallmouths. Each year, anglers take several in the 5- to 6-pound class, and occasionally someone lands one pushing 7.

Most of the big smallies are caught in spring, just after the season opens in late May or early June. In a normal spring, the opener falls near the spawning peak.

Smallmouths are easy to find during the spawning period. On a calm day, put on a pair of polarized sunglasses and drift or motor slowly over a shallow rocky reef. If the fish are there, you'll see them.

The most productive reefs are 3 to 10 feet deep and connected to shore. The bottom consists of sand, gravel and a mixture of softball- to basketball-sized boulders.

When you find the fish, keep your boat a short distance away and cast to them. In water this shallow and clear, trolling over the fish will probably spook them. A surface lure such as a small propbait works well in calm weather, especially early and late in the day. On windy days, you'll do better with a small crankbait, a tube jig, or a slip-bobber rig baited with a leech.

The males stay in the same areas for a week or two after spawning and can still be caught on jigs, crankbaits and propbaits. The females, which are larger, may drop into water as deep as 18 feet. They're often finicky so you may have to use live bait. At these depths, you can troll over the fish using a quiet electric motor and a slip-sinker rig baited with a leech, nightcrawler or shiner.

For fishing propbaits and crankbaits, carry a medium-power baitcasting outfit with 8-pound mono; for jigs, slip-bobber rigs and slip-sinker rigs, a light- to medium-power spinning outfit with 6-pound mono.

Once the fish abandon their spawning areas and move deeper, they're much tougher to find. During the summer, walleye anglers catch an occasional smallmouth by accident, but the fish are too scattered to catch consistently.

By late August, however, smallmouths begin to bunch up along the breaks of rocky reefs projecting from the shoreline or from Horseshoe Island. Most of them relate to points along the breakline that drop gradually into water at least 35 feet deep.

In early fall, you'll find the fish at depths of 15 to 25 feet, but as the water cools, they go deeper. By late September, most of them retreat to depths of 30 to 40 feet. They school more tightly as the season progresses. A good graph can be a big help in locating them.

Fall fishermen commonly use a slip-sinker rig baited with a 3- to 4-inch redtail chub. With winter coming, the fish feed heavily and seem to prefer larger baits than in spring or summer. Often these big baits produce a bonus walleye or northern pike.

During most of the year, smallmouths bite best on overcast days with a slight chop, preferably after a period of stable weather. You'll probably catch more fish in the morning and evening than in midday. In late fall, however, the reverse is true. Fishing is best on sunny, Indian summer days, with the fastest bite right in the middle of the day.

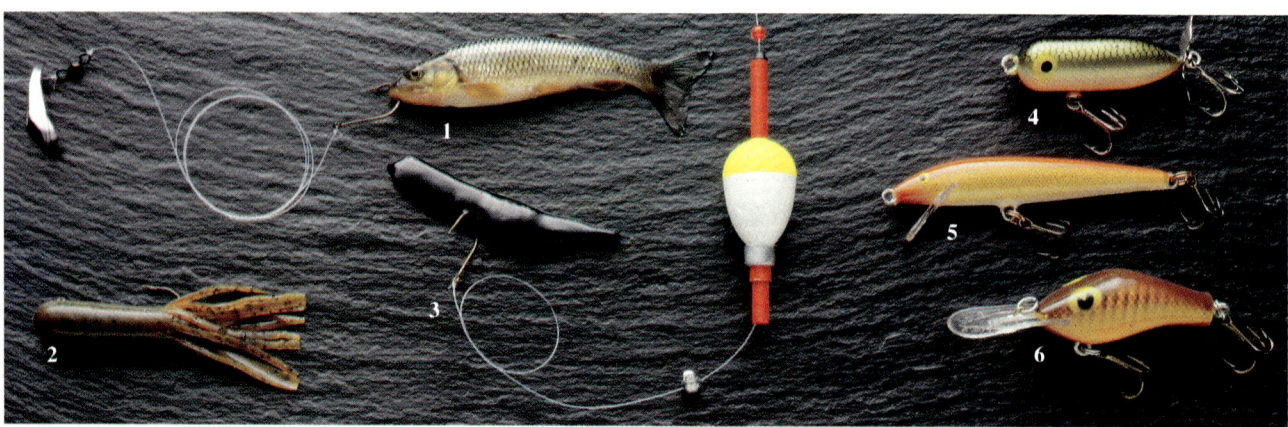

LURES AND RIGS for smallmouths include: (1) slip-sinker rig with a size 2 hook and a 3- to 4-inch redtail chub, (2) 1/16-ounce tube jig, (3) slip-bobber rig with a size 4 hook and a leech; (4) Bill Lewis Rat-L-Top propbait, (5) Floating Rapala, (6) Poe's Series 1100 crankbait.

How to Twitch a Minnow Plug for Smallmouths

CAST a floating minnow plug into the shallows and let it rest until the ripples subside. Some anglers wait as long as a minute.

RETRIEVE with a series of sharp twitches, keeping the lure on the surface. It should dart to the side, hesitate, then dart to the other side.

WATCH carefully or you may miss subtle strikes. Often a fish barely noses the lure, as if pushing it out of the way.

If you see the lure twitch or move unexpectedly, set the hook immediately.

Woman Lake:
Largemouth Bass

You'll seldom catch a largemouth in the main body of Woman Lake, but there are plenty of them in its shallow bays and connecting lakes, including a few that tip the scales at 7 pounds or more.

In the main lake, the vegetation is too sparse to hold many largemouths. The bays, however, have thicker vegetation and warmer water. Bays with only a narrow connection to the main lake hold the most bass. If the connection is too wide, the bays attract few bass in spring because the wind blows in water from the lake, greatly reducing the water temperature.

Like smallmouths, largemouths bite best early in the season. Their springtime activity centers mainly around spawning. Depending on the progress of the season, they may be in a prespawn, spawning or postspawn mode when the season opens in late May or early June.

In an early spring, most fish have completed spawning by the opener. But in a late spring, they're still on the beds and highly vulnerable. They're easy to see, and will hit almost anything tossed their way. Look for the beds in 1 to 5 feet of water around sunken logs, lily pad roots, or old mats of vegetation. You'll also find beds in bulrushes, beaver trenches and man-made boat canals.

By mid-June, the new vegetation becomes thick enough to provide overhead cover. Bass move into the "slop," where the water is slightly cooler and the young, as well as the adults, are protected from predators. On Woman Lake, this heavy, matted vegetation consists mainly of lily pads and wild rice, with a mixture of submerged plants.

Before the slop develops, spinnerbaits, weightless worms or topwater lures such as buzzbaits or stickbaits are the best choice. When the slop really gets thick, you'll need a totally weedless lure, such as a rubber frog, Texas-rigged plastic worm or weedless spoon. Carry a medium-heavy 7-foot flippin' stick with 17-pound mono for casting buzzbaits, spinnerbaits and weedless spoons; a medium-heavy 5½-foot baitcasting outfit with 12-pound mono for the other lures.

Once the slop develops, the pattern changes very little through late September. The fish move way up into the thickest slop on sunny days, and they cruise the outside edges of the weeds on cloudy days, but they're never far from the heavy vegetation.

LURES include: (1) Zara Puppy stickbait, (2) Snag Proof Frog, (3) 4-inch ring worm, (4) 6-inch Producto Worm, (5) Moss Boss weedless spoon, (6) ⅜-ounce J-Mac jig and Guido Bug, (7) Blue Fox spinnerbait, (8) Bill Norman Triple-Winged Buzzbait, (9) Bomber Fat A crankbait, (10) Slug-Go worm.

Docks also hold a lot of bass in summer and early fall. Bass prefer docks in water at least 3 feet deep and near the inside weedline; with the weeds this close, the fish can easily move back and forth.

The techniques for bass in summer and early fall are much the same as those used after the slop develops in spring. But when bass are in the deeper wild rice, try a jig-and-pig or a 4-inch Texas-rigged plastic worm. These lures will penetrate small crevices in the rice to reach the bass that lie below.

By early October, the slop has deteriorated. It will still hold a few bass, but most of them seek cover in deeper, submerged weeds. Look for the greenest weeds you can find, which will usually be coontail, and fish along the outside weedline at a depth of 10 to 14 feet.

Weedline bass usually hold in tight schools, so if you can find them, you'll have some fast fishing. Effective late-fall lures include a jig-and-pig, a ½-ounce spinnerbait and a deep-diving crankbait.

Bass feed most heavily on warm, overcast days with little or no wind, particularly if the weather has been stable for several days. Although slop bass may bite any time of the day, mornings and evenings are generally best. In late fall, bass activity gradually increases through the day as the water warms.

How to Catch Largemouths in Slop

CAST a weedless spoon into the slop; keep your rod tip high and retrieve slowly so the spoon slides over the weeds. Pause when it comes to an opening and let it flutter down (inset). If a bass hits, set the hook and lift to keep the fish out of the thick vegetation.

SLIDE the bass over the slop while holding its head up. If you let the fish dive, it may wrap around a weed and shake the hook. A flippin' stick with heavy mono (at least 17-pound test) is a must to get enough upward pull to keep the fish on top of the weeds.

Tips for Fishing in Slop

EQUIP your push pole with a duckbill to move your boat through heavy slop. Tip your outboard up so it doesn't drag in the weeds.

ADD a trailer hook if you're getting short strikes on a weedless spoon. Slide a piece of surgical tubing over the eye of the trailer, then push the trailer over the main hook.

CAST "with the grain" of the wild rice so your lure stays in the slots. If you retrieve across the grain, your lure is much more likely to foul.

BUZZ weeds off your trolling motor by lifting it out of the water and spinning the prop at high speed. A weed-cutter prop (inset) reduces weed buildup.

CARRY several pre-rigged rods; when you want to fish a different type of cover, such as a dock or an opening or edge in the slop, you don't have to change lures.

Bass-Panfish Lakes

These fertile farm-country lakes produce more fish than any other type of natural lake

If you're looking for seclusion and picturebook scenery, you won't find them on the typical bass-panfish lake. Although some of these lakes are surrounded by undeveloped woodlands, most are found in agricultural regions or heavily populated areas. But for anglers who aren't into aesthetics, these lakes have a lot to offer.

Most bass-panfish lakes are eutrophic. Runoff carries in nutrients from cities and farm fields, causing heavy growths of plankton, which result in an abundance of food. Consequently, these lakes can support more and faster-growing fish than lakes with lower nutrient levels.

High nutrient levels also cause lush growths of aquatic vegetation. In extremely fertile lakes, however, the plankton becomes so thick it keeps sunlight from reaching the bottom, preventing plants from taking root.

The basins of these lakes are so shallow that the water gets very warm in summer. Although a thermocline may form, there is seldom enough oxygen in the depths to sustain gamefish. As a result, they're found in shallow water most of the time.

Because of the warm water and dense weed growth, bass and panfish are the dominant gamefish species. The silty bottoms and periodic oxygen sags allow roughfish, especially bullheads and carp, to gain a foothold.

Many of these lakes also support northern pike and walleyes. As a rule, the walleyes must be stocked; there is not enough clean rubble bottom for successful spawning.

Even though gamefish may be plentiful, they're seldom easy to catch. The abundant supply of food means that feeding periods tend to be short. And the thick, weedy cover makes it difficult to get your bait to the fish.

The best time to fish these lakes is in spring, before the heavy weed growth develops. Food is least abundant in spring, too, so the fish must spend more of

their time feeding. Fishing usually slows in summer, after the weeds develop and young-of-the-year forage fish grow large enough to interest the gamefish. The action picks up again in fall after the weeds die back and a good share of the young forage fish have been eaten.

Some of these lakes, particularly the shallower ones, suffer winterkills in years of heavy snow cover, especially if the snow comes early. Gamefish die from lack of oxygen. If winterkills are too frequent, the lake becomes dominated by roughfish, which can better tolerate low oxygen levels.

To alleviate the problem, some natural resources agencies have installed aeration systems to agitate the water and restore oxygen. Many aerated lakes now offer outstanding fishing.

Case Study:

Big Round Lake, Wisconsin

Like thousands of other bass-panfish lakes around the country, Big Round was formed when a glacial ice block melted. Over time, the lake has become much shallower as sediment has filled in most of the original basin and obscured all but a few irregularities on the bottom. As its name suggests, the lake has a rounded shape, although there are a few subtle bays and points.

The lake is fed by the Straight River, a small stream draining farmland to the northwest. The stream carries in nutrients from the heavily fertilized fields, resulting in a "pea-soup" algae bloom in summer.

Despite the high fertility level and a maximum depth of only 17 feet, Big Round has never frozen out. The river carries in enough oxygenated water to prevent winterkill even in years of heavy snow cover.

Because the lake is so shallow and the basin so exposed to the wind, the water mixes from top to bottom and no thermocline forms in summer. After a few hot, still days, however, the bottom is usually a few degrees cooler than the surface.

Round is clearer than most eutrophic lakes, with a Secchi disk reading of 5 to 6 feet most of the year. In

midsummer, however, the reading dips to about a foot because of the heavy algae bloom.

The shoreline and shallows of Big Round are primarily sand or a sand-gravel mix, but the main basin is silt and muck. Large stands of bulrushes grow in the shallows, and thick beds of coontail, milfoil and cabbage flourish down to a depth of 8 feet.

As in most lakes of this type, largemouth bass are the dominant predator fish, and there are healthy populations of panfish, in this case, bluegills, black crappies and perch. The perch run small, but they make excellent forage.

Walleyes are stocked regularly in Big Round, and there's a remnant population of muskies, the result of past stockings. Although few anglers intentionally fish for muskies in Big Round, the lake produced a 50-pound, 4-ouncer in 1989. You may catch an occasional good-sized northern pike, but there aren't enough of them to generate much interest among anglers.

Although Big Round has no resorts, there are more than 100 private cabins, so fishing pressure is quite heavy. The lake's reputation for good bass fishing and wintertime walleye fishing also draws anglers from the surrounding area.

Big Round Lake Physical Data

Acreage	1,015
Average depth	10 ft
Maximum depth	17 ft
Clarity	1 to 6 ft
Color	green
Total phosphorus (parts per billion)	120
Thermocline	none
Average date of freeze-up	December 1
Average date of ice-out	April 14

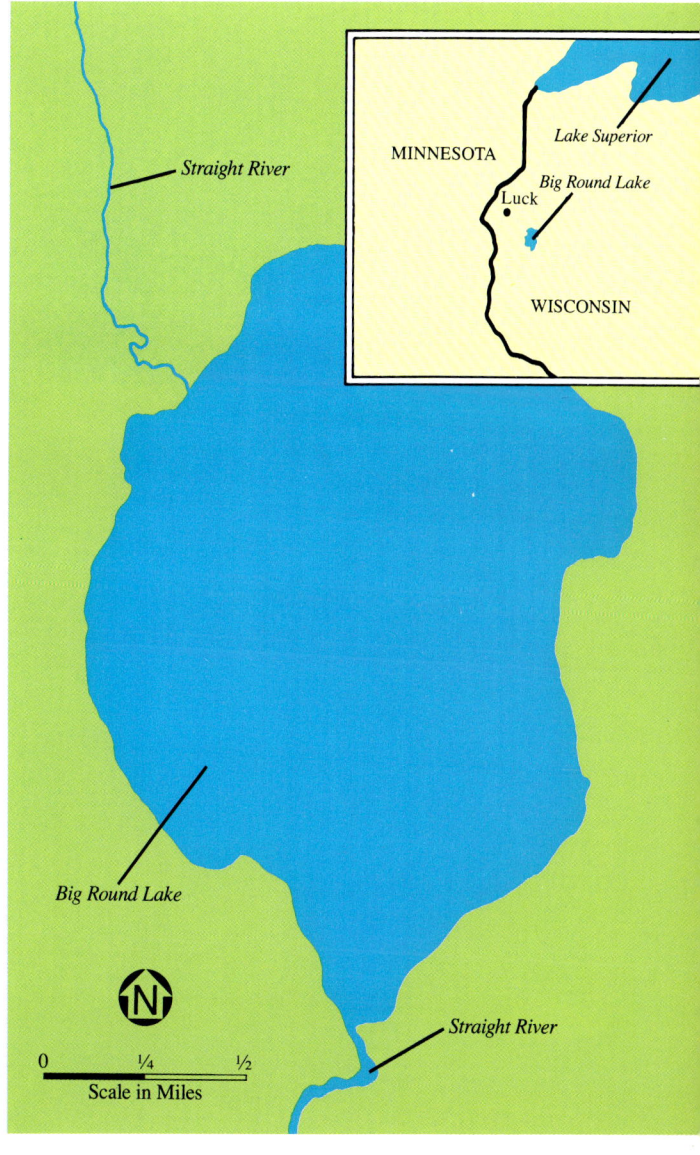

Round Lake Habitat (sample locations of habitats are marked on NASA photo)

1. BULRUSH BEDS draw bass, bluegills, crappies and walleyes in spring and fall. The deepest beds hold some bass through the summer.

2. LILY PADS grow on a dark, mucky bottom, and the water around them warms rapidly in spring, attracting prespawn largemouths.

3. BARS AND FLATS in midlake attract walleyes most of the year. Bass, bluegills and crappies use the bars and flats in summer and winter.

4. DOCKS, especially the deepest ones, hold largemouths and bluegills from summer through early fall. Docks are best in normal to high water.

5. BAYS, though not deeply indented from the rest of the shoreline, warm quickly in spring, so bass, bluegills and crappies move in to spawn.

6. POINTS in the outside weedline hold bass in summer and walleyes in early winter. Follow the margin of the matted weeds to find the points.

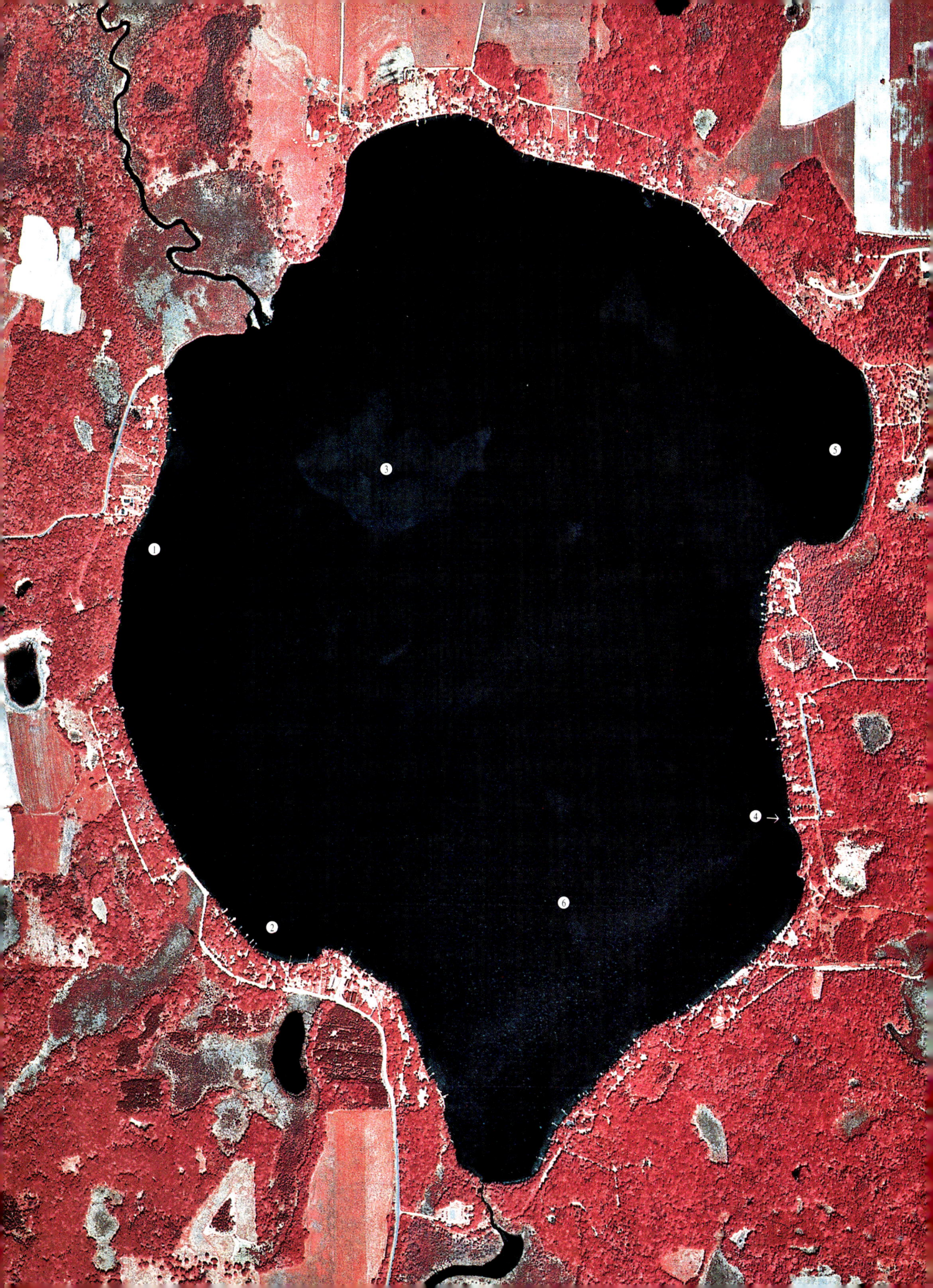

Big Round Lake:

Largemouth Bass

The shallow, weed-choked waters of Big Round are heaven for largemouth bass. Better known for numbers than size, the lake has hordes of 11- to 13-inchers. On a good day, you can catch two or three dozen, along with a few 2- to 3-pounders. And there's an outside chance of connecting with a 5- to 7-pounder. Largemouths start to feed heavily in mid-May, about two weeks before they spawn. You can find them almost anyplace in the shallows where there are old bulrushes or lily pads, or new growths of coontail or cabbage.

The main draw this time of year is warm water. If you have a temperature gauge, motor along the shoreline and look for warmwater zones. Usually, the bays have the warmest water and draw the most bass. If the water temperature is below 50° F, the fish probably won't be in the shallows.

Another attraction in late spring is spawning sunfish. If you can find a colony of spawning beds, you're likely to find the bass. They move in to feed on

How to Work Matted Weeds

TOSS a jig-and-pig or a Texas-rigged plastic worm on top of a dense weed mat. Hold your rod tip high as you retrieve so the lure slides over the weeds. Sometimes bass come out of the weeds and grab the lure on the surface.

PAUSE and lower your rod tip when the jig reaches the edge of the weeds or comes to a pocket. Be sure to keep the line taut as the jig sinks so you can feel the fish strike. Set the hook immediately.

How to Skip a Worm Under a Dock

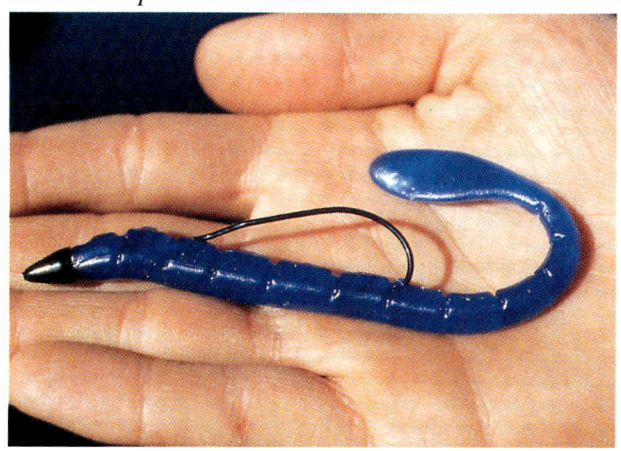

SELECT a fat-bodied worm; the broader surface makes it skip better than a skinnier worm. Rig the worm Texas style and peg the sinker so it doesn't separate from the worm when you cast.

SKIP the worm into the shadiest area under a dock. Using a spinning outfit with 10-pound mono, cast the worm with a sharp sidearm motion so it lands close to the dock, then skips underneath.

crayfish, minnows and other sunfish-egg predators, as well as on the sunfish themselves.

To locate springtime bass, use a shallow-running lure that allows you to cover water quickly, such as a ¼-ounce tandem spinnerbait. In morning or evening or under other dim-light conditions, try a ¼- to ⅜-ounce buzzbait or a propbait fished with a reel-and-pause retrieve. When you locate some fish and want to work the area more thoroughly, switch to a ¼-ounce jig-and-pig.

In spring, largemouths bite best from midafternoon to dusk, the period of highest water temperature. You'll catch the most fish on warm, still, cloudy days, especially after several days of warm, stable weather. Sunny days with a light breeze can be good too.

By mid-June, the water temperature has risen into the 70s and the weeds are almost fully developed. Under bright conditions, look for bass right in the thickest submerged weedbeds or in the shadiest areas under docks. In low-light conditions, you'll find bass in openings in the weeds, points along the outside weedlines, and around the docks. A few bass remain in the deeper bulrushes.

Use a buzzbait to "call up" bass in the thick weeds; or work a jig-and-pig or Texas-rigged plastic worm through the weeds and along the weedline. Fish the docks with a fat-bodied plastic worm.

When the water greens up during an algae bloom, many of the bass in deep water move shallower. The blanket of algae is so thick it provides shade.

LURES for largemouths include: (1) ¼-ounce Arkie Jig with a crawfrog, (2) single-spin spinnerbait with a curly-tail grub, (3) ⅜-ounce J-Mac Jig with a jumbo pork frog, (4) Fleck Spinnerbait with a curly-tail grub, (5) Northland Buzz-ard with a curly-tail grub, (6) Culprit Worm, Texas rigged with a ³⁄₁₆-ounce bullet sinker, (7) Producto Worm, Texas rigged with a pegged ¹⁄₁₆-ounce bullet sinker, (8) A.C. Shiner 00, (9) Devil's Horse.

Summertime bass bite best in the same type of weather as in spring. Morning and evening fishing is most productive, especially when you're working the dense weeds; the bass move out of the thick mats and feed along the edges.

By late September, most of the shallow submerged weeds have died. Many bass move into deep clumps of green coontail, although you'll find some in the deeper bulrush beds, particularly those nearest the edge of the break.

Work the edges of a bulrush patch with a ¼- to ⅜-ounce jig-and-pig, occasionally casting back into the rushes to catch less active bass. Use a jig-and-pig, a ½-ounce single-spin spinnerbait or a medium-diving crankbait to fish the deeper coontail clumps.

Through most of the fall, fishing is best in cloudy weather, just as in spring and summer. But starting in early October, largemouths bite better on sunny, Indian summer days, often right in midafternoon.

Because of the dense weeds in Big Round, most anglers use medium-heavy baitcasting outfits, 5½ to 6 feet long, with 12- to 20-pound mono, depending on the cover. For worm fishing, carry a 6-foot, medium-heavy spinning outfit with 10-pound mono.

Anyone can catch small bass on Big Round, but the big ones are hard to come by. Small bass race after any lure that comes by. The big bass are lazy; they hold tighter to cover and aren't anxious to go out of their way to get food. If they ignore a fast-moving buzzbait, for instance, try slowly retrieving a jig-and-pig in or alongside the weeds.

A jig-and-pig is a good choice for big bass

"Pitchin'" a Jig-and-Pig in the Bulrushes

1. REDUCE your spool tension by loosening the adjustment knob. The spool must turn freely in order to get enough distance when you pitch the jig.

2. ANGLE your rod tip downward, push the thumb bar, and thumb the spool. Hold the jig with your other hand so there is slight tension between the jig and the rod.

3. PITCH the jig toward a pocket in the weeds using a smooth, upward, shoveling motion; at the same time, release the jig.

4. STOP the jig in the exact spot by thumbing the spool. The jig should set down gently. With practice, you should be able to pitch 30 feet with good accuracy.

Tips for Catching Bass in Fertile Lakes

SWITCH to a larger pork chunk when bass refuse to strike your jig-and-pig. The bulkier pork keeps your jig on top of the weeds, and when the jig reaches a hole, it will sink more slowly, giving bass extra time to strike.

SELECT a plastic worm with metallic flecks when fishing in low-clarity water. The flecks reflect light in different directions, so there's a better chance that largemouths will notice the worm.

Florida Bass Lakes

The promise of a 10-pounder draws bass anglers from all over the country to Florida's lake region

Among the "snowbirds" that migrate southward each winter are tens of thousands of northern anglers eager to sample Florida's renowned bass lakes.

Most northerners have heard about Florida's famous natural lakes — Okeechobee, Kissimmee, Orange-Lochloosa and possibly several others. But few realize that the state has thousands of natural lakes, 7,783 to be exact.

Many have the mistaken idea that Florida's lakes are all shallow, swampy and weed choked. While quite a few fit that category, others are deep and clear with only a narrow fringe of shoreline vegetation. Although 90 percent of the lakes are small (less than 20 acres), some are huge. Okeechobee, the state's largest lake, covers 690 square miles.

Florida's natural lakes fall into three major categories: solution lakes, lakes formed in old seabed depressions, and riverine lakes.

Solution lakes formed when surface or groundwater seeped through and dissolved underground limestone, creating cavities that eventually collapsed and filled with water. Also called "sinkhole" lakes, solution lakes normally have a round, cone-shaped basin

Florida bass reach mammoth size, as this 15-pounder proves

with no inlet or outlet. Most are small (less than 250 acres) and deep (more than 25 feet).

Florida's natural lake region is an uplifted seabed, and some of the lake basins are simply depressions in the old sea bottom. These lakes are larger and shallower than solution lakes, and their bottoms are usually flatter. Florida's riverine lakes include oxbows and lakes that are actually wide, shallow portions of rivers.

Although most Florida lakes have the greenish to brownish color typical of highly fertile lakes, about two-thirds of the lakes have low to moderate fertility, so they are not as productive as widely believed. The deepest solution lakes are the least fertile.

Water clarity varies widely, but in most lakes is 5 feet or less. In a few lakes, however, clarity exceeds 25 feet. Florida's spring lakes are among the clearest in the world.

The allure of Florida's lakes stems mainly from a fish that inhabits them, the Florida bass. A subspecies of largemouth bass, the Florida bass grows considerably larger than its northern cousin. Northern largemouth seldom exceed 10 pounds; Floridas may surpass 20.

Not all bass that live in Florida lakes are purebred Florida bass, however. There are "intergrades" between northern and Florida largemouths, and even taxonomists have difficulty determining whether a given specimen is a pure Florida or an intergrade. To anglers, it doesn't really matter. The intergrades seem to get just as big. In fact, many believe that the current world-record largemouth, a 22-pound 4-ounce giant, was an intergrade.

But Florida bass aren't the only attraction. Many of the lakes have black crappies, or "speckled perch" as they're often called; redear sunfish, or "shellcrackers"; bluegills; chain pickerel and even channel catfish. Some lakes are stocked with striped bass and some with striped bass-white bass hybrids, called "sunshine bass."

Because of the year-round growing season, most of the fish in Florida lakes grow faster than their northern counterparts. But they don't live as long, so they aren't necessarily larger.

The fishing season in Florida stays open all year, but angling pressure is heaviest in late winter and early spring, when there are more fishermen around and the bass are concentrated in spawning areas.

There's one major difference in fishing Florida lakes versus lakes in the northern part of the country. Because the water temperature in Florida lakes seldom drops below 55° F in winter, the spring warm-up is more gradual than in northern lakes.

Consequently, all fish species spawn over a much longer period. Largemouths, for example, complete spawning in a week or two in northern lakes. But in Florida, spawning may last as long as four months. Some bass may be spawning while others have finished and moved back to their normal haunts. Still others have not yet started to spawn. As a result of this pattern, you'll find bass scattered over a wide range of habitat, even though spawning is under way.

While Florida lakes offer many outstanding fishing opportunities, a number of waters face serious problems. Florida's population explosion, combined with rapid industrial and agricultural expansion, has led to dramatic increases in the amount of organic pollutants entering some lakes. Algae blooms have increased, causing diminished growth of the rooted aquatic plants that gamefish require for cover. In a few lakes, bass have almost disappeared.

As the human population grows, more and more gamefish spawning and rearing areas are destroyed. Developers fill in wetlands to build homes, and property owners cover shoreline vegetation with sand to make swimming beaches.

Anyone who has driven through Florida and crossed dozens of man-made canals knows the practice of channelization runs rampant in the state. Many canals, supposedly built for flood control, are a guise to drain bottomland for property development. Some

A maze of drainage canals covers some parts of Florida

lakes have lost more than half of their surface area because of drainage.

Water-control devices on the canals are intended to maintain lake levels. But most lakes are now being held at a lower level than in years past. The lower water leads to increased plant growth. When the plants die, decomposition produces sediments that fill in and shrink the lake basin at a faster-than-normal rate.

Compounding this problem is the rapid spread of exotic plants, particularly hydrilla and water hyacinth. Besides further increasing the sedimentation rate, exotics can choke a lake to the point where boat travel is nearly impossible. And they often crowd out the native plants.

In some lakes, however, the invasion of hydrilla has been a blessing for fish. It provides excellent cover, and concentrates baitfish, aquatic insects and other fish foods. Although hydrilla caused navigation problems, knowledgeable fishermen quickly noted the advantages and took steps to discourage the complete chemical eradication advocated by many lakeshore property owners.

Perhaps some balance can be struck to control vegetation while leaving enough for the fish.

Case Study:
Lake Istokpoga, Florida

In Seminole, the name Istokpoga has a grim meaning — "Man who goes on water dies." Numerous drownings in years past gave the big, windswept lake its reputation. Today, the lake has a reputation for something else — first-rate bass fishing.

Lake Istokpoga (pronounced Is-ta-po´-ga) lies in an old seabed depression. The lake basin and surrounding land are flat, providing no protection when the wind blows.

Although considerably larger than the average Florida natural lake, Istokpoga has many of the qualities of Florida's other prime bass lakes. Its shallow, fertile, tannin-stained waters offer plenty of weedy cover and teem with bass foods such as small sunfish, shad, killifish and golden shiners.

Because Istokpoga averages only 4 feet deep, weeds grow almost everywhere. The shallows have cattails, pickerelweed, bulrushes, maidencane and lily pads.

As in many other Florida lakes, water hyacinth has been a long-standing problem, but has been kept under control with chemicals.

Hydrilla gained a foothold in the early 1980s and spread so rapidly that it crowded out most other kinds of submerged plants. It can take root anywhere, from the shallows to the deepest water, and deep beds may grow nearly to the surface.

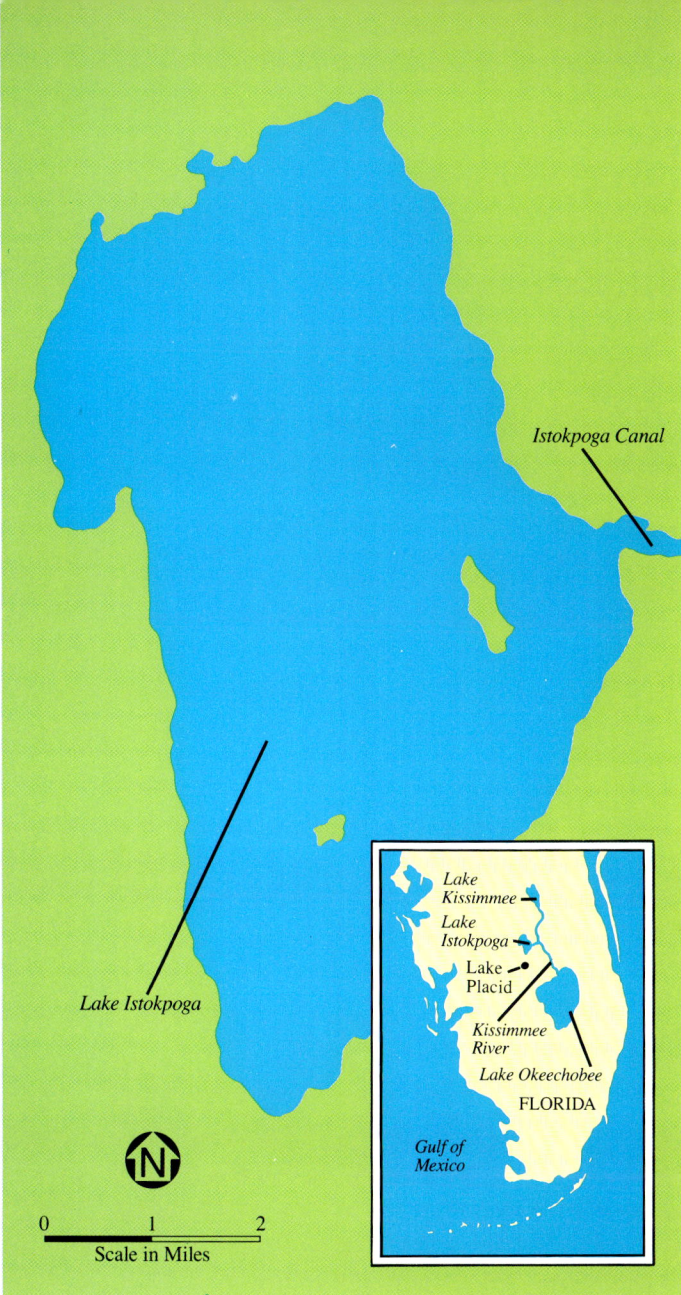

Water hyacinth (top) and hydrilla (bottom) are being controlled by chemicals in Istokpoga

Complaints by boaters and property owners led to an extensive chemical treatment program, but some large hydrilla beds remain. Ongoing chemical control will be necessary to prevent exotic weeds from overrunning the lake.

While hydrilla may be a headache for boaters, it's paradise for largemouth bass. It provides shade and ambush cover for the adults and hiding cover for the young. Within five years after hydrilla got its start in Istokpoga, the bass population tripled.

The lake also supports plenty of good-sized redear sunfish and crappies. Although there are reasonable numbers of bluegills, chain pickerel and channel catfish, these species aren't as popular with anglers.

Istokpoga's water level is regulated by a U.S. Army Corps of Engineers control structure on the canal draining from the southeast corner of the lake. As in many other Florida lakes, the control structure keeps the water lower than in years past, so the density of vegetation in the shallows has increased. Sediment produced by the decomposing plants is filling in the basin at a much faster rate.

Compared to most Florida lakes, angling pressure on Istokpoga is light. Most anglers fish for bass, with only about half as many pursuing sunfish and crappies.

Lake Istokpoga Physical Data	
Acreage	27,692
Average depth	4 ft
Maximum depth	10 ft
Clarity	2 ft
Color	brownish
Total phosphorus (parts per billion)	50
Thermocline	none

Lake Istokpoga Habitat (sample locations of habitats are numbered on NASA photo)

1. LILY PADS, called "bonnets," make good spawning habitat for bluegills, redears and crappies. They sometimes draw a few bass.

2. BULRUSH BEDS are spawning areas for bass, sunfish and crappies. You'll find bass in the rushes from October through May.

3. SHELL BEDS hold the small clams and snails (shown) that redear sunfish feed on. The best beds are in 5 to 6½ feet of water, on a slight break.

4. HYDRILLA BEDS hold bass, bluegills, redears and crappies all year. Look for the beds with the lushest, greenest weeds.

5. BOAT CANALS in lakeshore property make good year-round bass and sunfish habitat. Look for the fish around docks and tree roots.

6. CHANNELS cut through stands of emergent vegetation to provide boat access draw largemouths and sunfish at spawning time.

7. CATTAILS (shown), eelgrass and peppergrass attract largemouth bass all year, except during the hottest part of the summer.

8. MAIDENCANE grows only on a sandy bottom and is a good indicator of largemouth spawning habitat. You'll find some bass in it all year.

9. CYPRESS TREES have a complex underwater root network. They hold sunfish all year; bass from April through November.

NASA High Altitude Photograph →

Lake Istokpoga:
Largemouth Bass

Bass anglers flock to Florida with one thing in mind: catching a trophy bass. Even though bass over 10 pounds are getting harder and harder to find, there's still a reasonable chance of connecting — if you know when, where and how to go about it.

The biggest bass are caught from mid-December through late March, when the fish concentrate near their spawning areas. They spawn on hard, sandy bottoms in stands of emergent vegetation, particularly bulrushes. Most beds are in water from 1½ to 3 feet deep, with at least 4 feet of water nearby.

Spawning activity is light in December but rapidly gains momentum, peaking a few days either side of the first full moon in March. As with all largemouths, the male moves in first and builds the nest; the female hangs back from the nesting area until just before spawning time. Then she swims onto the nest, accompanied by one or more males, and deposits her eggs. Females remain on the nest no more than four days.

Unlike northern largemouths, the female Florida may assist with nest-guarding duties, especially if the male is caught. Many of the largest Florida bass taken are nest-guarding females.

Because the spawning period is so long and not all bass in the lake spawn at the same time, it's possible to catch some bass in the spawning areas and some in typical summertime habitat on the same day.

Golden shiners probably account for more big Floridas than any other bait. They're most effective in winter, but they'll catch bass anytime. Wild shiners work better than those raised in hatcheries. Bass prey on wild shiners in nature, so a hooked shiner gets very nervous when a bass approaches. It skitters to the surface and thrashes about wildly, attracting even uninterested bass. A hatchery shiner, on the other hand, has never seen a bass, so it remains much calmer and triggers fewer strikes.

Shiner fishing can be frustrating. Normally, you'll be fishing in heavy cover, either on the edge of a bulrush or cattail bed, over a mat of hydrilla, or in a weed-fringed canal. A lively shiner will tangle your line around the vegetation, and a hooked bass will swim far back into it, so you'll need heavy tackle. A 7- to 9-foot heavy-power fiberglass rod and a good-sized

LURES for largemouths include: (1) Cordell Boy Howdy, (2) A.C. Shiner 375, (3) Rat-L-Trap, (4) Bomber Model A, (5) tandem spinnerbait, (6) Blue Fox Floyd's Buzzer, (7) 5-inch Ditto Gator Tail, Florida rigged (p. 161).

MAKE a golden shiner rig by sliding on a 3-inch cylinder float and tying on a special weedless shiner hook. Push the hook through the bottom jaw and out the nostril of the shiner (inset). Set the weedguard.

baitcasting reel spooled with 25- to 40-pound abrasion-resistant mono make an ideal combination.

Wild shiners are expensive, but you can catch your own if you know how. To locate shiners, chum shallow weedy areas with oatmeal until you see them dimpling the surface. Then catch them with a cane pole and size 12 hook baited with a tiny doughball, or throw a cast net over them.

Winter fishing usually peaks in midday, when the water temperature is warmest. A slight chop is better than a calm surface; an overcast day better than a sunny one. A warming trend increases feeding activity; a cold front slows feeding and pushes the bass farther back into the rushes or out of the rushes into deeper water.

Fishing for Florida bass on the spawning beds is a highly controversial topic. Many blame this practice for the decline in big bass. When a female bass is on the bed, any disturbance from anglers may cause her to permanently abandon the spawning area. Of course, bass guarding the nest are very aggressive, so many question the sporting ethics of anglers who catch bass when they're most vulnerable.

When the weather warms in summer, wild shiners are tough to keep alive, so almost all anglers use artificials. Most any kind of proven bass lure works — the choice depends on the type of cover, the mood of the bass and personal preference. Serious anglers usually carry several rods rigged with different lures, then experiment to find what the bass want on a given day.

Locating bass in summer can be a challenge in Istokpoga because the lake is so large and has little structure to concentrate the fish. There are thousands of acres of hydrilla-covered flats, any of which may hold bass.

Your best chances of catching bass are early in the morning, when the temperature is coolest. The fish seem to bite better whenever there's a light to moderate wind.

During an intense heat wave, you'll find largemouths in the thickest hydrilla beds and the deepest bulrushes, where the shade keeps the water a few degrees cooler.

The best summertime approach is to cover a lot of water using a "locator" lure, such as a vibrating plug. Once you catch a fish or two, work the area thoroughly with a lure you can retrieve more slowly, such as a plastic worm or a jig-and-pig. On calm days, topwater lures such as propbaits, buzzbaits and minnow plugs twitched along the surface will draw bass out of the weeds. This artificial lure strategy works just as well other times of the year.

When fishing artificials, use medium- to heavy-power baitcasting or spinning gear with 14- to 17-pound mono. Stout tackle helps extract largemouths from the heavy vegetation. When fishing in hydrilla, for instance, it's not unusual to pull in a bass along with a clump of weeds weighing considerably more than the fish.

Starting in October, you'll see bass busting into schools of shad on the surface. A flock of gulls can be a tipoff; they follow close to pick up the injured shad. It pays to carry an extra rod rigged with a topwater lure or a Rat-L-Trap, should this opportunity present itself.

How to Locate Bass in Hydrilla

CAST a Rat-L-Trap over a hydrilla flat. The weighted lure lets you cast a long way and retrieve rapidly, so you can find active bass quickly.

TOSS a marker when you catch a fish. Continue to work the area with the Rat-L-Trap as long as it continues to produce.

CATCH less aggressive bass, which are often buried deeper in the weeds, by switching to a plastic worm or jig-and-pig.

How to Fish Bass With Golden Shiners

SOUND the outside edges of the bulrush beds with your depth finder, looking for water at least 6 feet deep. Bass prefer the deeper beds.

LOB a shiner rig (p. 159) into pockets in the rushes after anchoring the boat on both ends. If you cast where the rushes are thickest, the shiner will swim around the stems.

PULL your bobber out and try to make it catch on a bulrush stem. This prevents the minnow from pulling the rig far back into the weeds and tangling.

POINT your rod at the fish (left) when you get a bite; reel up slack until you feel weight. Set the hook hard (right) and don't let the fish swim back into the weeds.

Largemouth-Fishing Tips

UNTIE the anchor rope if the bass gets into the weeds. Tie a float to the rope so it doesn't sink. Now you can follow the bass, grab it, then reanchor.

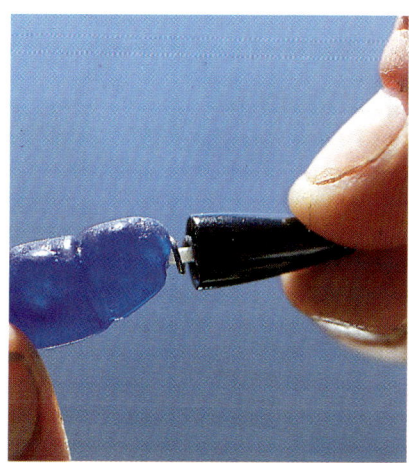

FLORIDA-RIG a worm by twisting a screw-in weight into the head. The weight can't separate, so it pulls the worm deep into the weeds.

TOUGHEN bread for shiner fishing by microwaving a damp, crustless slice for 30 seconds. Roll into a ball and bait a size 12 hook with small bits.

Oxbow Lakes

These river-channel lakes offer first-rate fishing, but anglers must contend with constantly changing water levels

If you live near a big, winding river, you're probably not too far from Horseshoe, Crescent or Half-Moon Lake. Dozens of lakes with these names are found throughout the country, remnants of riverbeds left behind when the river changed course.

The term "oxbow" originates from the name of the U-shaped device used to collar oxen to their yoke. Oxbow lakes have the same shape because of the way they were formed.

A river flowing over loose materials continually erodes the outside bends and deposits silt on the inside bends, causing the channel to wind, or meander. The river forms a series of loops, some of which erode completely through at the neck. The crescent-shaped body of water that remains is usually isolated from the river, though some remain connected on the downstream end.

Most oxbow lakes form naturally, but sometimes man speeds up the process for purposes of navigation or flood control. Meander loops are often cut off to shorten the channel or to allow flood waters to pass more quickly, reducing upstream flooding.

Oxbow lakes have a very short life span, sometimes less than 50 years. A few persist for as long as 1,000 years, still a short life compared to other types of natural lakes. When the river tops its banks, it deposits silt in the upper end of the lake. The lake gradually fills in until it becomes too shallow for fish. Eventually, it becomes nothing more than a swampy scar on the landscape.

Rivers constantly change and new oxbows form as fast as old ones fill in. But on many of the country's largest rivers, the banks have been stabilized and the channel has been straightened for commercial navigation. The rivers cannot meander, so no new oxbows form as old oxbows die.

Because of their short life span and their tendency to flood, oxbows are not as heavily developed as other natural lakes. Government agencies and private investors are reluctant to spend money on a lake where the future is so uncertain. Most oxbow lakes have few, if any, resorts or private cabins, and some lack public accesses.

You may be able to motor into the lake from the river, if there is a connection at the lower end. If not, consult a U. S. Geological Survey quad map or Corps of Engineers river chart to determine where the lake comes closest to the present river channel. Then, you can portage a canoe or small boat from the river to the lake.

Oxbow lakes rise and fall with the river. Even without a connecting channel, the lake level follows the river level because of seepage through the highly porous soil. If the seepage rate is slow, however, the change in lake level may lag considerably behind that of the river.

In oxbow lakes that connect to the river, fish swim freely between the two so they usually have the same kinds of fish. In oxbows that do not have a connecting channel, fish from the river swim into the lake during floods.

Oxbow lakes will challenge anglers who aren't accustomed to constantly changing water levels. When the water is high, the fish scatter into newly flooded lowlands. When it's low, they're often confined in small, deep basins of the lake. Veteran oxbow lake anglers know where to look for fish at different times of year at different water stages.

But oxbows offer some advantages over other types of lakes. Because of their crescent shape, you can always find a spot out of the wind. Another bonus: the lack of access and resort facilities means relatively light angling pressure, so oxbow lakes still in their prime offer outstanding fishing. Even if the lake is heavily fished, it is restocked every time the river overflows its banks.

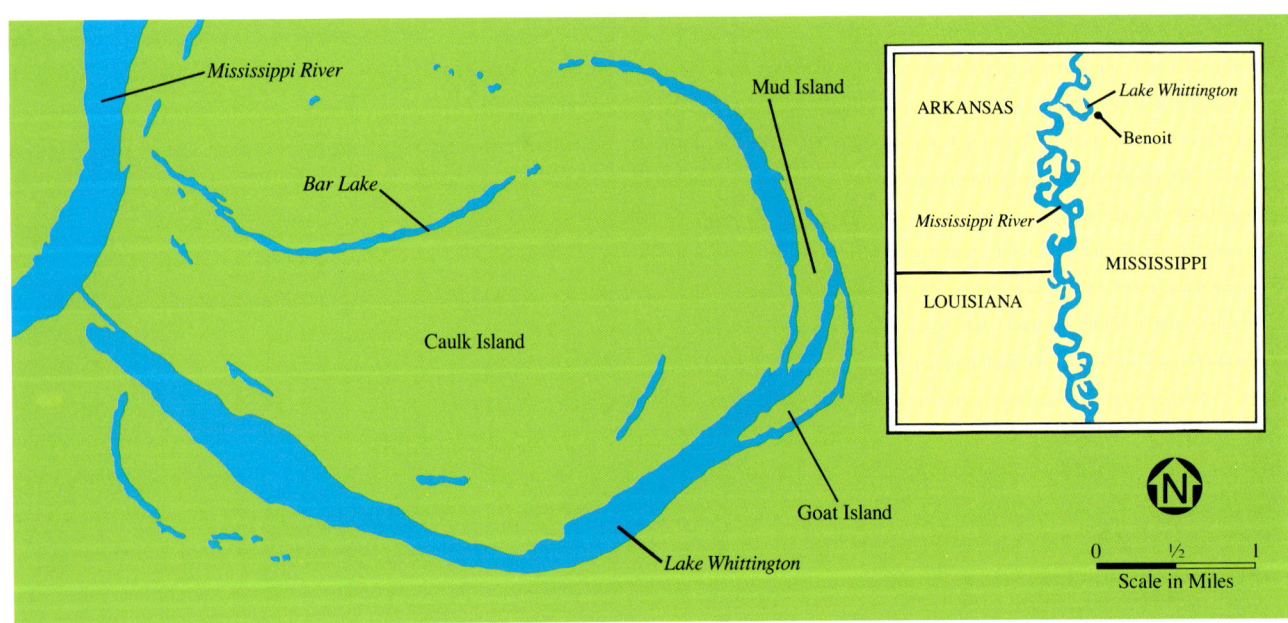

164

In 1937, the Corps of Engineers bulldozed a channel (arrow) to cut off Lake Whittington from the Mississippi River

Case Study:

Lake Whittington, Mississippi

Oxbow lakes abound in the lower Mississippi River valley, particularly from southern Missouri south to the delta. Here, the flood plain is very flat and sandy, so the river can easily erode its banks and change course. Because the river has such a large flow in its lower reaches, its cutting ability is great.

Between Cape Girardeau, Missouri, and New Orleans, are 37 major oxbow lakes. Typical of these is Lake Whittington, a 2,350-acre oxbow near Benoit, Mississippi. Like many of these waters, Whittington is a "cutoff" lake. It was isolated from the river when the Corps of Engineers cut through the neck of a 15-mile meander loop to create a shortcut for barge traffic. Erosion would have cut off the loop in another decade or two; the Corps simply sped up the process.

Lake Whittington is bounded on the south and east by the Mississippi River levee, and on the north and west by Caulk Island, the piece of land left behind after the cutoff. As in most oxbows, the upper end of the lake has silted in and is completely separated from the river unless the water gets extremely high. The lower end is open, and the channel to the river is navigable unless the water is very low.

In an average year, the water level in Lake Whittington fluctuates about 30 feet. The water level usually peaks in April, rising about 25 feet above normal summer levels. It may rise 45 feet in a severe flood. The level is usually lowest in September and October, when it drops about 5 feet below normal. Levels 10 feet below normal have been recorded.

During floods, water covers much of Caulk Island, and fish spread out over thousands of acres of partially submerged trees and brush. Fishing can be good during high water, but navigating through the timber requires a maneuverable, shallow-draft boat. Most local anglers prefer 14- to 16-foot jon boats powered by 15- to 25-hp outboards. A push pole is a must for crossing shallow spots and breaking through logjams.

Because the clarity is so low and the water level changes so often, aquatic vegetation does not have a chance to take root. Fish rely on logs, brush and rip-rap for cover.

In summer, water more than 20 feet deep lacks sufficient oxygen for gamefish. Most of the lake is so shallow that wind circulation keeps the temperature the same from top to bottom.

The lake supports good populations of crappies, bluegills, largemouth bass, white bass and channel catfish. There's also a fair number of longear and redear sunfish, some yellow bass, and a few sea-run striped bass. Although silt deposits have reduced the water volume by 60 percent since the lake was created, fishing has held up well.

Local fishermen are concerned about Lake Whittington's future because the lake has filled in so rapidly in recent years. Many believe that a dam is needed at the lower end to keep water levels higher during low-water periods. At present, however, neither state nor federal conservation agencies have any such plans.

Lake Whittington Physical Data

Acreage	2,350
Average depth	8 ft
Maximum depth	56 ft
Clarity	1 ft
Color	brown
Total phosphorus (parts per billion)	120
Thermocline	none
Average date of freeze-up	rarely freezes

Lake Whittington Habitat (sample locations of habitats are numbered on NASA photo)

1. THE OUTLET CHANNEL holds large schools of white bass, as well as some largemouths and catfish, from summer through fall.

2. CLEARINGS along shore indicate a clean bottom where crappies, bass and bluegills spawn. With no trees, the sun can easily warm the beds.

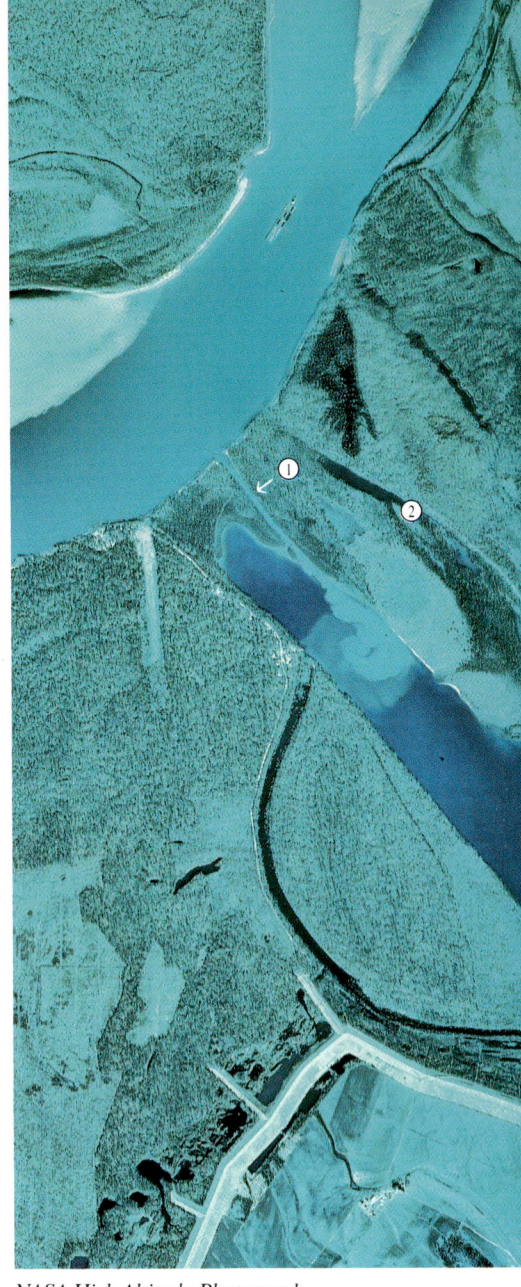

3. YOUNG WILLOWS sprout up when silted-in flats are exposed at low water. When the water rises, the flooded shoots make good gamefish cover.

4. RIPRAP banks along the main lake, especially those with submerged trees or brush for cover, draw largemouths from summer through fall.

NASA High Altitude Photograph

5. FLOATING DEBRIS loosened by rising water provides cover for bass and crappies. The wind determines where the debris will settle.

6. BUCKBRUSH clumps provide cover for all fish species in high water. Fish can easily hide among the tangle of branches and leaves.

7. POINTS in the main lake attract largemouths, crappies and sunfish in summer; the shallow flats atop the points hold white bass.

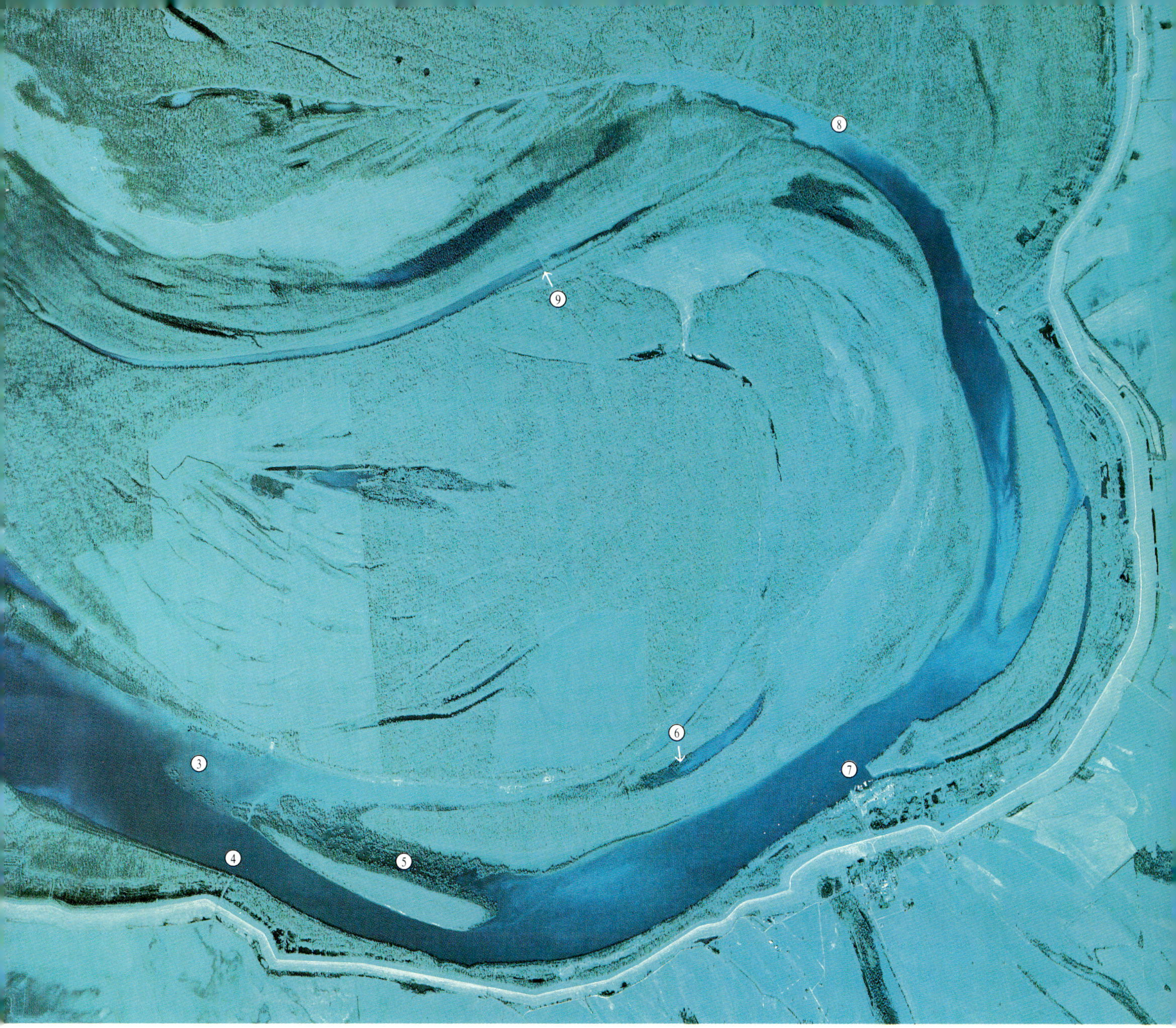

8. MATURE WILLOWS offer cover to largemouth bass, bluegills and crappies during high water. Most of the fish hold in the outer few rows of trees, rather than in the middle of the flooded stand.

9. EARTHEN DAMS are built to maintain water levels in backwaters during low-water periods. When flooded, the dams provide structure which attracts bluegills and largemouth bass.

Lake Whittington:
Largemouth Bass

Because of the rapidly changing water levels, largemouths in oxbow lakes have developed an unusual feeding pattern seldom seen by anglers on other types of lakes.

In spring, rising water floods thousands of acres of timber and brush, forcing terrestrial animals such as snakes and mice to swim for cover. Bass roam freely through the woody tangle, picking these animals off the surface.

Faced with the maze of cover, anglers tend to select snag-resistant lures such as plastic worms, brushguard jigs or spinnerbaits. But these offerings seldom work as well as surface lures, which better imitate the natural food.

Fishing really heats up in late April and stays hot through June. Most of the fish run 1 to 3 pounds, but there are plenty of 4- to 6-pounders and every so often, somebody lands one weighing more than 8 pounds.

Any propbait, stickbait or minnow plug will work, but one of the local favorites is a minnow plug with a propeller on the tail. You can buy the lures (Bagley's Spinner Tail) or make your own (p. 170). Using a medium-power spinning or baitcasting outfit with 8-

LURES for Lake Whittington largemouth bass include: (1) Bass Pro Shop Rocker Buzz buzzbait, (2) 6-inch T's Salt Hookers worm rigged Texas style with a 2/0 hook, (3) Strike King spinnerbait, (4) $5/16$-ounce Stanley Jig with pork frog, (5) Heddon Zara Spook, (6) Bill Lewis Rat-L-Trap.

to 12-pound mono, toss the lure past a tree or clump of brush and retrieve with twitches sharp enough to make the prop churn the surface. Pause occasionally and let the lure rest a few seconds, particularly when it reaches a pocket in the cover.

You'll improve your odds by selecting the right type of cover. Bare trees seldom hold bass, but those with a lot of vines or small branches around the trunk provide good ambush spots. Trees and brush near the edge of a flooded stand usually hold more bass than those deep within the stand.

You can score consistently with this surface-fishing technique, if the water is at the right stage. Lake Whittington anglers frequently check the closest water level gauge on the river. Fishing is best when it registers between 16 and 25 feet and is holding steady or slowly rising or falling. If it rises too rapidly, the water gets muddy; if it falls too quickly, the fish don't feed.

By early summer, the water has usually dropped enough to force bass out of the timber and brush and into the main lake. When the river gauge reads 10

How to Fish a Doctored Minnow Plug

REMOVE the rear screw from a minnow plug. Slip a propbait propeller and a pair of cup washers over the screw and reattach it.

CAST well past the cover where you suspect bass are holding. Angle your cast so the lure will track as close to the cover as possible.

TWITCH the plug sharply as you retrieve, letting it rest a few seconds between twitches. The erratic action will draw bass from several feet down.

CAST into patches of duckweed. The small floating plants attract bass if they're packed together tightly enough to provide heavy shade.

LOOK for viney trees or trees with lots of branches on the trunk. They're more likely to hold bass than are trees with a bare trunk.

to 15 feet, you'll find most fish near points, steep banks, riprapped shorelines, breaks along the old river channel or shoreline springs. The best spots have some type of woody cover and are usually less than 10 feet deep, with deeper waters nearby. Bass will stay in these locations as long as the water is stable or slowly falling.

In summer and fall, use standard largemouth-fishing tactics. When searching for bass, cast a spinnerbait or buzzbait. In dense woody cover, try a plastic worm or jig-and-pig. On points or other open-water structure with lighter cover, toss a crankbait. Most anglers use medium- to heavy-power baitcasting tackle with 12- to 20-pound mono, depending on the type of cover they're fishing. By the middle of December, the rapidly cooling water pushes largemouths deeper and fishing slows until the weather begins to warm again in mid-March.

Warm, stable weather and overcast skies spell fast bass action on Lake Whittington. Throughout most of the year, the fish bite early and late in the day, but springtime fishing is better from midday to late afternoon.

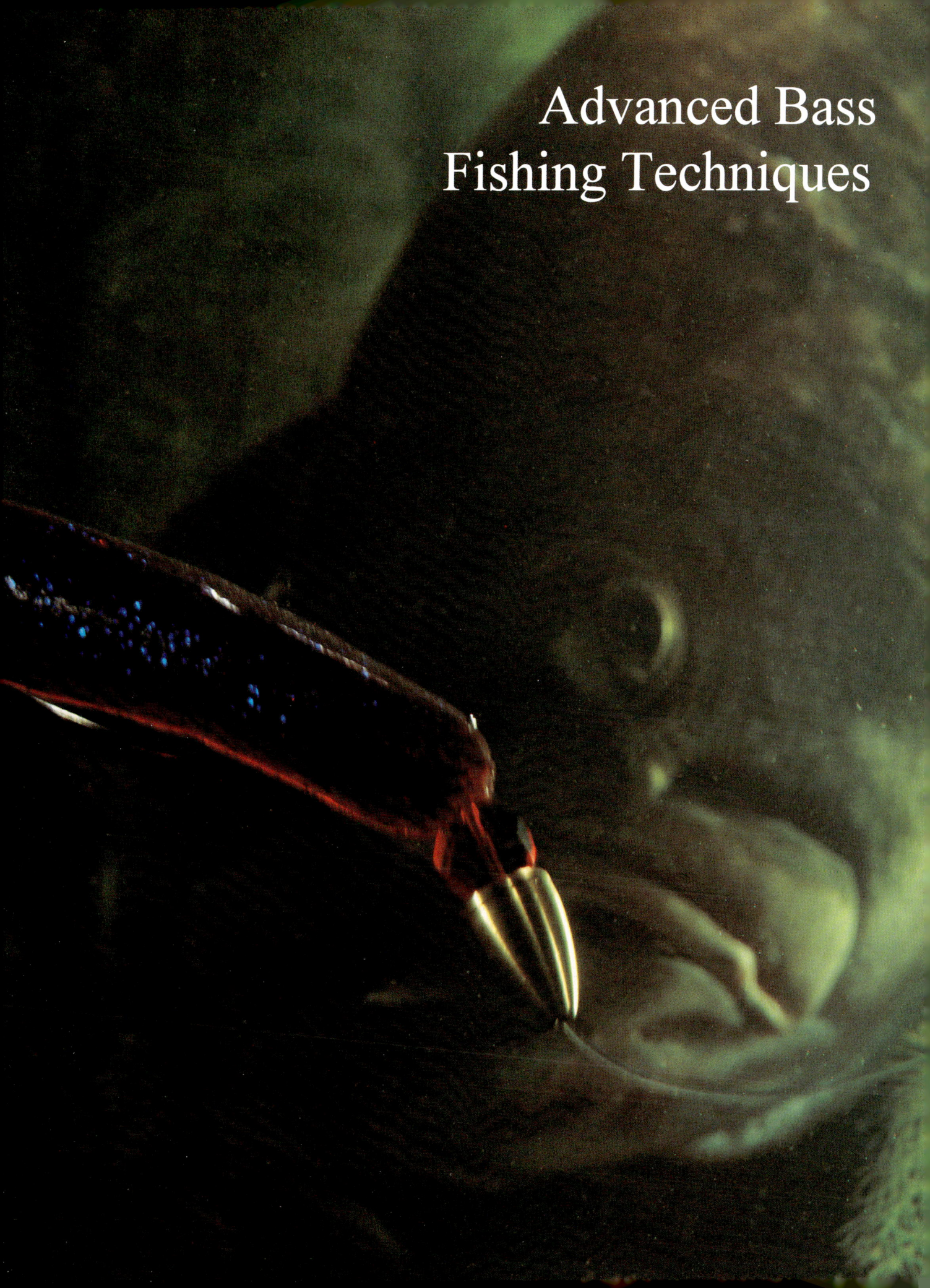

Advanced Bass Fishing Techniques

Advanced Soft-Plastic Techniques

Shaw's Sight-Fishing Secrets

Most veteran bass anglers cringe at the thought of fishing a clear lake on a calm, sunny day. The bass are either holding so tight to cover or hugging so tight to the bottom that you can't see them on a graph. And even if you do locate some fish, getting them to bite is a real challenge.

Optimal Conditions:
Type of Water: any clear body of water
Season: spring through fall
Water Temperature: doesn't matter, as long as bass are in the shallows
Weather: calm, sunny
Water Stage: any stage
Water Depth: depends on clarity
Water Clarity: 3 feet or more
Time of Day: mid-morning to late afternoon

But Shaw Grigsby, the famed bass pro from Gainesville, Florida, seldom has a problem finding bass – he simply goes out and looks for them. While scouting, he may do some blind casting, but his foremost intent is spotting fish, or subtle signs of their presence, such as fin movement, vague shapes and shadows. Then he makes precise casts to catch the fish he sees.

This may sound like a remarkably easy way to locate bass, but it's really not. "Most people I fish with don't see 'em," Grigsby says. "They're not really sight fishing, they're looking for something in the water to throw at. Even when I take them by the hand and tell them to look right there, they still don't see 'em.

"But once you learn to spot the fish, there's nothing like it. You know the fish are there, so you don't waste time in unproductive water or in areas that hold only small ones. And it's an adrenaline rush to watch the fish – how he takes the bait and how he handles it in his mouth."

Shaw Grigsby

Hometown:
Gainesville, Florida
Favorite Waters for Technique:
Sam Rayburn Lake, Texas; Lake Ontario, New York
Career Highlights:
Ranks fourth on B.A.S.S. all-time money list
Winner: 1984 Red Man All-American Championship; Texas BASSMASTER Invitational (3 times); 1993 Georgia BASSMASTER BP Top 100
Qualified for BASS Masters Classic 6 out of 7 years from 1988 to 1994

When and Where to Sight-Fish

Clear, calm water is best for sight fishing

Sight fishing obviously requires clear water. As a rule, don't try to sight-fish where you can't see the bottom.

For maximum visibility, the surface should be calm, the skies clear and the sun directly overhead. You won't see much on a breezy day because of the ripples, and cloud cover makes it harder to see detail. When the sun is at a low angle, much of the light reflects off the surface, rather than penetrating the water to illuminate the bottom.

If possible, do your sight fishing along a protected bank. Even a barely perceptible breeze creates enough surface disturbance to obscure visibility along a bank that is exposed to the wind.

You can sight-fish whenever bass are in the shallows, which could be from the pre-spawn period well into fall. In late fall, however, when the water temperature in the shallows drops below that in the depths, most of the bass head for deeper water. In the South, the critical fall water temperature is 55 to 60°F; in the North, 45 to 50°F.

How to Spot Bass Under Poor Sight-fishing Conditions

CAST into areas where the reflection from the shoreline darkens the water whenever glare is a problem.

LOOK for bass along the inside weed edge in waters that are too weedy or murky for good sight fishing. This inner zone is usually clearer and weed-free.

The best time to find bass in the shallows is after a few warm, sunny days in early spring. Bass move out of the main water body, which is still very cold, into shallow bays, coves or creek arms, which are a little warmer. And most of the fish are cruising, looking for food and spawning sites, so they're easy to see. Cold fronts drive fish out of the shallows, or they bury themselves in thick cover, where they can't be seen.

In reservoirs with shad populations, bass commonly herd the baitfish into the back ends of coves and creek arms in fall. The clearest creek arms are generally those nearest the dam. Try sight fishing in these areas if you see circling gulls or other bird activity, or lots of shad flipping on the surface.

Sight fishing is difficult in water deeper than ten feet, even if the clarity is adequate. Unless the surface is perfectly calm, which is rarely the case, distortion prevents you from clearly seeing the fish.

Dense bottom cover also reduces sight-fishing possibilities. It's easy to spot fish around rocks or fallen trees or even in brush piles, but not in a lush weedbed.

CHECK isolated bays that do not receive runoff when the main water body is too muddy.

Nest-robbers quickly move in when a nest-guarding bass is removed

Angling for Spawners: An Ongoing Controversy

Sight fishing can be deadly in spring, when bass congregate in the shallows to spawn. Often, the fish are protecting a nest and refuse to leave, even with a boat hovering overhead. If they do leave, they usually return a few minutes later.

Although nest-guarding bass can be extremely finicky, you can generally irritate them into striking by dabbling a tube bait or worm, or some type of live bait, in the spawning bed. In Florida, more than half of all trophy bass are taken during the spawning period, mainly by bobber-fishing with big golden shiners. Waterdogs, leeches and nightcrawlers also work well for nest-guarding bass.

Anglers and fisheries managers have long debated the subject of fishing during the spawning period. At present, only five northern states totally prohibit fishing around spawning time. Thirty-five states, mainly in the South, have year-round seasons. The remainder allow year-round fishing, but have special size limits, bag limits or catch-and-release regulations to control harvest.

Closed seasons appear to be justified in the North, where rapidly warming temperatures in the spring tend to compress the spawning season. Nest building, spawning and guarding of fry may all take place in a month or less, meaning all individuals that are going to spawn are doing so at about the same time. Because the fish are tightly concentrated in the shallows, they're extremely vulnerable to angling.

Several northern states have recently changed their regulations to allow catch-and-release fishing at spawning time. Some biologists, however, question whether a bass caught off the nest will return in time to protect it from predators. Studies are presently being conducted to answer this question. Other biologists maintain that it really makes no difference if the fish return to their nests in time, because it only takes a few successful nests to provide an adequate number of fry.

Fishing for bass during the spawning period is an age-old tradition in the South, and there seems to be little reason to change. Because the water temperature stays considerably warmer in winter, the spring warm-up is much more gradual, and the spawning period is greatly extended. A few fish spawn early and then leave, while others continue to trickle in, some as much as four months later. Consequently, spawning concentrations are lighter than in the North, lessening the need for protection.

Sight-Fishing Techniques

> **Equipment:**
> **Rod:** 6-foot, fast-action, medium-power graphite spinning rod
> **Reel:** spinning reel with long spool and gear ratio of at least 5:1
> **Line:** 6- to 8-pound-test, low-vis mono
> **Lures:** tube jig, rigged Texas-style

The major challenge in sight fishing is to spot the fish before it spots you. Otherwise, it will usually dart toward deeper water, and even if it doesn't, it will probably refuse your lure.

To minimize spooking, stand in the bow and move along with your troll motor. Wear drab clothing and be sure to avoid reds, yellows and whites. While blind casting with a minnow plug or soft stickbait, look as far ahead of the boat as possible. Move fast enough to cover a good deal of water, but not so fast that your momentum carries you over the fish. The easier it is to see them, the faster you can go. Always wear polarized sunglasses and try to keep the sun at your back so glare will not prevent you from seeing into the water.

When you see a bass, immediately reverse direction, switch to another rod rigged with a tube bait and cast to the fish before it sees you. Keep a low profile, stay far enough away from the fish that you can barely see it and don't make any sudden movements or unnecessary noises.

Bass in clear water tend to be superalert and not as aggressive as those in murky water. This explains why Grigsby prefers a tube bait. "It looks natural, and you can swim it like a minnow or slow-crawl it like a crayfish," he says.

Grigsby recommends injection-molded, rather than hand-dipped, tube baits. The hand-dipped models may look a little nicer, but the injection-molded type is bulkier, heavier and softer. The weight and bulkiness make it easy to skip-cast (below), and the softness means a bass will hold onto it longer.

The way the bait sinks also makes a difference. "When a baitfish dies, it spirals down," Grigsby points out. "I've found that a bait that does the same is much more effective than one that plummets straight down." An ordinary bullet sinker would not give the bait this spiraling action, so Grigsby rigs his baits with a special hook and internal weight he helped design. A clip on the hook secures the bait, and the weight (below) gives it the desired action.

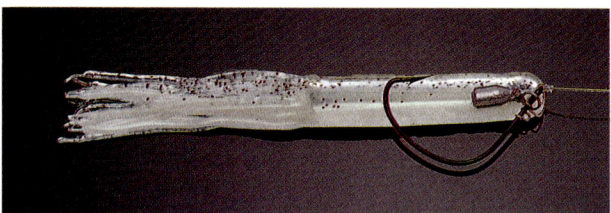

Cutaway of Luck "E" Strike G4 tube bait rigged with size 1 HP hook and internal weight

He normally uses a 1/16-ounce weight, but when it's windy or he wants to keep the bait on bottom to mimic a crayfish, he switches to a 1/8-ounce.

Don't cast right to the fish, or it may spook. If it's motionless, cast well past it and draw the bait 3 to 5 feet in front of it. If it's swimming, lead it accordingly. A skip-cast is best, because it mimics a skittering baitfish. Skip-casting these light lures is easiest with a spinning outfit, preferably with a long-spool reel, and light mono, no more than 8-pound test. A high gear ratio, at least 5:1, enables you to reel in quickly and cast to another fish you've sighted.

How to Sight Fish

LOOK for bass while moving along and blind casting.

SKIP-CAST ahead of a fish you've spotted.

SELECT the color of your polarized sunglasses based on light conditions. Compared to an unpolarized view (left), brown lenses (middle) enable you to spot fish better on a sunny day; yellow lenses (right) on a cloudy day. Blue lenses, or the gray ones used by most anglers, do not provide as much contrast.

Sometimes the fish will strike as soon as the bait hits the water, or it may grab the bait as it's spiraling down. But the vast majority of strikes come in response to an excruciatingly slow retrieve, accomplished by moving the rod tip no more than an inch at a time to crawl the bait along the bottom. Or, try barely jiggling the bait without moving it ahead.

After watching a few fish react to your bait, you'll learn to judge their catchability. If a fish bolts away or shows no response to the bait, keep moving, and try to find new fish. One that turns on the bait and tips down to inspect it, however, can probably be caught. Keep casting as long as it shows interest.

If the fish just keeps following, twitch the bait sharply to mimic a scooting crayfish; this last-ditch maneuver may draw a reflex strike.

You may have to change baits, sometimes more than once, to draw a strike. Try a small plastic crawfish or, when fishing for spawners, a 5-inch lizard. In fall, when fish are feeding on shad, a 4-inch ringworm is a good option.

There's no way to avoid spooking some fish as you motor through the shallows. But the fish that move away usually don't go far. Remember exactly where you saw them and come back a little later. Knowing where they are, you should be able to get within casting range without alarming them.

When you see a fish take the bait or feel a strike, reel down until your rod points at the fish, then pull back with a smooth sweep. The light-wire hook penetrates easily, so there is no need to risk snapping the line with a full-power hook set.

If it's obvious that you won't be able to keep the fish from swimming into a brush pile or around a dock pole, don't keep fighting it or it will wrap your line around the cover. Instead, back off on the tension and let it swim freely. After it stops running, try to ease it back out of the cover the same way it went in. The method is not foolproof, but it's the best way to land fish on light line.

Sight fishing has helped Grigsby claim numerous major tournament titles, including three wins in the Texas BASSMASTER Invitational, an unprecedented accomplishment. But there are other reasons he enjoys sight fishing. "It's highly intense," he explains. "You're one-on-one with the fish – it's totally you against him. And that's what does it for me."

CRAWL the bait just ahead of the bass. JIGGLE, then pause, to draw a strike. SCOOT the bait to mimic a crayfish.

Advanced Soft-Plastic Techniques

Draggin': Refinement of a Time-Proven Method

Optimal Conditions:
Type of Water: weedy reservoirs that are drawn down in fall and rise in spring
Season: spring
Water Temperature: low 50s to 70°F
Cover Type: clean to sparsely vegetated bottom
Water Stage: high
Water Depth: 5 to 15 feet
Water Clarity: at least 1 foot
Time of Day: anytime

In East Texas, it's called "draggin'" – most everywhere else, it's Carolina rigging. The technique originated in South Carolina decades ago, but never gained widespread popularity until Jim Nolan used it to claim the 1991 Texas BASSMASTER BP Top 100 tournament on Sam Rayburn Lake. Most of his record-breaking catch of 86 pounds, 6 ounces was taken on a Carolina-rigged lizard.

With the new soft plastics now available, draggin' is more effective than ever. According to Jay Yelas, one of pro bass fishing's elite, "There's no better way to put a quick limit in the boat. It's one of the simplest and surest ways to catch numbers of bass."

A Carolina rig differs from a Texas rig in that the bullet sinker is positioned well up the line (p. 184), rather than riding on the nose of the bait. This way, the bait sinks much more slowly and has a more enticing action. With a Texas rig, the hook is always buried in the bait; with a Carolina rig, it may or may not be, depending on the size of the cover. Texas fisherman have dubbed this technique draggin' because all you do is cast out and drag the bait in with short pulls.

Originally, a Carolina rig consisted of an egg sinker, a barrel swivel and an ordinary worm hook. Yelas modifies the rig somewhat by substituting a bullet sinker for the egg sinker and a wide-bend, locking-style hook for the standard worm hook. He adds a glass bead to prevent the sinker from damaging the knot on the swivel.

Yelas prefers a heavy bullet sinker, about 1 ounce. This much weight enables long casts, helps you "read" the bottom, and lets you fish practically any water depth. It also gets the bait to the bottom quickly and keeps it there, even on a fairly rapid retrieve or from a moving boat. As a result, you can cover more water in a given time than you could with a lighter Texas rig. The sinker may also attract bass by kicking up silt on the bottom and clicking against the glass bead.

Yelas, winner of the 1993 Maryland BASSMASTER BP Top 100 tournament on the Potomac River, always has one rod set up with a draggin' rig in tournament competition, and the technique has contributed to several of his high finishes.

Jay Yelas
Hometown:
Sam Rayburn, Texas
Favorite Waters for Technique:
Sam Rayburn Lake, Texas; Lake Seminole, Georgia/Florida; Lake Guntersville, Alabama
Career Highlights:
Winner: 1989 Red Man Tournament of Champions; 1993 Maryland BASSMASTER BP Top 100
3rd place 1993 BASS Masters Classic

Best Conditions for Draggin'

Yelas uses some variation of this technique throughout the year and in a wide variety of waters, but he relies on it most heavily in spring, from the pre-spawn through the post-spawn period. "Bass can be real fussy around spawning time," he says, "so they're more likely to grab a slow-sinking bait." Draggin' also has an edge over most other techniques in calm, sunny weather, for the same reason.

Draggin' works best on a clean to sparsely vegetated bottom. It is not recommended for use in heavy vegetation or woody cover; the unweighted bait will not penetrate the cover as well as a Texas rig or a leadhead jig.

Yelas contends that the very best situation for draggin' is in a reservoir that is routinely drawn down in fall. The weeds, usually hydrilla, milfoil or peppergrass, die off on structure exposed by the drawdown, and, when the lake refills in spring, many shallow points and bars are weed-free (below and opposite). "If you know how far the lake was drawn down, you know where the inside weedline will be," Yelas explains. "The depth of the weedline is the same all over the lake. You fish the clean-bottomed structure from the weedline on in, or the fringe of the weeds."

In early spring, before spawning begins, look for clean Vs (opposite) in the back ends of creek arms. The weedline of these Vs holds fish throughout the day, but the action is fastest in late afternoon, because of the warming water.

Around spawning time, you'll still find some bass along the weedlines, but most of them have moved into shallower bushes, where they will nest. Work the weedlines in the morning, but move to the bushes on a sunny afternoon, because the warming water draws females into the shallows. When the bass are bedding, a tube jig, a floating minnow plug or an unweighted lizard usually works better than a Carolina rig.

Once spawning is completed, a few stragglers remain in the spawning areas, but you'll find most bass on points, humps and flats closer to or in the main lake. Start fishing inside weedlines on these spots in the morning. Later in the day, you'll also find bass in deeper bushes, especially when the water is high.

Because this technique relies mainly on visual attraction, it's most effective where the water is fairly clear. The visibility should be at least one foot and preferably two or more. In murkier water, a noisier bait, such as a spinnerbait, would be a better choice than a Carolina rig.

How the Inside Weedline Forms in a Reservoir

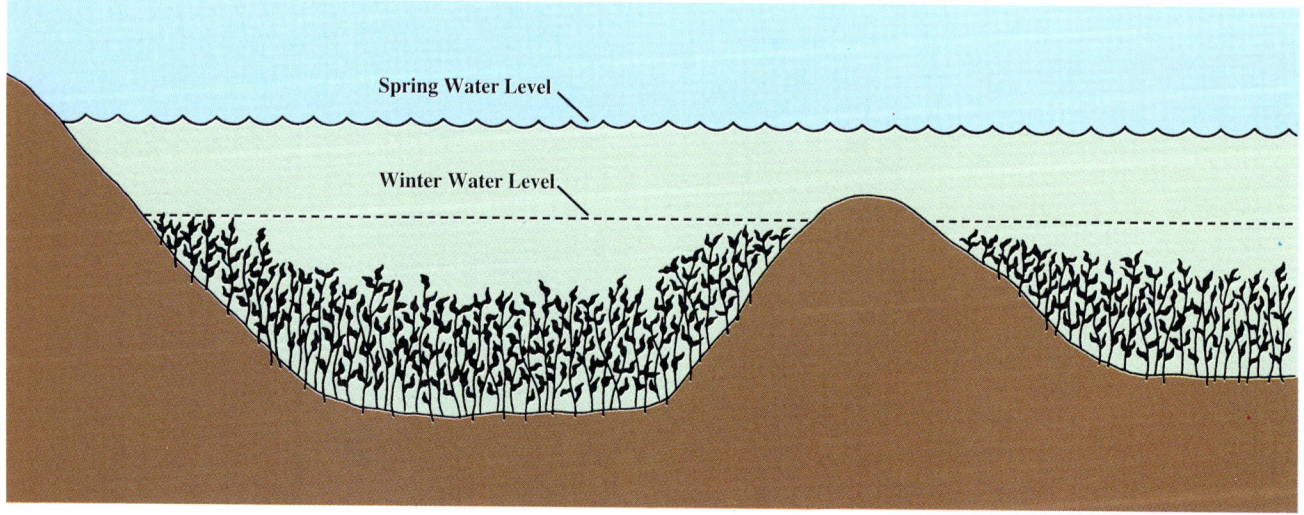

FALL DRAWDOWNS expose shallow, weedy structure, causing the vegetation to die. Weeds remain in areas still covered by water. When the water level rises in spring, bare spots remain on the shallow structure, and the adjacent deeper areas are heavily vegetated. Weeds develop on the shallow areas as the season progresses.

LOOK for bass where the fall drawdown creates shallow bare spots with deeper weeds nearby. Prime locations include (1) shallow humps, (2) points and (3) clean Vs (dotted line) in the back ends of coves and creek arms.

183

The Draggin' Technique

> **Equipment:**
> **Rod:** 7-foot, medium-heavy-power, fast-action graphite baitcaster with two-handed grip
> **Reel:** high-speed baitcaster
> **Line:** low-stretch 20-pound mono or 30-pound Spectra with 12-pound mono leader
> **Lures:** soft plastics, such as 6-inch lizard, 4½-inch crawworm and 4-inch French fry

"There's not a whole lot to fishing a Carolina rig," Yelas insists. "You don't have to be an accurate caster, and there's nothing special about the retrieve. In fact, there are times when you'll catch more fish by setting the rod down in the boat."

You can use practically any kind of soft-plastic bait. A lizard is a good all-around choice during the pre-spawn period. Bass are active then, so a big bait with good action draws the most strikes. During and after spawning, a smaller, less conspicuous bait, such as a "French fry" or crawworm (below) is a better choice. Normally, the bait is Texas-rigged so it doesn't foul with weeds and debris, but it can be fished with an open hook if the bottom is clean.

Yelas prefers pumpkin and green hues for most of his Carolina rigging. "Haven't been anyplace where I couldn't catch fish on these colors," he said. In clear water, he prefers translucent baits, but if the visibility is less than two feet, he switches to solid-colored baits, usually with a touch of chartreuse.

The taller the vegetation, the longer the leader you'll need. Bass in the weeds are less active than those along the weedline, and they often suspend near the weedtops. Some anglers use a leader up to seven feet in length to keep the bait high enough that the bass can see it.

In very clear water, you'll have better success with lighter line and a lighter sinker. Instead of 20-pound line and a 12-pound leader, use 12-pound line, an 8-pound leader and a lighter rod and reel. Instead of a 1-ounce sinker, try a ¼-ounce. With this lighter gear, the technique is more like split-shotting.

Although draggin' works on any structure with a fairly clean bottom, you'll maximize your odds by pinpointing the inside weedline, positioning your boat just outside of it and casting perpendicular to it. If you position the boat too far outside the weedline, you'll encounter dense weeds.

Using a 7-foot, long-handled rod, make a two-hand power cast. The long rod gives you extra distance and makes it easier to wield a long leader. Wait until the rig hits bottom, drag it about 4 to 6 inches with your rod tip, pause, then drag it again. How long you pause depends on the mood of the bass. As a rule, the closer to spawning time, the longer the pause.

Sometimes strikes are aggressive, but more often, you'll just notice a bit more or less weight on the rod tip. Spectra line helps telegraph these subtle takes. When you feel something different, reel up slack until you feel the rod "load," and set the hook. The high-speed reel makes it easier to take up the slack, and the long rod and low-stretch line give you a stronger hook set.

There is no need to horse the fish in open cover. Take your time and let the fish play itself out before you attempt to land it.

"Not only is Carolina riggin' simple," Yelas concludes, "it's the best way to milk a school of bass, because you catch both aggressive and inactive fish. What other technique will do that?"

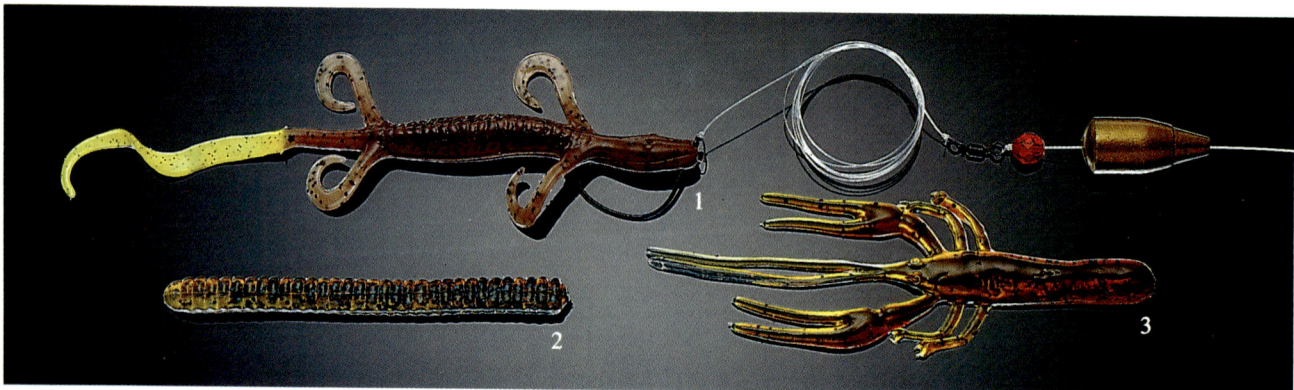

MAKE a Carolina rig by sliding a 1-ounce bullet sinker and a glass bead onto 20-pound mono or 30-pound Spectra, tying on a size 10 barrel swivel, then adding a 3-foot, 12-pound mono leader. Attach a 3/0 HP hook for a (1) lizard; 2/0 for a (2) French fry or (3) crawworm. The glass bead keeps the sinker from damaging the knot, and makes a clicking sound. The lighter leader prevents losing the entire rig should the hook get snagged.

Draggin' Tips

CUSTOM-COLOR soft-plastic baits by dipping them in a specially formulated dye, such as Dip-n-Glo.

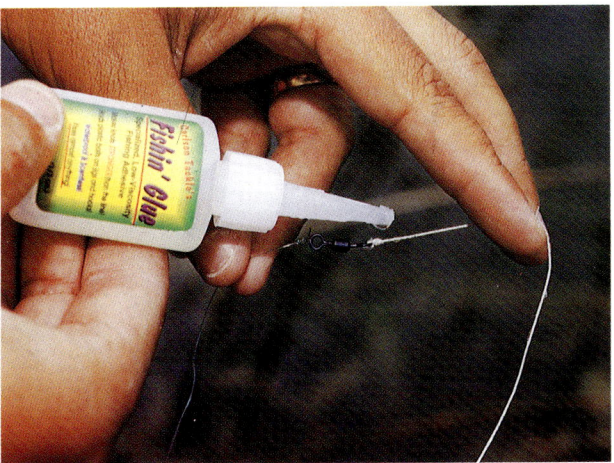

SECURE knots in Spectra or other braided line using waterproof glue, such as Fishin' Glue. It will prevent the knot from slipping and the tag end from fraying.

WORK the shady side of isolated bushes between the inside weedline and shore to catch bass that are moving toward their spawning areas.

SHAKE your sinker while moving the rig forward as little as possible. The commotion and silt stirred up by the sinker trigger strikes when fishing is tough.

CHECK your sinker for evidence of bottom composition. If you find mud in the sinker's hole, for instance, the bottom is probably too soft. Bass prefer a sandy bottom.

Advanced Soft-Plastic Techniques

Soft Stickbaits: Breakthrough for Stubborn Bass

At first glance, a soft stickbait is not much to get excited about. The plastic is harder and stiffer than most other soft-plastic baits, and it has no legs, tentacles or curly tail to give it action, so its appearance is certainly not lifelike. But many would argue that this bait is the most significant bass-fishing innovation in recent years.

David Vance, one of East Texas' best-known guides and a regular on the BASSMASTER tournament trail, is one such soft-stickbait proponent. "Its near-neutral buoyancy and enticing, dying-baitfish action work magic on big bass," he maintains, "even when they have the post-spawn blues."

Vance does most of his fishing on Lake Fork, the state's premier trophy bass factory, which produces astounding numbers of 10- to 18-pound "sows." He knows the best time to catch the giant bass is around the spawning period, but he also knows just how finicky they can be at that time.

"They turn up their noses at fast-moving baits," Vance says. "But you can put this bait right in their face and tease them into hitting it. And once they grab it, they won't let go."

Optimal Conditions:
Type of Water: any lake or river with clarity of at least 1 foot
Season: spawn through post-spawn
Water Temperature: 55 to 70°F.
Weather: calm, overcast
Water Stage: stable or slowly rising
Water Depth: 10 feet or less
Time of Day: all day if skies are overcast; otherwise, early and late in day

The major drawback to these baits is the difficulty of fishing them in windy weather. They can be a problem to cast, and when the wind catches your line, it pulls the bait through the water too fast. Because these baits must be fished so slowly at this time of year, they're not a good choice for covering lots of water.

The original soft stickbait, the Slug-Go, was introduced in 1990, and within a few years, its popularity swept the country. Today, fishermen can choose from dozens of different soft-stickbait brands.

David Vance

Hometown:
Winnsboro, Texas
Favorite Waters for Technique:
Lakes Fork, Sam Rayburn, Toledo Bend, all in Texas
Career Highlights:
Well-known guide on Lake Fork; 36 ten-pound-plus bass; 2nd place – 1991 Texas BASSMASTER BP Top 100

WORK any visible spawning beds in shallow, sandy areas to catch nest-guarding males; work the areas between the beds for cruising bass. Your chances of catching the larger females are better around woody cover just outside the bedding area; females stage there before and after spawning.

When and Where to Try Soft-Stickin'

Soft-stickin' excels once bass move onto the spawning grounds. They're much less aggressive than they were in the pre-spawn period, and they stay that way until late in the post-spawn. The bait's slow sink rate is a plus this time of year because the fish are in shallow water, usually less than 10 feet. Once they move deeper, however, soft-stickin' becomes less effective.

Concentrate on the creek arms where bass are known to spawn. The best ones tend to be long and narrow, so the spawning beds are protected from the wind. They have only small creeks feeding them, so they stay fairly clear. Avoid fishing creek arms with muddy water.

A soft stickbait produces practically no sound or vibration, so the water must be clear enough for bass to see it. As a rule, use soft stickbaits only when the visibility is a foot or more.

Soft-stickin' works best under low-light conditions – early or late in the day or under cloudy skies. Under high sun, the bass stick tight to the cover, where they're less aggressive and more difficult to reach with a soft stickbait, which won't penetrate the cover as well as a jig or Texas-rigged worm. Evenings are usually better than mornings, because warming water makes the fish more aggressive.

The Lone-Star Lunker Program

The chances of catching a 10-pound Texas largemouth have skyrocketed in recent years, thanks in part to the "Operation Share a Lone-Star Lunker Program," or "LSL." This coop venture between the Texas Parks and Wildlife Department, various corporate sponsors and anglers, provides TPWD with wild brood stock bass used to improve their propagation program.

Anglers who turn in a bass weighing 13 pounds or more to TPWD are given a fiberglass replica of their fish, courtesy of the corporate sponsors. Taking eggs from large, wild bass not only selects for large size, it increases genetic variability. If only captive brood stock are used, inbreeding can be a serious problem. Using wild brood stock also increases the chances that the offspring will spawn in the wild. And the fact that the parent was caught on hook and line increases the likelihood that the offspring will be catchable.

To date, more than 125 lunkers have been turned in by anglers, including a former state-record 17.65-pounder, and the present state record, an 18.18-pounder (right). Although a relatively small percentage of these fish have spawned in captivity, TPWD officials are confident that new facilities and techniques will improve spawning success. A new hatchery recently opened to care for these lunkers and to better duplicate natural conditions by precisely controlling water temperature and photoperiod.

Once TPWD is finished with the fish, they are returned alive to the anglers who caught them. Most are then released back into the waters from which they came. Several of the fish have been caught again, and one fish was entered in the program a second time.

Not only has the LSL program created a positive relationship between anglers and fisheries managers, it has boosted public awareness of the importance of catch and release of largemouth bass. The program has also taught many fishermen how to properly handle big bass; tournament and recreational anglers are successfully releasing more bass than ever before.

Texas angler Barry St. Clair donating his 18.18-pound Texas-record bass to LSL

Slot Limits: The Perfect Fishing Regulations?

Slot limits protect a given-size class of fish. On Lake Fork, for instance, a slot limit of 14 to 21 inches was established in 1989. This means you can keep bass under 14 inches and over 21, but those in between must be returned to the water. In 1993, the regulation was altered slightly to allow only one bass over 21 inches.

A study conducted by the Texas Parks and Wildlife Department showed that the number of bass over 18 inches long more than tripled from 1988, before the regulation was imposed, to 1993.

Of all possible types of size regulations, slot limits make the most biological sense for protecting waters with good fish populations. Other regulations, such as minimum size limits, may work better when fish populations are low. Here's why slot limits are so effective:

• They protect the prime spawning stock, fish that have just reached sexual maturity. The large, old fish that most people assume are the prime spawners may be well past their spawning peak, and their eggs often have a very low hatch rate.

• They ensure a continuing supply of fish that will grow to trophy size in the next few years. If anglers harvest the small fish, as the regulations allow, competition among fish in that size class is reduced, resulting in faster growth of those that remain.

• The width of the slot can be adjusted to suit existing fish populations. It can be widened when populations are low, narrowed when they're high and moved up or down to allow harvest of strong-year classes.

RIG a stickbait, such as a Lunker City Slug-Go, so it rides straight, with head angled upward (opposite). The lighter the cover, the more you can push the hook point through the plastic without risk of fouling. The point is protected by the bait's concave back (inset of cross-section) or, in some brands, a slot.

The Soft-Stickin' Technique

Equipment:
Rod: 6½-foot, fast-action, medium-heavy to heavy-power graphite baitcaster
Reel: narrow-spool baitcaster
Line: 15- to 20-pound, clear, low-stretch mono
Lures: 6-inch soft stickbait

The secret to catching bass on a soft stickbait is to keep your presentation slow. Just cast the bait and retrieve it with short twitches followed by pauses, varying the cadence until you find the right combination. The bait should dart randomly with each rod twitch, rather than veer from side to side in a predictable fashion. Between twitches, it will suspend momentarily, then slowly sink.

The bait is rigged with a long-shank offset hook, which keeps the center of gravity toward the middle of the bait and ensures that it sinks in a horizontal position. With a shorter-shank hook, the bait would nosedive and sink much faster. Heavy line, 15- to 20-pound mono, helps keep the nose up.

When rigged properly, the bait should have a slight upward bend at the head (opposite). This way, the bait will plane upward when you twitch it, then glide back down.

Vance normally favors a natural greenish shiner color, but he uses darker colors in muddy water or on cloudy days. In clearer-than-normal water, he often switches to a blue-back shiner color.

Soft stickbaits may be difficult to cast. If you cast into the wind, for instance, they slow down quickly and you end up with a backlash. Try to cast straight downwind and keep your rod tip low when retrieving to minimize the bow the wind puts in your line.

Bass usually grab the bait on the pause, as it settles. You may feel a tap, see the line jump or move off to the side, or just feel extra resistance. Then, quickly reel up all your slack and set the hook with a hard wrist snap. A beefy rod is a must to drive the big hook into the jaw, and to horse a fish from the cover once it's hooked.

"You got to be on your toes at all times when you're soft-stickin'," Vance explains. "If you're not paying attention, a bass may grab the bait and you won't even know it. But once you learn the system, you'll catch more big fish than you ever dreamed about."

Soft-stickbait Tips

STORE soft stickbaits so they stay straight by laying them one by one in long-enough compartments. If they warp, they won't dart randomly.

PUSH a lead insert or nail into the bait just ahead of the hook bend. The bait will cast better and run deeper, and the wind won't move it as fast.

How to Fish a Soft Stickbait

1. INSERT the hook as shown so the head of the bait has a slight upward bend.

2. TWITCH the bait, with your rod angled downward, to make it dart.

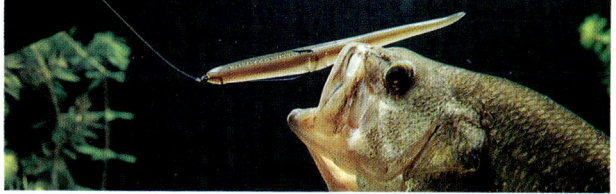

3. PAUSE to let the bait glide on a slack line; finicky bass like long pauses.

4. SET the hook sharply so the thick hook will penetrate the bass's jaw.

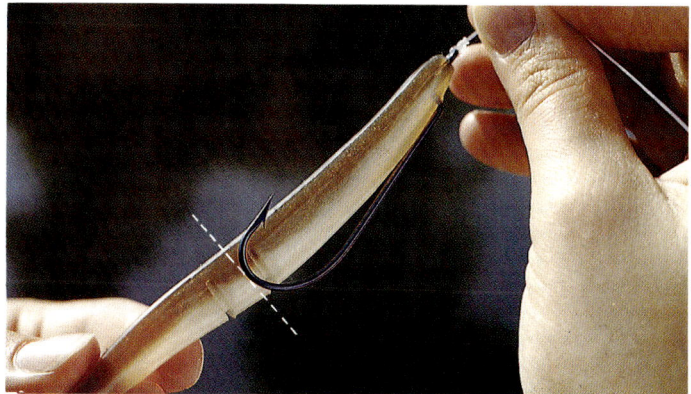

LAY the hook over the bait and draw an imaginary line at the rear of the bend. Push the hook through the body along this line to ensure that the bait rides straight.

BOIL warped baits for about 30 seconds. Lay them on their back to dry, making sure they're straight. Boiling them too long softens them too much.

Advanced Jigging Techniques

Yo-Yoing for Bass in Dense Milfoil

> **Optimal Conditions:**
> **Type of Water:** any lake with deep milfoil beds
> **Season:** post-spawn through early fall
> **Water Temperature:** upper 60s or higher
> **Weather:** calm, sunny
> **Water Stage:** normal, stable
> **Water Depth:** 15 feet or less
> **Water Clarity:** 2 feet or more
> **Time of Day:** late morning to early evening

Eurasian water milfoil – the very mention of it causes panic among boaters and lakeshore property owners. As its name suggests, this fast-growing aquatic plant is native to Europe and Asia, as well as northern Africa. It was found in the Chesapeake Bay area in the late 1800s, and since that time has spread to 37 states and 3 Canadian provinces.

The plant infests natural and man-made lakes, growing to depths of 15 feet or more and forming a dense canopy at the surface or several feet below it. The matted plants interfere with boating and crowd out other aquatic plants. And fragments of them wash in and foul the beaches.

For bass and bass fishermen, however, not all the news about milfoil is bad. "The thick canopy provides shade, security and cooler temperatures for largemouth," explained Pat Martin, a successful tournament angler who spends a lot of his time fishing Minnesota's Lake Minnetonka, a 14,000-acre natural lake infested with Eurasian water milfoil. "There's been a big increase in the number and size of the bass since the milfoil explosion." Many other natural and man-made lakes around the country also underwent a bass boom soon after milfoil was established. "But milfoil is tough to fish," Martin says. "With so much of it, most fishermen don't know where to find the bass. And even if they can find them, they have trouble getting a lure to them."

With the rapid spread of Eurasian water milfoil, anglers coast-to-coast are having the same problems. The bass may not be in the traditional spots, and the old techniques may no longer be as effective. But by understanding the locational patterns and using the angling techniques that follow, you'll catch more bass than ever.

These techniques will work on any milfoil-ridden natural lake with clear water, but they can also be used on man-made lakes and on lakes overrun with other dense weeds, such as hydrilla.

Pat Martin

Hometown:
Chanhassen, Minnesota
Favorite Waters for Technique:
Lake Minnetonka and Clearwater Lake, Minnesota
Career Highlights:
1991 Minnesota Team of the Year on both the American Scholarship and Minnesota/Wisconsin Pro-Am circuits
Winner of 6 tournaments on the same circuits

Sprig of Eurasian water milfoil, and leaflets of Eurasian (top inset) and northern (bottom inset) water milfoil

Midsummer milfoil canopy provides ideal cover for largemouth bass

Understanding Milfoil

Eurasian water milfoil is easily confused with several native North American milfoil species. But it can usually be distinguished by its finer, more closely spaced leaflets. While native milfoil species seldom grow in water deeper than 10 feet, Eurasian milfoil thrives in water as deep as 30, so it covers a much greater portion of a lake bed.

Considered one of the most aggressive and troublesome of all aquatic plants, Eurasian milfoil may interfere with swimming and boating, detract from a lake's aesthetic appeal, clog water intakes, interfere with fish spawning, lower oxygen content of the water and even increase mosquito populations. But despite all these adverse impacts, many milfoil-infested lakes are producing more and bigger bass than ever. A number of old reservoirs, where the woody cover has deteriorated, have been rejuvenated by establishment of milfoil.

Milfoil provides hiding cover for small bass and ambush cover for big ones. And the dense vegetation makes an ideal surface for aquatic invertebrates, an important link in the aquatic food chain.

The plant flourishes in a wide variety of lakes, but reaches its highest density in those with fine-textured, inorganic sediments. It is not as abundant in highly fertile lakes with turbid water and an organic ooze bottom, or in deep, infertile lakes.

Eurasian milfoil grows rapidly in spring, beginning when the water temperature reaches the upper 50s. There may be a second growth spurt in late summer. When the shoots reach the surface, they branch profusely and flower, forming heavy mats in the shallows. Even before the mats form, the dense growth prevents the lower leaves from getting enough sunlight, so they begin to drop off. By midsummer, the mats remain, with surprisingly little vegetation below.

In deep lakes, the milfoil canopy may be several feet beneath the surface, and dense surface mats form only near shore. The tendency of the plant to mat in shallow water means that the densest growth takes place in low-water years.

Wind and currents move leaf fragments from one part of a lake to another, where it quickly reroots. Outboard motors also rip up milfoil beds, producing fragments that are likely to spread. Milfoil fragments are transported from one body of water to another via boat trailers and water birds.

Once Eurasian milfoil gains a foothold in a lake, it soon overwhelms other native aquatic plants, sometimes crowding them out completely. The milfoil generally maintains its dominance for 5 to 10 years, then gradually declines in density.

Attempts to eradicate or control the spread of Eurasian milfoil have been only minimally successful. Chemical treatments have never shown long-term results, although growth can be controlled with regular applications. Methods such as harvesting, dredging and derooting may actually promote milfoil growth. In some lakes, milfoil growth has continued unabated in disturbed areas but declined in undisturbed areas. In British Columbia, the spread of milfoil from lake to lake was slowed only slightly by a major public education and road-check program.

Research is currently underway to test "selective" chemicals, those that kill only certain plants, including milfoil. But even if such treatments prove successful, they would be too expensive for wide-scale use. Other possible control measures include introduction of a variety of insects that damage milfoil. There is evidence to suggest that some natural declines have been insect-related.

When and Where to Find Milfoil Bass

Bass use milfoil throughout the year. They often spawn along the inside edges of shallow milfoil beds at depths of 1 to 4 feet, either in sheltered bays or along protected shorelines. After spawning, when the males have abandoned the fry, you'll find bass on milfoil flats adjacent to spawning areas. Look for dense clumps of milfoil that grow nearly to the surface, usually in water from 8 to 12 feet deep.

"Let's say you're fishing a flat with a blanket of milfoil 4 feet beneath the surface," Martin proposed. "Then you come across a small area with milfoil 1 to 2 feet under the surface – that's where you want to fish in the post-spawn."

Often, these milfoil clumps are found on a slight rise, but they may also grow where the bottom is perfectly flat. On a calm, sunny day, the clumps are easy to spot. Those with schools of sunfish in or around them are the most likely to hold bass.

The depth at which you find post-spawn bass depends on their activity level. As a rule, the more active they are, the higher they'll be in the milfoil. Feeding bass cruise just beneath the milfoil canopy or even on top of it; bass in a neutral or negative mood stay near the bottom and move very little.

As summer progresses, largemouth move closer to the break at the outer edge of a milfoil bed, usually holding in 10 to 15 feet of water. There, the sharp drop-off gives them easy access to deeper water.

Bare spots on points or inside turns, or anywhere along the weedline, are the hub of summertime bass activity. These bare spots, most of which are less than 20 feet in diameter, are simply hard-bottomed areas where milfoil can't take root.

When bass are most active, usually during low-light conditions, they move about and feed right on the bare spots. When they're less active, as is often the case on sunny days, they tuck into thick weed clumps near the bare spots and move about much less.

Bass using these bare spots in summer provide the year's best and most consistent fishing. A school of bass may hold on the same spot for weeks at a time. They remain in these locations until the milfoil begins to turn brown in late summer or early fall. Then the consistency of the pattern breaks down; the fish begin to move about more and spend more of their time feeding in shallower water.

By fall turnover, most of the bass have abandoned the deep bare spots. You'll find them relating to shallower bare spots or areas of sparse milfoil growth, usually from 5 to 8 feet deep but sometimes as shallow as 3. Check bare spots within milfoil beds or along their sandy inside edges. Don't overlook such weed-free areas as boat channels or rock piles within a milfoil bed.

This locational pattern grows even stronger as the water drops below 50°F. Late-season fishing is best when a few warmer-than-normal days stabilize the water temperature. Bass remain in these areas until freeze-up.

How Milfoil Growth Affects Seasonal Bass Location

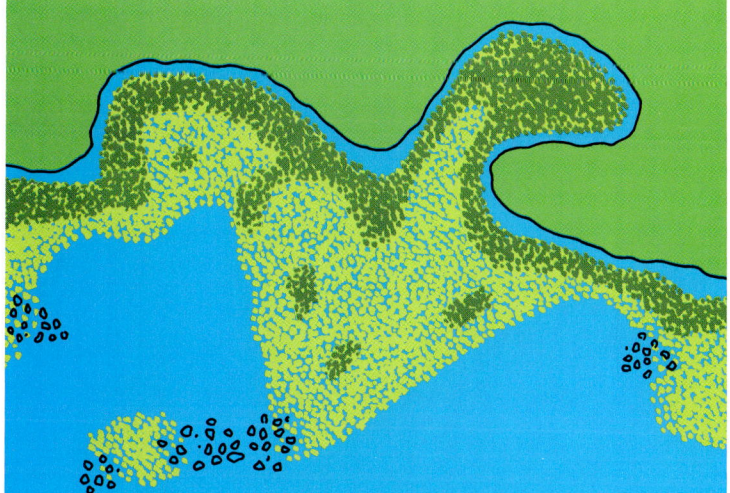

LATE SPRING/EARLY SUMMER. Milfoil growth is heaviest near shore and on shallow humps, with only a few scattered clumps of tall milfoil in deeper water on adjacent flats. Bass relate to the densest milfoil clumps.

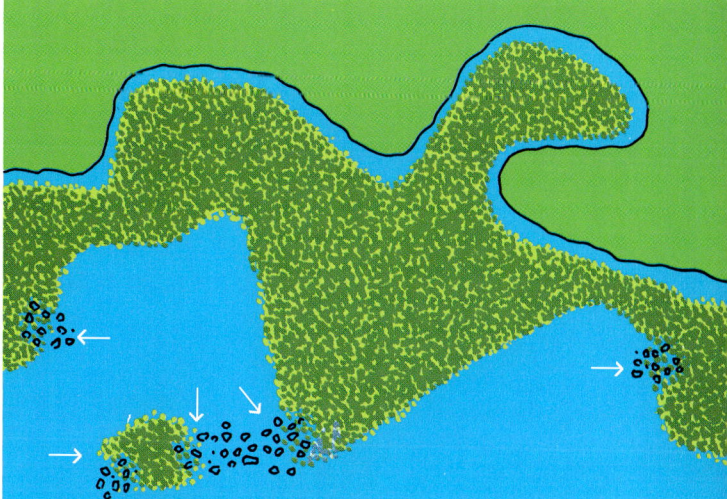

MIDSUMMER. Heavy milfoil growth covers the shallows and extends onto deep flats. Only small holes separate the tall milfoil clumps. Look for bass in holes and bare spots (arrows) around the outer edge of the milfoil.

POPULAR LURES for milfoil fishing include (1) Texas-rigged worm, such as a Berkley Power Worm, with a 5/16- to 5/8-ounce bullet sinker and a heavy size 3/0 worm hook; 5/8- to 1-ounce, weedless, bullet-head jig, such as a J-Mac, tipped with (2) Gene Larew Electric Salt Craw or (3) Berkley Power Grub.

How to Yo-Yo the Milfoil

Equipment:
Rod: 6½- to 7- foot, long-handled, medium-heavy-power, fast-action, graphite baitcaster
Reel: baitcasting reel with gear ratio of at least 6:1
Line: 25-pound, low-vis green mono (not low-stretch)
Lure: 5/8- to 1-ounce, weedless bullet-head jig with plastic or pork trailer; Texas-rigged plastic worm

Most anglers detest fishing in milfoil because it's nearly impossible to pull a lure through it without fouling. And if you do hook a fish when casting, it will almost surely tangle in the weeds and escape.

Martin helped develop a unique technique which solves the problem. Called yo-yoing, it involves jigging vertically in the milfoil, using a stiff rod and high-speed reel to horse the fish to the surface before it can tangle.

The best jigs for yo-yoing have a bullet-shaped head with the attachment eye at the tip to minimize fouling, and a large, strong hook that will improve your hooking percentage but won't bend when you hoist in the fish. Use the lightest jig practical for the conditions and a bulky trailer that will slow the sink rate. Dark colors or those that match common foods, such as crayfish, perch or bluegills, work best.

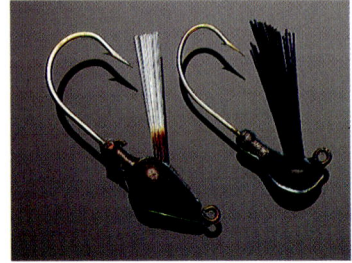

Head with eye at tip (left) is better than one with eye at top (right)

If jigs aren't working, try Texas-rigged plastic worms, and fish them the same way.

To locate bass, start at the downwind edge of the cover and move slowly into the wind. Then, flip the jig into an opening in the milfoil, from a few inches to a few feet in diameter. To keep your line as vertical as possible while you're moving forward, flip into openings slightly ahead of the boat.

Flip just ahead of moving boat

Always fish close to the boat, little more than a rod length away. This way, you can easily feed line and jiggle your rod tip to make the jig sink through the weedy tangle, and you can horse a hooked fish straight up, so it won't wrap in the weeds.

When the jig hits bottom, experiment with different jigging tempos until you find the pattern that works best. The more active the bass, the faster the tempo. When the bass are fussy, try "dead-sticking" them, letting the jig lie motionless for several seconds between each lift. Keep flippin' into different openings as you work into the wind.

Rod should be low when jig touches bottom, ready for hook set

With two anglers in the boat, both should stand on the front deck and work water ahead of the boat. If one stands in the back, he will be working water that the boat has already passed over. But an angler in the back of the boat may want to try casting spinnerbaits or crankbaits to pick up any fish cruising high in the milfoil.

Active bass usually inhale the jig on the drop, so you'll feel a tap or notice the jig stop sinking. But when the bass are finicky, they'll just pick up the jig off the bottom, and all you'll feel is a little extra weight. Set the hook hard and crank the fish out of the cover as quickly as possible. If you give the fish a chance to swim around the weeds, it may escape by tangling your line or spook other fish in the school by tearing up the weeds. If you don't hook the fish, flip the jig into the same spot, and try to coax another strike.

Place one hand a foot up the rod for extra hoisting leverage

"Sometimes you have to catch one bass to trigger others in a school to start feeding," said Martin. "It's not unusual to see a school follow a hooked bass to the surface in a wild frenzy."

If this happens, drop your jig back into the same hole, let it fall to bottom, then bring it up and work it just beneath the canopy, where the active bass are most likely to be. You may want to switch to a lighter jig, about 1/2-ounce, that will sink through the upper zone more slowly.

Once activated, some bass in the school begin feeding above the canopy. In this case, you may have better success by fan-casting the area with a spinnerbait, vibrating plug, minnow plug or shallow-running crankbait. Plugs with internal rattles work best; bass can home in on them more easily, so you get more strikes and better hookups.

You'll catch many more bass if you're careful not to spook the school. Put the fish you catch in your live well until you're done fishing a spot. A fish you release or one that breaks your line may alarm the school, and they'll quit biting. Working into the wind also reduces spooking; when you hook a fish, the boat will blow away from the school, not over it.

Temporarily store the fish in your live well

When you find a school of bass, note the precise location, toss out a marker and keep working it until the action stops. Then, you may want to switch to a jig of a different size or color, or to a Texas-rigged plastic worm. The change may trigger a few more fish to bite.

Leave your marker in place when you're done working the school, then come back and try the spot again later; there may be a few rocks, taller milfoil, a deeper slot or some other structural element that will draw bass back to the same spot.

High winds make it difficult to jig openings in the submerged milfoil. Not only will you have trouble seeing them, it's difficult to keep your boat in the right position. The wind also buffets your rod tip and deadens your feel, making it necessary to use a jig weighing at least 1 ounce.

Tips for Fishing in Milfoil

BEND the hook shank as shown so the point has a better angle to penetrate a fish's jaw. Touch up the point with a file or hone.

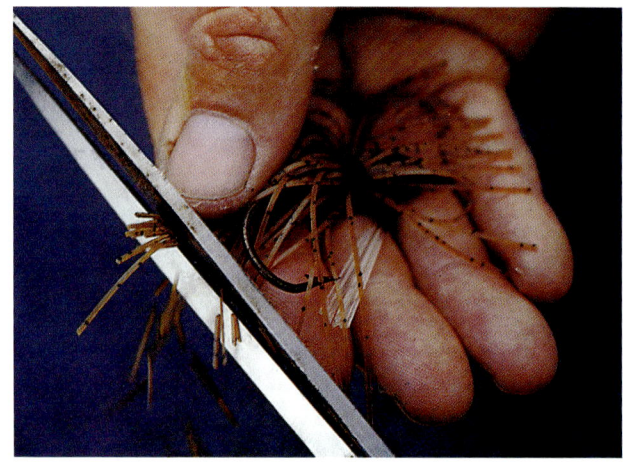

TRIM the rear of the skirt so it is even with the hook bend; trim the front so the strands stand out to form a collar whose fibers will quiver even when the jig is at rest.

SHORTEN the weedguard as shown to improve hooking; the long bristles cover the hook. The tip of the trimmed bristles should stop just short of the hook point.

PUSH the hook into a fat-bodied grub so it rests just under the skin (dotted line). This way, the hook gap stays open, improving your hooking percentage.

SHAKE the jig, then let it rest, to trigger a strike. Sometimes the frantic action draws the attention of bass that ignore an ordinary lift-and-drop presentation.

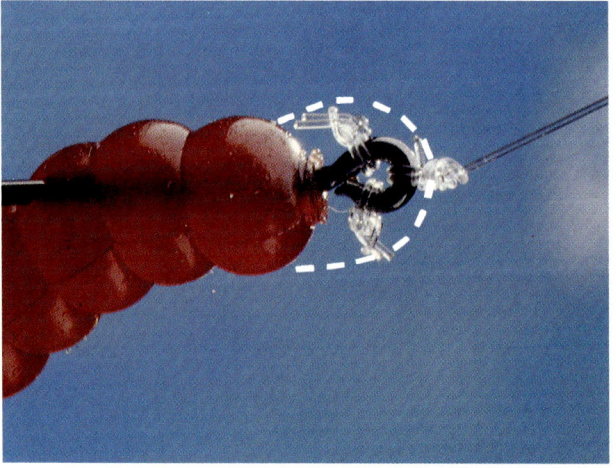

SECURE a worm with pieces of stiff mono tied to the hook eye. When the worm is pushed over the eye (dotted line), the tag ends prevent it from slipping back.

Work matted milfoil with a surface lure, such as a weedless spoon, on a warm day

Other Milfoil Techniques

After a few warm days in spring, when pre-spawn bass are holding in shallow water along the inner edges of milfoil beds, they'll hit practically anything you throw at them. It pays to use lures that cover a lot of water. Buzzbaits and spinnerbaits are ideal for working pockets in the milfoil and paralleling the edge. When the bass are not as aggressive, try a slower presentation, such as twitching a soft stickbait (p. 190).

In summer and early fall, bass cruise the outer edges of milfoil beds when they're active, and they tuck back into the milfoil when they're not. When they're along the edges, you can catch them on a variety of baits, including medium- to deep-running crankbaits, ribbontail worms on mushroom-head jigs, deep-running spinnerbaits, and the same bullet-head jigs discussed earlier. It's possible to use baits with open hooks, because milfoil growth along the edges is sparse enough that fouling is not a big problem. Try to hold your boat right over the drop-off and cast parallel to the break.

Another good summertime pattern is fishing surface clumps of matted milfoil. Work edges and holes in the clumps with buzzbaits and spinnerbaits; the clumps, themselves, with weedless spoons and hollow-bodied rats and frogs.

When bass move onto shallow milfoil flats in midfall, try slow-rolling a tandem-blade spinnerbait so it just bumps the weedtops, letting it helicopter into openings and slots. Or slowly retrieve a high-buoyancy, shallow- to medium-running crankbait over openings and along shallow edges of the flats. A buoyant plug is more likely to float off of the weeds should it foul. If you feel resistance, set the hook. A strike doesn't feel much different than hooking a milfoil stem. This technique produces fewer but bigger bass than you'd normally catch in summer.

"We're still discovering new ways to fish the milfoil," Martin explained. "When you get milfoil in a lake, it's literally a whole new environment for the fish, and you have to modify your techniques to stay competitive."

Try paralleling the inside weedline with a buzzbait

Advanced Jigging Techniques

Football Jigs: Magic for Pre-Spawn Bass

Optimal Conditions:

Type of Water: deep, clear, rocky reservoirs with steep structure
Season: pre-spawn, late fall
Water Temperature: 50 to 60°F
Weather: cold, windy, rainy is best
Water Stage: any stage; falling is best
Water Depth: 10 to 35 feet
Water Clarity: moderately clear to very clear
Time of Day: early morning, late afternoon best

When pre-spawn largemouth congregate along steep bluffs before moving into their spawning areas, they can be tough to catch. They're still in deep water and not very aggressive, and the sharp-breaking structure makes fishing a real challenge.

But Ted Miller, winner of the Arizona BASSMASTER Invitational on Lake Havasu in 1989, has devised an unusual technique that triggers these uninterested bass to strike. He's been onto the method for years but, until now, hasn't been doing much talking.

"There are times when this method stands head-and-shoulders above any other," Miller maintains. "In a spring Redman tournament on Lake Havasu, my draw-partner and I both used the technique. We finished one-two."

Miller has now retired from tournament competition, explaining why he agreed to reveal the details of the jigging technique that accounted for much of his tournament success.

Unlike the methods used by most tournament anglers, Miller's technique excels when the fish are holding on steep structure, particularly during the pre-spawn period. But the technique also works well when bass move to steep structure in late fall. The heavy jig with its unusual football-shaped head clinks against rocks and darts rapidly as it bounces down a steep bank, and the bulky, wriggling "spider-jig" body moves a lot of water.

The heavy football jig head enables you to stay in contact with the bottom – a near impossibility on the steep structure if you use a lighter jig head or one with the attachment eye near the nose. The quick-sinking action is opposite to that recommended by most pros, but is remindful of the darting movements of crayfish, which abound on the steep, rocky structure. Miller believes the wild action triggers "reflex" strikes from bass that are attempting to pick off crayfish before they zip under a rock.

The football head has some other advantages. Its shape keeps the jig head and hook riding upright, and when the jig is worked slowly over a gravelly bottom, the head pivots each time it bumps into a pebble, making the body move up and down and creating an enticing action.

Although the technique evolved on western reservoirs, it will work wherever the bass are holding in deep, clear water and feeding on crayfish.

Ted Miller

Hometown: Apache Junction, Arizona
Favorite Waters for Technique: Colorado River reservoirs
Career Highlights: Winner: 1987 U.S. Bass World Championship; 1989 Arizona BASSMASTER Invitational; 1989 Lake Mead Golden Blend Diamond Invitational; Three-time qualifier, Red Man All-American

Where and When to Find Pre-Spawn Bass in Deep Western Reservoirs

The key to finding pre-spawn bass is knowing where to find their spawning areas and concentrating on adjacent deep water. In reservoirs of this type, largemouth spawn in the back ends of coves. Before they spawn, you'll find them along steep bluffs leading into the back ends.

Early in the pre-spawn period, when the water temperature reaches about 50°F, look for bass along bluffs at the junction of a cove and the main lake.

Features that Concentrate Pre-spawn Bass

IRREGULAR POINTS plunging into deep water are best.

STEEP BLUFFS lead bass into spawning coves.

SHADED INDENTATIONS hold bass on sunny days.

As the water warms and spawning time nears, they work their way farther into the cove, hugging the bluff until they're adjacent to the spawning area. They'll stay there until the water temperature reaches the low 60s.

Bass tend to hold near any irregular features along the bluff. Look for rock slides, points, indentations and ledges with some kind of cover, such as a rubble pile or brush clump.

Typical depths during the pre-spawn period are 10 to 35 feet, but the fish can be considerably deeper if the water is extremely clear. The best spots have water much deeper than that in which the bass are holding; this way, the fish can easily retreat to whatever depths they wish.

The spots that draw bass during the pre-spawn period also attract them in fall. But the fall pattern is not as reliable, because the turnover scatters the fish about the lake.

The technique works best in cold, raw weather, as evidenced by an experience Miller had in a bass tournament on Nevada's Lake Mead. "First day, the rain would hit your raincoat and freeze," he recalled. "I caught 16 pounds, next closest guy had 6. Next day, it cleared up and I blanked. Still won the tournament though."

In sunny weather, the fish usually bite best in the morning, before sunlight begins to hit the bluff face. Afterward, look for any shaded indentation.

Water stage is not a major consideration, although the technique tends to be most effective under stable or falling conditions. In rising water, bass move onto shallow flats or into flooded brush where you would probably do better using other methods.

RUBBLE PILES on underwater ledges make ideal cover.

ROCK SLIDES indicate good underwater structure.

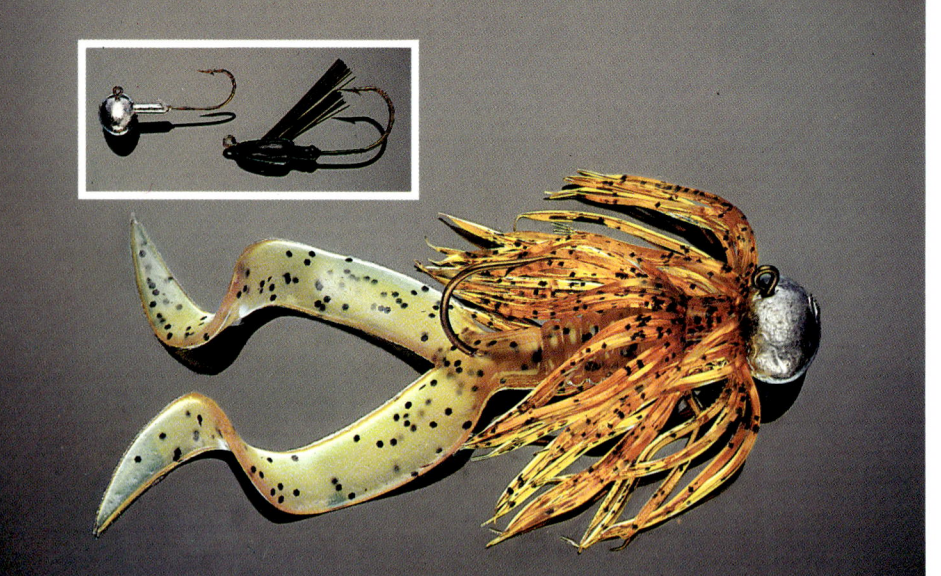

Miller's Football-Jigging Techniques

Equipment:
Rod: 6½-foot heavy-power, fast-action graphite baitcaster
Reel: high-speed baitcaster
Line: 12- to 14-pound mono
Lures: football-head spider jig

MILLER'S FAVORITE JIG has a ¾- to 1-ounce football head (contact Jerry's Jigs, Peoria, Arizona or Do-it Molds, Denver, Iowa), a Yamamoto Tease Skirt and a Bass'N Man 4-inch Double-tail. A football head (left in inset) is a better choice than a standard brushguard jig head (right in inset). Because of its more compact shape, vertical attachment eye and fine-wire hook, it sinks more vertically, hugs bottom tighter, has a more enticing, rocking action and hooks fish better.

Miller's jigging technique involves casting a football-head spider jig (left) toward a steep-breaking bluff or shoreline. He normally uses a ¾-ounce jig head, but for windy weather or deep water, he switches to a 1-ounce. His favorite color is

How to Jig the Bluffs

1. CAST to the base of the bluff wall, quickly lift your rod to spin off extra line, engage the reel and allow the jig to free-fall to the bottom on a semislack line.

2. HOP the jig with a 6- to 12-inch vertical twitch, raising your rod to about 10 o'clock. Then let the jig sink again, feeding more line, if necessary.

3. FOLLOW the jig with your rod tip as it free-falls again. Keep the line taut enough to feel strikes, but not so taut that the jig won't sink vertically. The rod should stop at about 8 o'clock.

4. CRANK-SET the hook by reeling as fast as you can while lifting your rod high. A crank-set takes up the slack created by the rapidly sinking jig. Play the fish with steady pressure, allowing it to tire in deep water.

pumpkin-pepper, because it closely matches the color of a crayfish.

Position your boat within 25 or 30 feet of the bluff and cast perpendicular so your jig lands near the base. If you attempt to fish parallel to the bluff face, as most anglers normally would, you'll be snagged constantly.

The trickiest part of this technique is working your jig precisely the right way. You may have to vary your retrieve, using longer or shorter hops, until you find the action the bass prefer.

This type of jigging is tough on monofilament line, because the heavy jig is constantly dragging the line over rocks. Retie often, and check your line frequently by giving it a sharp tug.

A jig this heavy sinks much faster than the line, so you're always fighting a bow in your line. This may cause a problem when trying to set the hook, unless you use a fine-wire hook, a long, stiff rod and a high-speed reel, and "crank-set" the hook (opposite).

Let the fish tire out in deep water, then land it as shown below. The heavy head and fine-wire hook make the jig easy to shake and if you horse the fish, it's more likely to jump and throw the hook.

Nestle the gunwale in your armpit for maximum reach when lip landing

"I'm surprised this technique hasn't really caught on," said Miller. "You can catch a good limit of bass on a blustery day when guys throwing light jigs and crankbaits just give up."

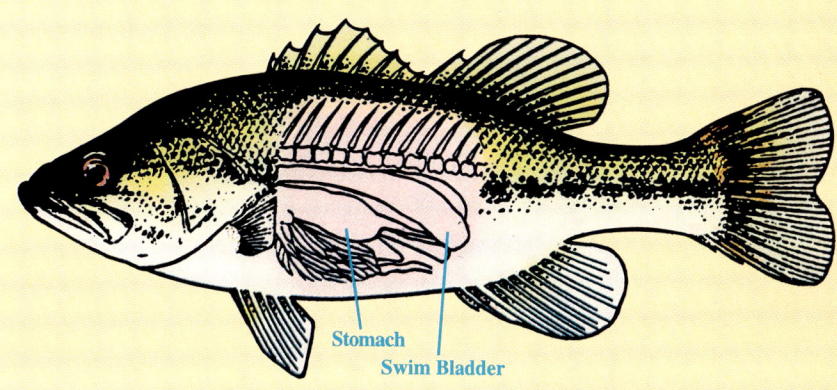

Position of swim bladder in a largemouth bass

How to De-Gas a Largemouth

When you pull a fish from water deeper than 30 feet, its swim bladder (above) inflates as a result of the reduced water pressure at the surface. Sometimes the swim bladder swells up enough to force the stomach out the mouth. Because of the added buoyancy and exhaustion from the fight, the fish may not be able to descend or right itself, so it flounders upside down on the surface.

These symptoms are seldom seen in *physostomous* fish, such as trout and salmon, because they have a duct connecting the swim bladder and esophagus. They can rapidly eliminate excess gas by "burping" it up, and can easily swim back down when released.

The symptoms are most noticeable in *physoclistous* fish, like largemouth bass, which do not have a duct connecting their swim bladder and esophagus. To eliminate excess gas, they must metabolize it, which can be a slow process, especially when their metabolic rate is low due to cold water. Use the following procedures to successfully release these fish:

Reel the fish in quickly to avoid sapping its strength. If the stomach is not protruding from the mouth, release the fish immediately. Dropping it nose-first will help give it the momentum it needs to return to the depths, where increased water pressure compresses the swim bladder. If you do not release the fish immediately, gas bubbles will accumulate in the blood, as well, lessening survival chances.

If the fish is not strong enough to overcome the buoyancy of its swim bladder, it will float back to the surface. The body will look swollen, and the stomach may be protruding from the mouth. Retrieve it and de-gas it as shown below.

Remove a scale and insert an 18- or 20-gauge hypodermic needle at the point indicated below, then listen for the escaping gas. You may have to push on the belly to force out the gas. If the stomach does not retract from the mouth, poke it down the throat with a blunt object.

When you release the fish, watch to make sure it doesn't float back up. If it does, de-gas it again, or keep it.

Fish pulled from water more than 50 feet deep may have more serious problems including ruptured blood vessels and gas bubbles in vital organs. If you see blood spots on the body or fins, or bugged-out eyes, the fish will probably die; it makes no sense to throw it back.

Insert needle 3 to 5 scale rows below lateral line, on line between notch in dorsal fins and vent

Advanced Plug Techniques

Zell's Topwater Tricks

Optimal Conditions:

Type of Water: any body of water with ample shallow-water bass habitat
Season: spring through fall
Water Temperature: above 55°F
Weather: cloudy and calm
Water Stage: stable or rising slowly
Water Depth: usually less than 5 feet, but sometimes deeper in clear lakes
Water Clarity: at least 1 foot
Time of Day: all day in cloudy weather; early and late in sunny weather

Ask an old-timer to recount his early bass-fishing memories, and he'll more than likely talk about lunkers slurping Hula Poppers or Jitterbugs off the surface around dawn or dusk. But you don't hear much topwater conversation among the modern generation of bass pros unless, of course, you're speaking with Zell Rowland – "Mr. Topwater."

Considered the best all-around topwater man in professional bass-fishing circles, Rowland to date has won nearly one million dollars using surface baits, far more than any other bass pro. "Lucky for me, most fishermen still think of topwaters strictly as morning and evening baits. I catch fish on 'em all day, sun or no sun. There's just something about a bait floundering on the surface that really turns the bass on."

When asked why more pros don't use topwaters, Rowland replied, "It takes a long time to learn to fish 'em, and each type of topwater has to be worked a little differently. Over the years, I've spent thousands of hours learning tricks that help me put fish in the boat.

"Course, topwaters aren't always the answer. You need lots of good shallow water cover and water temperatures above 55°F. If the water is too cold, too rough or too muddy, I usually go to other types of baits."

On the pages that follow, we'll show you Rowland's presentation strategies for each of his favorite types of topwaters. He rarely fishes a bait without somehow modifying it, so we've also included a complete collection of his personal bait-doctoring tips.

Zell Rowland

Hometown:
Montgomery, Texas
Favorite Waters for Technique:
Sam Rayburn Lake, Texas; Buggs Island Lake, Virginia/N. Carolina; Santee-Cooper Lake, S. Carolina
Career Highlights:
Winner: 1986 BASSMASTER Super-Invitational; 1991 Alabama BASSMASTER Invitational; 1992 Golden Blend Diamond Invitational World Bass Fishing Championship (all-time record prize of $150,000)

ROWLAND'S FAVORITE TOPWATERS include chuggers, such as (1) Rebel Pop-R; propbaits, such as (2) Smithwick Devil's Horse; stickbaits, such as (3) Heddon Zara Spook; buzzbaits, such as (4) Strike King Buzz King.

How to Fish Topwaters

> **Equipment:**
> **Rod:**
>   **for chuggers, propbaits and stickbaits:** 6½-foot, medium-power, medium-action graphite baitcaster
>   **for buzzbaits:** 7½-foot, medium-heavy-power, fast-action flippin' stick
> **Reel:**
>   **for slow retrieves with chuggers:** narrow-spool baitcaster with gear ratio of 4:1 or less
>   **for all other topwater retrieves:** narrow-spool baitcaster with gear ratio of 5:1 to 6:1
> **Line:** see individual lure sections

"You've got to let the fish tell you what they want on a given day," says Rowland. "Do they want a bait that makes more noise, or one that has a quieter, more subtle action? You have to have all the different topwaters and go through an elimination process.

"And there is no right or wrong way to fish a topwater. You have to vary your retrieve until the fish let you know the right combination of speed, intensity of twitches and time between them.

"The beauty of surface fishing is that you can see how the bait is working and how the fish are reacting. I start with a fast retrieve to cover some water, but if that's not working, I'll slow down. And if they don't like sharp twitches, I'll try gentle ones."

One of the most common mistakes in topwater fishing is setting the hook too soon and missing the fish (opposite). Rowland prefers a fairly soft rod that doesn't offer much resistance when a fish bites; this way, it will take the bait deeper.

A softer rod also helps in casting lightweight topwaters. It's important to make long casts, because bass in shallow water are easily spooked by angler movement and boat noise.

Another frequent mistake is attaching a topwater with a heavy snap-swivel, so the nose rides too low (opposite) and ruins the action. Line that is too light may also dampen a topwater's action, because it sinks faster than heavier line and causes you to pull the bait under when you twitch the rod.

Some of the baits Rowland uses require major modifications; others, only minor tinkering. He pays extremely close attention to little things when preparing his baits. For instance, he always replaces chrome hooks with high-quality bronze hooks (opposite), not only to improve his hooking percentage, but to ensure that the chrome doesn't spook fish on a sunny day.

Tips for Fishing Topwaters

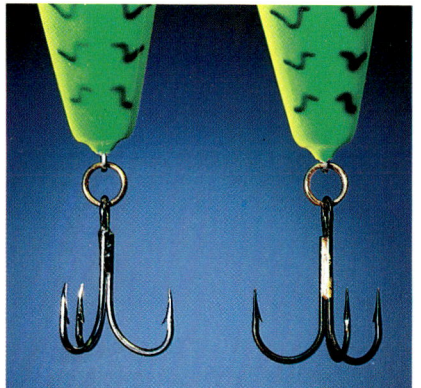

REPLACE thick-wire, chrome-plated, curved-point hooks (left) with extra-sharp, thin-wire, round-bend bronze hooks with straight points (right).

WAIT for the fish to pull the bait down before setting the hook (left). This increases your hooking percentage, because you're pulling the bait back into the fish. If you set too soon (right), you'll probably pull the bait away from the fish.

WATCH the bait very closely for any indication of a strike. Often, you won't see an obvious splash or swirl, just a slight ripple as the fish sucks the bait beneath the surface.

AVOID attaching the bait with a heavy clip or snap-swivel. The nose will sink (left) and the bait won't chug, walk or skitter as it should. Always tie directly to the attachment eye (right) so the nose is above water.

How to Reduce Backlashing

Everyone who uses baitcasting gear gets backlashes, or "professional overruns" as the pros jokingly call them. The problem is most serious with light baits, such as topwaters and unweighted soft plastics.

Many fishermen shy away from baitcasting gear to avoid the headache of untangling backlashes. Although there's no way to eliminate the problem, you can minimize it with the following steps:

- Try not to cast into the wind when using a light bait. The wind slows the flight of the bait, but the spool keeps spinning, producing a backlash.

- Select a narrow-spool reel. Because a narrow spool is lighter, it has much less momentum than a wide one, so it is less likely to backlash. And you'll find it easier to cast light baits with a narrow-spool reel.

- Adjust your spool tension properly. Here's a good rule: set the tension so the weight of the bait can barely turn the spool with the rod held horizontally.

- Learn to thumb the spool; even the best baitcasting reel will overrun once in a while if you don't. Depending on the reel you're using, you may have to feather the spool in mid-cast, and you must stop the spool with your thumb just before the bait hits the water.

- Don't throw the bait too hard. Cast with a smooth motion, letting the rod do the work. An intense arm motion gets the spool spinning too fast, so it's more likely to overrun.

- Make a long cast, then lay a strip of electrical tape over the spool. This eliminates severe backlashes, because the spool can overrun no deeper than the tape.

- Don't overfill the spool with line; the line level should be no less than 1/8 inch from the top of the spool. The more line that comes off with each turn of the spool, the greater the chances for a backlash.

Tape spool to stop backlashes

Chuggers

"I've thrown the Pop-R more than any other human being alive," Rowland contends. "If you use an ordinary Pop-R right out of the box, it makes a low-pitched chugging or burping noise, which isn't bad. But you'll catch a lot more fish if you sand it down."

Sanding (opposite) makes the bait float higher and at a different angle, about 45 degrees. So it's easier to skitter, has more lateral action and sounds like a shad flicking on the surface.

"It takes me almost two hours to sand one," Rowland says. "But they work so well, I've actually had guys steal them off my rods at weigh-ins." If you don't care to sand a Pop-R, select a "Pro" model. It has thinner walls, and an action more like a sanded one. But Rowland far prefers the action of his own sanded baits.

Start with a fast retrieve to mimic a skipping shad, but if that doesn't work, slow down. Make the head swish from side to side by throwing slack into the line between twitches. But don't expect as much lateral motion as you get with a stickbait.

Use 17- to 20-pound mono. Lighter line tends to sink, pulling the head down and resulting in a burping, rather than skipping, sound. But 12- to 14-pound line may be needed in clear water or when using a slower retrieve, because the fish may be line-shy.

How to Fish a Pop-R

CAST toward likely cover, then begin your retrieve with the rod at an angle of about 45 degrees. This will keep your line up so it can't sink.

LOWER the rod as the bait nears the boat. You'll get more splash (inset) with the rod tip low, and you won't pull the nose of the bait out of the water.

SET THE HOOK with a firm sweep. With the small hooks, you don't want to jerk too hard. Set at whatever position the rod is in when the fish strikes.

How to Doctor a Pop-R

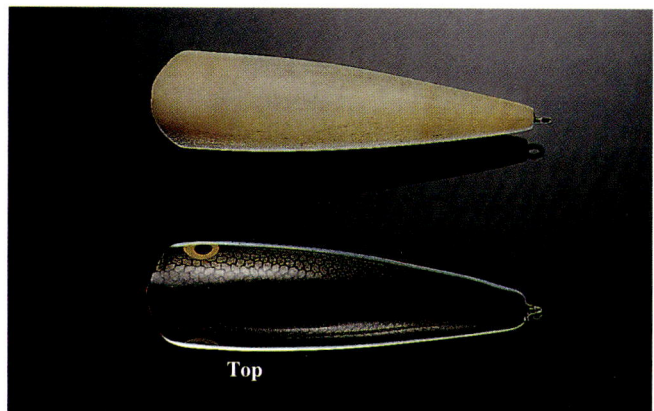

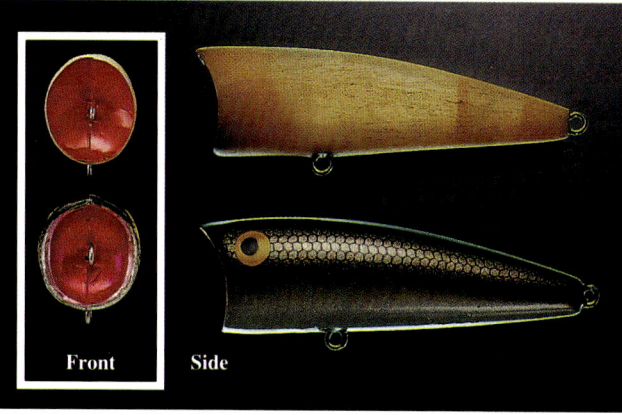

REMOVE the hooks. Using 60-grit sandpaper, sand the bait evenly until it tapers smoothly from front to back. Sand the belly only enough to remove the paint; do not sand the cupped face. Use emery cloth to smooth the surface. The sanded bait should have a smaller bulge in the middle than an unsanded one (top view) and a smaller hump on the back (side view). The edge of the cupped face should be much sharper (front view). The bait should be so thin you can feel it give when you squeeze it and you can see light through it.

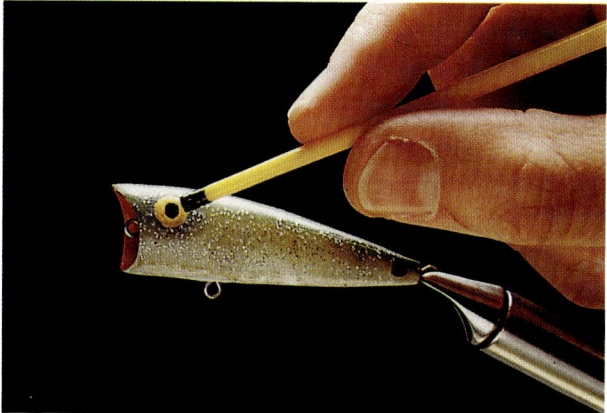

PAINT the sanded bait to match the predominant baitfish. An olive-green back and pearl belly, for instance, is a good match for shad. Sprinkle glitter onto the wet paint, if desired.

DAB on eyes and body spots using tapered handles of small paintbrushes. Cut off one handle at a wide spot for dabbing on eyes; another, near the tip, for the pupils. For round spots, the ends must be perfectly flat.

SPRAY the painted bait with clear lacquer to protect the finish and strengthen the thin walls.

REPLACE the rear hook, which is dressed with bucktail, with a better-quality bronze hook (p. 209) dressed with feathers similar in color to the forage. Tie six 1- to 1½-inch feathers to the hook, two per gap, so they curve outward. The feathers give you a more enticing action.

Propbaits

When bass are holding tight to cover, especially in murky water, Rowland relies heavily on a propbait. His favorite is the Smithwick Devil's Horse, which has propellers at opposite ends to create a lot of commotion. It may take the noise of a propbait to draw the fish out.

Propbaits are normally fished with a twitch-and-pause retrieve, varying speed and length of twitches, and the duration between them. To get the most from a propbait, you should modify the blades for different types of retrieves (below).

Use 17- to 20- pound mono with twin-bladed propbaits. Lighter line is limper and tends to curl around the front propeller. For smaller propbaits with a single rear propeller, use 12- to 14-pound mono.

Some propbaits have the old-style hook hangers that restrict hook movement. Remove them and substitute screw eyes and split rings, as you would with a stickbait (opposite).

How to Modify a Propbait for the Conditions

STANDARD PROPBAIT. Best for normal fishing conditions

PROP BLADES BENT FORWARD. Best for finicky bass, because the bait does not move forward as much when you twitch it

REVERSED END FOR END. Helps casting accuracy and distance in windy weather, because the bait has a more aerodynamic shape

FRONT PROP REMOVED. Gives the bait more of a side-to-side "walking" action, for extra attraction under tough conditions

Stickbaits

In extremely clear water, Rowland often uses a stickbait, his favorites being the Heddon Zara Spook, and its smaller cousin, the Zara Puppy.

"A Zara Spook is one of the world's best big fish baits," he contends. It's balanced and tapered exactly right for the enticing "walk-the-dog" retrieve, riding with the nose slightly out of the water for maximum lateral action.

The secret to getting good side-to-side action from a Zara, or any other stickbait, is to throw slack into the line after each twitch (below), so there is no resistance to lateral motion.

To get maximum action out of a Zara, however, you'll have to make some modifications, like repositioning the attachment eye (below). Use 17- to 20-pound mono with a Zara Spook; 12- to 14- with a Puppy. Line that's too heavy restricts the action.

"Zaras are one of the worst baits for holding fish," Rowland says. "The old-style hook hangers work like a crowbar in a door, so a fish can get the leverage it needs to throw the hook. Be sure to replace these hook hangers with split rings and screw eyes (below). Then, if they touch it, they're hung."

How to Doctor and Work a Stickbait

REPLACE old-style hook hangers (left) that restrict movement of the hooks, making it easy for bass to throw the bait. Substitute screw eyes and split rings (right), which will not allow the hooks to bind.

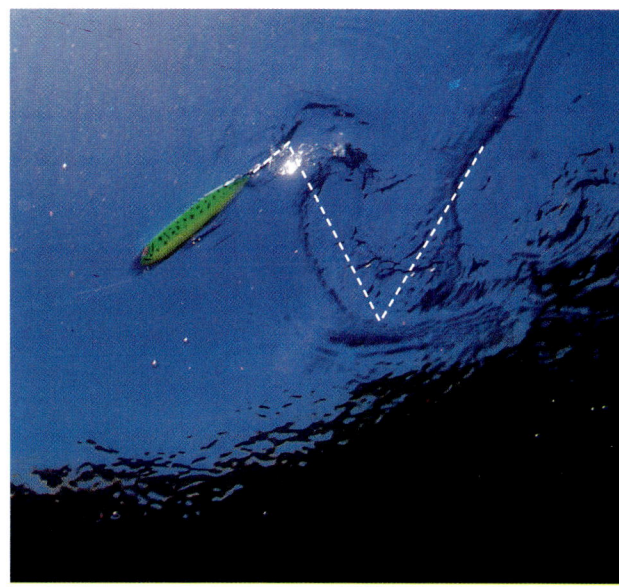

WALK THE DOG in a wide "Z" pattern by throwing slack into the line after each twitch. This way, the bait can glide freely to the side after the twitch, and you'll get a sharper jerk on the next twitch.

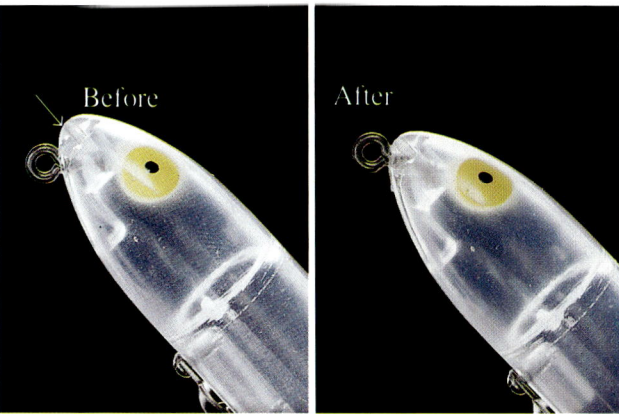

REPOSITION the front screw eye to make walking the dog easier. Drill a small hole halfway between the hole at the tip of the nose (arrow) and the old screw eye, and switch the eye to the new hole.

VEER your bait toward cover by alternating soft and hard twitches. It will glide farther one way than the other, so you can lead it in the desired direction. To help the bait veer to one side, bend the front screw eye the opposite way (inset).

BUZZBAIT STYLES. Safety-pin buzzers (left) have an L-shaped arm extending above the body to support the blade; in-line buzzers (right) have the blade on the main shaft. The in-line style rides higher in the water, so it's a better choice for fishing over matted weeds. But you can modify a safety-pin bait so the blade clacks on the main shaft (opposite), making it noisier, and because it rides lower in the water, it tends to hook fish better.

Buzzbaits

Buzzbaits are a good choice for locating fish, because you can cast them farther and retrieve them faster than most other topwaters. They work well around dense cover because of the single, upturned hook. They come in two basic styles: safety-pin and in-line (above).

"I like a ¼- or ½-ounce buzzbait," Rowland says. "Don't pay much attention to blade style – any blade is fine, just so it makes a lot of racket." To make the bait louder, he files grooves in the rivet or adds a "clacker" (opposite). He prefers old baits to new ones, because the blade tends to squeak more as it becomes worn.

Rowland usually adds a single-hook trailer to his buzzbait, because he feels his hooking percentage is too low with only the main hook. In dense weeds, the trailer is turned up so it won't foul as easily. In light cover, it's turned down to improve hooking odds and increase the chances of hooking the fish in the lower jaw, so they're less inclined to jump and throw the hook. Removing the skirt (opposite) also improves your hooking percentage, especially when the fish are fussy, because they tend to strike farther forward on the bait.

Start fishing a buzzbait at medium to fast speed. Using a fast-action flippin' stick (p. 208) and 20-pound mono, make a long cast and begin reeling immediately, with your rod top held high. The long rod improves casting distance, makes it easier to steer the bait around cover, and helps keep the head of the bait riding high when you start the retrieve. Gradually lower the rod tip as the bait nears the boat; otherwise, you'll pull the head too far out of the water, and the blade won't spin properly. You may get more strikes if you shake the bait periodically during the retrieve.

If the fish aren't responding to a rapid retrieve, try slowing down. To get the blades to turn at this slow speed, cup them a little more (opposite). Sometimes, bass will only hit a bait when it stops. A buzzbait is not a good choice when the fish are in this kind of mood, because it sinks when you stop reeling.

When a fish grabs the bait, hesitate until you feel resistance before setting the hook, just as you would with other topwaters. Because of the heavier hook on a buzzbait, however, you'll have to pop the rod a little harder to sink the barb.

Rowland's topwater prowess is a direct result of his dedication to topwater fishing and his attention to detail. "I'm constantly taking baits apart and putting them back together to see what makes them work," he explained. "And I'm always trying new ways of doctoring baits and new retrieves. Most guys aren't willing to spend the time. They take a bait out of the box, make ten casts and put it away. Whether it's a Pop-R or any other topwater, you've got to completely understand the bait if you want to catch fish consistently."

How to Modify a Buzzbait

 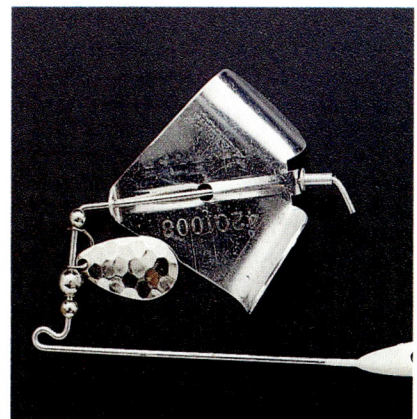

REMOVE the rivet (arrow) holding on the buzzblade, then file grooves in it as shown in the inset, and reassemble. The blade spinning against the grooved rivet makes a lot of commotion. For even more noise, replace the standard aluminum rivet with a steel rivet that has been grooved. Another way to add noise: bend the shaft so the edge of the blade just ticks it.

ADD a "clacker" by removing the buzzblade and sliding some beads, a clevis and a Colorado blade onto the vertical arm. Replace the buzzblade; when it turns, it will clack against the Colorado blade.

ADJUST the amount of blade cupping to accommodate different retrieve speeds. The slower the retrieve, the more the blade must be cupped to keep it spinning.

DRILL holes in a buzzblade as shown; the holes leave a bubble trail in the water, which helps draw bass. Also, a bait with drilled blades does not veer to the side as much as a standard model.

SELECT a buzzbait with a flat head (left) when you want to retrieve more slowly. The flattened shape planes the bait upward much more than a standard head (right).

REMOVE the skirt from your buzzbait (left) when you're getting too many short strikes. With the skirt in place (right), the bait's center of attention is farther to the rear, so a fish is more likely to strike behind the hook.

Advanced Plug Techniques

Weighted Stickbaits: Rx for Coldwater Bass

Optimal Conditions:
Type of Water: any reservoir with fairly clear water
Season: winter through pre-spawn
Water Temperature: 40 to 60°F
Weather: winter: sunny days; pre-spawn: cloudy, windy days
Water Stage: any stage
Water Depth: bass must be within 12 feet of the surface
Water Clarity: at least 2 feet
Time of Day: afternoon

Stickbaits, jerkbaits, minnow plugs – it makes no difference what you call them – these lifelike minnow imitations have long been standard items in the tackle boxes of most freshwater anglers.

The first minnow plug was imported to the United States from Finland in 1959 by Ron Weber, now President of the Normark Corporation. "At first, I couldn't get the tackle industry to take the Rapala seriously," Weber recalled. "A store owner would pick one up and hand it right back. Too light to cast, he'd say. That was probably true with the heavy line they used back in those days. But as lighter tackle and lines became popular, the lures began to catch on. It soon became obvious they were terrific baits for practically any kind of gamefish."

A slow, steady retrieve gives the lure a unique wobble that closely mimics a swimming shiner. After these lures were introduced, bass fishermen quickly added a retrieve variation. They found that the plug's high buoyancy made it possible to use an erratic, twitch-and-pause surface retrieve that worked magic on shallow-water bass. When given a sharp twitch, the lure dives a few inches, then quickly pops back to the surface, where bass strike it at rest. This retrieve has now become a standard bass-fishing technique.

Innovative southern anglers added yet another effective twist. They discovered that the twitch-and-pause retrieve worked considerably better with the lure weighted to make it neutrally buoyant. This way, it would "hang" in the face of the fish, rather than immediately floating up – a major advantage in tempting uninterested bass to strike. The weighted stickbait technique is the focus of this article.

Stacey King, a professional bass angler from Reeds Spring, Missouri, began using weighted stickbaits in nearby mountain lakes, such as Table Rock and Bull Shoals. Now he uses them regularly on the B.A.S.S. tour. "Found out about 'em years ago when some guys from Oklahoma and Arkansas came up here and started winning tournaments on Table Rock. They just drilled a hole in the bait and let it fill with water.

"It's definitely a big-bass technique. When the water's cold, a hawg bass just doesn't want to chase – you've got to put the bait right in its face. That's when a weighted stickbait really shines."

King, generally considered "the stickbait man" in pro bass circles, has perfected the weighting technique to get maximum performance from his lures. "The idea is to make it look like an injured baitfish," he says. "It's a visual deal – they see a quick flash, like a shad struggling to right itself, and they run up and hit it."

Stacey King

Hometown:
Reeds Spring, Missouri
Favorite Waters for Technique:
Table Rock and Bull Shoals lakes
Career Highlights:
Qualified for BASS Masters Classic 5 out of 6 years, from 1989 to 1994
Guided 25 years on Ozark Mountain lakes

When and Where to Use Weighted Stickbaits

Weighted stickbaits are most effective at water temperatures from 40 to 60°F, particularly from late winter through the pre-spawn period. In winter, however, it takes sunny weather to activate the bass and draw them up into stickbait range, which generally means a depth of 12 feet or less. The fish don't move horizontally to reach shallow water, they simply rise vertically to feed on baitfish drawn to the sun-warmed surface layer.

Because the weighted stickbait technique relies on visual attraction, it's most productive in waters where visibility is at least 2 feet. King does most of his stickbait fishing in deep, clear reservoirs, but the technique can be used in any man-made or natural lake with adequate clarity.

The exact location of the bass depends on the type of water you're fishing. In Ozark Mountain lakes, for instance, most bass spend the winter relating to sharp-breaking structure along the main river channel or major creek channels. They move vertically along the steep breaks, rising to depths of 5 to 15 feet on warm days and dropping into 25 feet or more on cold days.

Structure with flooded timber is most likely to hold largemouth. The fish suspend high in the branches in warm, stable weather and use deep branches under cold-front conditions.

As the water starts to warm in spring, bass move up on the structure, feeding on shallow flats adjacent to the steep breaks where they spent the winter. Cold fronts may push them back to the steep breaks. As spring progresses, they begin working their way toward the small coves and shoreline pockets where they will spawn.

Cloudy, windy weather is better once the fish begin moving to the vicinity of their spawning areas. Choppy water makes them less wary, and they feed aggressively along windswept shorelines, where windblown plankton draws and collects baitfish.

The technique's effectiveness fades by the onset of spawning, which usually begins a few weeks earlier in the creek arms than in the main lake coves.

Weighted stickbaits work well not only for largemouth, but also for smallmouth and spotted bass. But the locational patterns vary somewhat for the three species. Largemouth can be found on suitable structure throughout the lake, even ranging into the back ends of small creek arms. But smallmouth inhabit only the main basin and large creek arms. Spots have intermediate locational tendencies.

Weighted stickbaits produce a mixed bag of largemouth (left), smallmouth (center) and spotted (right) bass

Where to Fish Weighted Stickbaits

UNDERWATER EXTENSIONS. Gradually sloping points often have long underwater extensions or large flats projecting from their tips. The most productive extensions or flats have plenty of 5- to 20-foot-deep water.

PEA-GRAVEL POINTS. Pre-spawn bass seek out a pea-gravel bottom for spawning. They stage on gradual points with this type of bottom, then move into nearby shoreline pockets with the same type of bottom to spawn.

CHANNEL SWINGS. Places where the main-river or creek channel abut a steep shoreline concentrate bass in winter. The fish prefer staying close to the break when making their vertical movements.

CHUNK-ROCK POINTS. Points with plenty of large, broken rocks usually indicate a sharp-sloping breakline. They attract bass, particularly largemouth and spots, during the winter months.

SADDLES. Underwater connections, or saddles, between structural elements, such as a point and island, draw all three bass species. The most productive saddles level off at 10 to 20 feet.

Techniques for Fishing Weighted Stickbaits

Equipment:
Rod:
   for open water: 6½-foot, medium- to medium-heavy-power, fast-action, long-handled baitcaster
   for woody cover: 5½-foot, pistol-grip baitcaster with same power and action
Reel: baitcaster with gear ratio no higher than 5:1
Line:
   for light cover: 8- to 10-pound, low-vis, abrasion-resistant mono
   for heavy cover: 12- to 17-pound, low-vis, abrasion-resistant mono

A glance at Stacey King's tackle box reveals a wide selection of weighted stickbaits, consisting of shallow (less than 5 feet), medium (4 to 8 feet) and deep (more than 8 feet) runners. But deep runners normally aren't needed in clear water, because a medium runner will pull the deep fish up.

"When I'm fishing over weedy or brushy cover, I use plugs that are just a little less than neutrally buoyant," King says. "This way, they rise slowly when you stop reeling, so they'll float away from the cover. But when cover is not a concern, I prefer a bait that suspends motionless. I may even use a sinking plug if I'm trying to reach deep water.

"Weighting is a painstaking process. I like to drill a hole, insert a lead tube and leave a little extra sticking out. Then I can keep filing it off until the weight is perfect." King weights most plugs in the belly, but some have internal wire connectors, so they must be weighted in the side or top.

"Most people don't realize that water temperature changes a plug's buoyancy. The colder the water, the more weight you need. If you're going to be fishing in cold water, test your bait in cold water."

Water temperature is also important in selecting plug size. As a rule, King prefers 5-inch baits in water of 50°F or less; 5½- to 7-inchers in water warmer than 50°.

Using a long-handled rod for extra casting distance and keeping the wind at your back, make a long cast and reel quickly to get the plug down to, or just above, the level of the fish. Then slow down and retrieve as shown below; a reel with a low gear ratio keeps you from reeling too fast. When you're fishing in standing timber, a shorter, pistol-grip rod is a better choice because you can cast more accurately.

You may have to experiment to find the presentation that best suits the mood of the fish. Try starting with a basic stop-and-go retrieve. With your rod tip low, twitch the bait sharply to make it dart and flash, then hesitate a few seconds. That's when most fish will strike. Vary the hesitation length; you may have to wait as long as 30 seconds between twitches, but sometimes a series of steady twitches works best. If sharp twitches aren't working, try 3- to 5-foot sweeps. Or, combine sweeps with twitches.

Bass may hit the lure hard, or you may just feel a subtle tick or a little extra weight. Crank-set the hook by making a firm, sideways sweep and reeling faster.

Weighted stickbaits are no longer the secret they once were, and as preweighted models become available from manufacturers, their popularity is likely to soar. Stacey King's advice: "If you like to catch big bass, this is a technique you need to perfect and add to your fishing arsenal."

How to Retrieve a Weighted Stickbait

TWITCH the lure one to three times, after reeling it to the desired depth. The more active the fish, the harder and faster the twitches should be.

PAUSE after twitching, letting the line go slack. If there is any tension on the line, the bait will continue to glide forward.

UNWEIGHTED baits (top) float up during pauses, away from sluggish fish. Weighted ones (bottom) track deeper and stay at the same depth.

How to Weight a Stickbait

HANG a piece of lead tubing on the front hook, and trim the weight so the plug barely sinks.

SINK the plug with a weighted noose. Move the noose so the plug floats as shown; mark noose position on belly.

DRILL a hole at the mark on the plug's belly. Dab in epoxy glue. Implant lead so it protrudes slightly.

FILE off the lead until you achieve the desired buoyancy, then cover the lead with epoxy glue.

Other Weighting Methods

WRAP hooks with lead wire or solder to achieve the right buoyancy. Try to keep the wire from filling the hook gap, reducing the "bite."

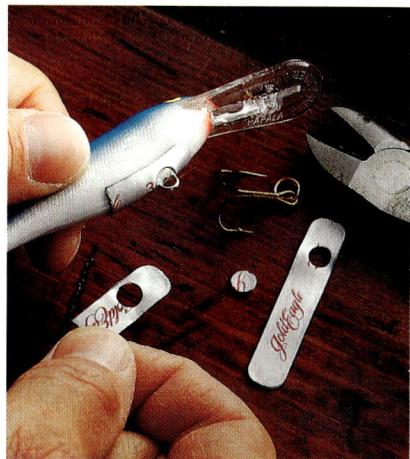

APPLY strips of golfer's tape to the bottom of the plug to achieve the desired buoyancy. Seal in the tape with epoxy glue.

REMOVE rubber inserts from Rubbercor sinkers. Pinch one onto the front hook and a smaller one onto the middle. Trim lead for correct buoyancy.

Advanced Spinnerbait Techniques

Calling Up Clearwater Smallmouth

Optimal Conditions:
Type of Water: ultraclear lakes
Season: summer and fall
Water Temperature: 50°F or higher
Weather: windy or rainy
Water Stage: any stage
Water Depth: as deep as 40 feet
Water Clarity: at least 10 feet
Time of Day: anytime, if weather is favorable

Ask most any smallmouth expert to outline his strategy for catching the fish in ultraclear lakes, and here's what he's likely to say:

- use smaller-than-normal baits
- select natural or drab colors
- use lighter-than-normal line
- fish deep

But Rick Lillegard, a veteran guide and tournament angler from Atkinson, New Hampshire, doesn't always heed this standard advice. In fact, a technique he uses in Lake Winnipesaukee violates every one of the usual clearwater smallmouth rules. "It may sound crazy," he says, "but it puts a lot of fish in the boat in a hurry and allows me to cover a lot of water."

Pioneered in the early 80s by Keith Kline of the Fleck Lure Company and Danny Correia, a B.A.S.S. touring pro, the technique involves "calling up" smallmouth over water as deep as 40 feet by retrieving big, often bright-colored, spinnerbaits just beneath the surface. "It's becoming more popular," says Lillegard, "but it doesn't seem logical to most people, so they won't even try it."

Some top pros, however, have been trying it. Rick Clunn used big spinnerbaits to call up enough smallmouth to win the 1992 New York BASSMASTER Invitational on Lake Ontario. And the technique has become one of the favorites of 1992 B.A.S.S. Angler of the Year, Kevin Van Dam, who routinely uses it to catch smallmouth in clear Michigan lakes.

Clearwater smallmouth often pursue suspended forage in open water, and this technique takes advantage of that behavior. Lillegard knows the bass are suspended, because they often grab the bait as soon as it hits the water. The main reason the technique works so well is that it doesn't require a pinpoint presentation; all you have to do is cast over an area known to hold fish, and they'll come up for the bait.

Rick Lillegard

Hometown:
Atkinson, New Hampshire
Favorite Waters for Technique:
Winnipesaukee, Squam and Sunapee lakes, New Hampshire
Career Highlights:
1989 and 1991 Angler of the Year, North American Bass Assn. Team Trail; 1992 American Bass Assn. Team Champion

When and Where to Call Up Smallmouth

You can call up smallmouth over deep water in most any clear lake, but the technique works best in those with high smallmouth populations and pelagic baitfish that roam open water in large schools.

In the Northeast, for instance, smallmouth have plenty of pelagic forage in the form of smelt and small white perch, which scour open water for zooplankton and small minnows. The bass also eat yellow perch, which have pelagic tendencies in these lakes. In clear Canadian-shield lakes, smallmouth patrol open water to find ciscoes.

The technique is effective in waters of this type because smallmouth that feed on pelagic baitfish tend to be highly aggressive and willing to chase baits they've spotted from a considerable distance.

Evidence that open-water smallmouth eat yellow perch

Best Places to Call Up Clearwater Smallmouth

NARROWS. A narrows may be a channel between two islands, an island and shore, or two basins of a lake. Current induced by the wind funneling water through a narrows draws baitfish and smallmouth.

SADDLES. These subsurface connectors link two pieces of structure, such as two humps, or an island and shore. They serve as underwater highways for bass moving between structures.

BIG BOULDERS. Boulders the size of a car, or even larger, make prime year-round smallmouth cover. The best boulders lie on a break between shallow and deep water. Look for fish along the shady side.

SUNKEN ISLANDS. Large sunken islands that top out at 10 feet or less, with a clean, sand-boulder bottom, irregular shape and variable depth, make excellent summertime smallmouth habitat.

After smallmouth finish spawning, look for them around big boulders or beds of cabbage or sandgrass just outside the shoal areas where they spawned. Others lie suspended in open water, but still relating to the breakline or deeper sandgrass beds. Once the fish set up in these locations, they'll remain there until cooling water drives them deeper in mid-fall and makes them less aggressive.

Lillegard has his best success calling up bass relating to points and weed flats connected to shoreline breaks, but it's also possible to call up bass relating to isolated structure, such as a sunken island.

As summer progresses, young pelagic baitfish grow large enough to interest smallmouth and draw them from the breakline. The bass spend more and more of their time relating to deep water, either holding on the bottom or suspending. But some smallmouth remain on points and weed flats until mid-fall.

In shield lakes or other clear waters with a lot of exposed bedrock, smallmouth are strongly drawn to sandy structure, because it offers the only available weed growth. You'll find the fish on sandy humps and points, along sandy shoreline breaks, and even in sandy bays. An exposed sandy shoreline provides a visual clue on where you're likely to find sandy structure in the lake.

Calling up smallmouth is easiest in windy weather. "Get out where there's wave action," Lillegard advises. "It's easier to fish the calm water, but you'll catch more fish along the windy shores." Another good time for calling them up is in rainy weather; raindrops break up the calm surface.

SANDY SHORELINES. Good smallmouth weeds, such as sandgrass and cabbage (right), grow on sandy bottoms. A sandy shoreline is a good indicator of a sandy, weedy bottom farther out from shore.

WEEDY FLATS. Sandgrass (left), a short, stringy weed that grows in water as deep as 25 feet, is a smallmouth magnet from spring through fall. Cabbage (right) does not grow as deep, but is equally attractive to the fish.

SPAWNING FLATS. Large, shallow flats with a sand-rock bottom are hubs of early season smallmouth activity. Try the top of the flat when they're spawning; otherwise, you'll find them where the flat slopes into deep water.

EXTENDED LIPS. Look for smallmouth around the ends of underwater extensions of major points from early summer through fall. In many lakes, these extensions are easy to find because of buoys (arrow) at their tips.

How to Call Up Clearwater Smallmouth

LILLEGARD'S FAVORITE BAITS for calling up smallmouth include (1) tandem Colorado-blade spinnerbait, such as a Hog Sticker, with size 7 to 8 rear blade and size 3 to 4 front blade. Add a size 2/0 to 3/0 trailer hook tipped with a 3- to 5-inch grub as shown; (2) stickbait, such as a Zara Spook, about 4½ inches long; (3) floating minnow plug, such as a Bomber Long A (model 15A).

> **Equipment:**
> **Rod:** long-handled, 6½- to 7½-foot, medium-heavy- to heavy-power, fast-action, graphite baitcaster
> **Reel:** high-speed baitcaster
> **Line:** 14- to 17-pound-test, low-visibility mono
> **Lure:** ¾- to 1-ounce tandem Colorado-blade spinnerbait tipped with curlytail grub

A smallmouth that will charge to the surface from deep water to grab a bait is obviously in a highly aggressive mood. As Lillegard puts it, "These fish are really supercharged and bustin', so you don't have to put the bait in their face and you don't have to tease them into hitting it.

"You know when you're bit – it's a solid reflex strike. They try to tear the blades off the bait. Lots of times, they're on it just as it hits the water."

This level of aggression means you can work a likely spot very quickly. If the fish are going to bite, they'll bite right away, so the idea is to move rapidly and keep hitting new water.

Lillegard's usual strategy is first casting to visible shallow-water cover, such as boulders and weed patches, then casting over the deep water adjacent to them. Simply cast a big, tandem-blade spinnerbait as far from the boat as you can and retrieve rapidly so it tracks about a foot or so beneath the surface. Long casts not only increase your coverage, they allow you to reach smallmouth that haven't been spooked by the boat.

You'll need a long, powerful rod for distance casting with such a heavy, wind-resistant bait. For two-handed power casting, choose a rod with an extra-long handle. A 6½-foot rod is adequate most of the time, but in a strong wind a 7½-footer works better. It helps you punch your casts into the wind, and quickly take up slack for strong hook sets. A high-speed reel starts the bait moving before it can sink, and keeps it riding high in the water.

Despite the clear water, Lillegard normally uses bright colors. "Seems like high visibility is the key," he theorizes. "I use an all-chartreuse spinnerbait most of the time, but when it's calm and sunny, I may go with a white body and nickel blades."

If the water is calm and spinnerbaits aren't working as well as you'd like, try a stickbait, such as a Zara Spook. Under low-light conditions, use a black one; other times, a minnow or frog pattern. A good-sized bait, about 4½ inches long, works well for big bass, but when the fish are fussy, you may do better with a 3-incher.

Cast the bait as far as you can, let it rest motionless for 30 seconds or so, then walk it from side to side (p. 228). After retrieving about 15 feet, reel in and make another cast. The fish usually strike while the bait is at rest or just after you start to reel.

Another option is a floating minnow plug. Lillegard prefers a gold or silver plug with a green back. On a rippled surface, retrieve with rapid sharp jerks to give the plug an erratic action. When the surface is calm, let the plug rest for a few seconds, nudge it a few times (p. 228), then switch to the fast, jerky retrieve. With minnow plugs and stickbaits, use light line, about 10-pound test; heavy line may spook fish in the clear water.

"I don't know of any other technique as exciting as calling up smallmouth," says Lillegard. "When a bass spots your bait, he doesn't want to eat it, he wants to kill it – that's why I love this kind of fishing."

How to Call Up Smallmouth with a Spinnerbait

WORK the structure by holding your boat well away from the break and making long casts over the lip using a spinnerbait. This way, you won't spook bass in the shallows. Then turn around and cast over deep water for suspended bass.

START reeling even before the bait hits the water. Cruising smallmouth are drawn by the frantic action and often strike immediately.

RETRIEVE your spinnerbait fast enough to keep it running no more than a foot beneath the surface. Cruising smallmouth look up for their food. If you don't get a strike within the first 10 feet, quickly reel in and cast again.

How to Call Up Smallmouth with a Stickbait

MAKE a long cast to reach smallmouth that haven't been spooked by the boat; the fish seem drawn by the big splashdown.

WAIT for the ripples to subside before starting the retrieve. This gives any smallmouth in the vicinity time to swim over, inspect the bait and possibly strike it.

WALK the bait by giving it a series of rapid downward twitches. How hard you twitch determines how far the bait will veer to the side.

SWITCH to a smaller stickbait, such as a Zara Puppy, when smallmouth are making passes at the bait, but not grabbing it.

How to Call Up Smallmouth with a Minnow Plug

SOFTLY NUDGE the bait a few times after casting and letting the ripples subside. On each nudge, the nose of the bait should dip beneath the surface, and the tail should come out of the water. Then, rip the bait toward you; the change of speed may draw a strike.

LOOK for followers; smallmouth tend to chase minnow plugs without striking. Should you spot a fish behind your bait in the clear water, try to trigger a strike by slowing down and twitching the bait gently, so it barely moves ahead yet maintains its depth.

Tips for Calling Up Smallmouth

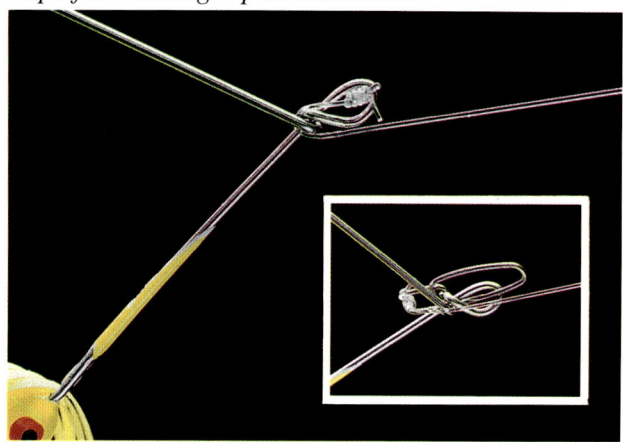

CHECK a twist-eye spinnerbait after each cast; your line will be damaged if it fouls around the arm and catches in the twist as shown. Attaching the bait with a clip (inset), minimizes damage when the line does foul.

WATCH closely when landing your fish. Clearwater smallmouth have a tendency to chase each other, possibly to steal whatever food one has captured. Even if you can't catch the followers, they tell you the spot has potential.

AVOID light-wire, R-bend spinnerbaits. Aggressive smallmouth can easily bend them, and the metal will eventually fatigue and break.

LOOK for subtle features, such as a buoy and its chain, that will attract smallmouth in open, coverless water. Even if the feature does not provide cover, it gives the fish something to which they can relate.

MODIFY a standard tandem spinnerbait (top left) to make it helicopter better. Remove the blades, cut an inch off the wire shaft, add a ball-bearing barrel swivel (arrow) and replace the blades as shown (bottom left). Reel the bait steadily, briefly stopping a couple of times

during each retrieve (right) and throwing slack into the line so the bait stops abruptly and starts to helicopter. Then snap the bait back into motion and resume the retrieve. Try this change of pace when smallmouth are just nipping at the bait.

The final weigh-in at the BASS Masters Classic is a spectacular show

Tournament-Fishing Basics

Tournament fishing is not for everyone, but if you're the competitive type, you'll probably enjoy it. Not only will you learn a great deal from experienced tournament anglers, you'll meet new friends and may even win a little money.

But don't get into tournament fishing with the idea of making a career of it; only a very few top pros could make a decent living solely from tournament winnings. Much of their income comes from product endorsements, seminars and other public appearances.

The best way to get started in tournament fishing is to join a bass-fishing club. Most of them conduct low- or no-entry-fee tournaments on close-to-home waters. After you develop confidence in your tournament-fishing skills, you may want to consider money tournaments and statewide competition, which sometimes earns you qualifying points for national events.

There's more to tournament fishing than paying your entry fee and showing up. To be competitive, you'll have to do some research, particularly if the event will be held on an unfamiliar body of water. You need to know locations, depths, cover types and patterns that have worked well in the past. We'll show you how to gather this crucial information.

Everyone you talk to – bait-shop operators, local anglers, guides and other tournament entrants – will offer you advice on how to proceed. But the only sure way to collect reliable information is to do some pre-tournament scouting and fishing on your own. We'll give you some tips on making the most of your time.

When formulating your tournament strategy, consider the type of event you're fishing. A single-day tournament, for instance, may require a different strategy than a three-day tournament. We'll provide some recommendations for each popular tournament type.

Tournament Tips from the Pros

Regulars on the pro bass-fishing circuit know what it takes for consistent tournament success. Whether you fish tournaments for fun or have aspirations to become a professional tournament angler, it pays to heed the advice of pros who have spent many years competing at the highest level.

But don't get hooked on tournament fishing to the point where it affects your job and family life. Look at it as a competitive sport that can help you improve your fishing skills.

Shaw Grigsby

"I firmly believe that anyplace in the lake holds fish – I mean anyplace! If you only have a day or two to practice, pick out a small section of the lake, fish everything you can fish, and try to develop a pattern. Then apply it to the rest of the lake. Most people run all over the lake, trying this and that. But they never figure out what the fish are doing because they're skipping around too much."

Zell Rowland

"I like to figure a lake out for myself, rather than rely on information from other fishermen. I collect some basic information from local sources, like water color and type of cover and structure; then I take it from there. All a guide will do is show you the community holes and how to run the lake. I prefer to run the whole lake myself; I just take along extra props."

Ken Cook

"To separate yourself from the crowd, you have to have a different mindset than the average tournament fisherman. You've got to think differently – not only about lure and presentation strategies, but also about locational patterns. I generally look at a lake map and pick out the most obvious spots. Then I avoid them, because everybody else has a map and will key on those same spots."

Mike Folkestad

"To be a successful tournament fisherman, you must have tremendous confidence in your ability and *know* you can win. The best way to build confidence is to go out by yourself and figure out a pattern on your own. Finding your own fish is a lot of work, and there'll be days when you catch nothin'. But fishing somebody else's fish won't help your confidence."

Jay Yelas

"It's important to gain experience by fishing a lot of small tournaments before entering the big ones. Fishing a tournament is a lot different from just going fishing. You have to learn how to deal with a partner, how to put time restrictions on your day, and all that. I see a lot of guys jumping into big tournaments too soon and they usually struggle."

Stacey King

"It's critical to have a thorough knowledge of the bass itself and what he does year-round. A good understanding of different lake types is also important. Always remember – you'll never learn it all, so keep an open mind and try to pick up something from everyone you fish with, regardless of the level of their knowledge."

Pretournament Research

Tournament fishermen must learn to analyze information collected from many sources and weigh it in light of what they know about bass behavior in a particular body of water. They put the most stock in first-hand accounts, realizing that hearsay from tackle-shop operators, resort owners and weekend anglers could be outdated, and are skeptical of information offered by other tournament entrants, which could be intentionally misleading.

When you enter a tournament, it pays to collect the following information before you begin to practice:

Tournament Rules

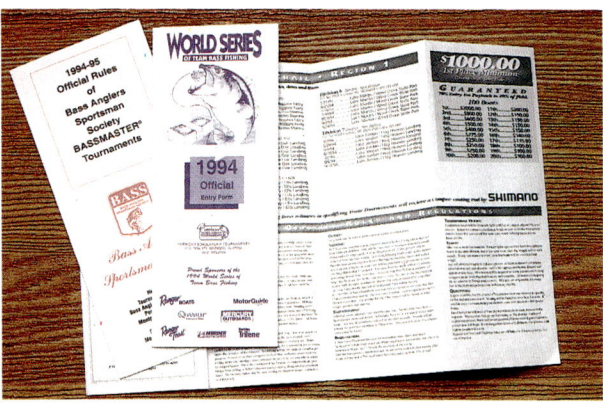

Tournament rules are varied and may be complex

Obtain a copy of the tournament rules and study it before doing your on-the-water research. It may limit pretournament fishing dates and prohibit use of some techniques, such as trolling. It may also specify certain areas that are off-limits to fishing, such as fish refuges, private waters, tributaries and release sites from recent tournaments. If you are unsure of a particular rule, consult the tournament director.

Lake Information

Information from local fisheries personnel can be helpful in planning your fishing strategy. Request a contour map, and ask for other maps, which may offer different information. Obtain a copy of the latest lake survey, which usually includes information on gamefish and forage fish populations, water quality, and aquatic vegetation types in different sections of the lake. If there is more than one bass species present, get specifics on which sections of the lake are best for each. Knowing what the predominant forage fish is can be helpful in selecting baits and planning your fishing strategy. If the lake has pelagic forage, such as shad, the bass tend to move and suspend more than in lakes with nonpelagic forage.

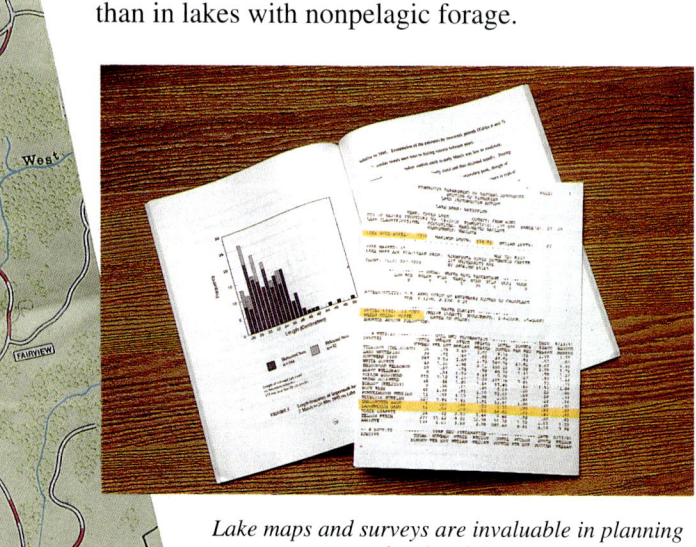

Lake maps and surveys are invaluable in planning strategy on an unfamiliar lake

Navigation Rules

Collect information on special waterway regulations, such as slow zones. You can save lots of fishing time by avoiding closed-throttle areas. Be sure to ask how water level affects access to various parts of the lake. State fisheries or reservoir personnel should have this information.

Past Tournament Results

Check results of past tournaments held on the same body of water at the same time of year. Assuming that conditions are similar this year, those results can help you determine the most productive depths, general locations, cover types, and the most effective techniques. Past results may be available from tournament organizers or from fishing newspapers or magazines.

Tournament results will also give you an idea of what species of bass is most likely to give you a win, and what the winning poundage will be. Knowing this will help you formulate an overall tournament strategy, gauge your pretournament fishing success and determine when you need to change locations or techniques.

Current Conditions

Monitoring weather conditions in the weeks before the tournament helps you determine how the season is progressing. For example, if the tournament is scheduled during what is normally the post-spawn period, but the weather has been abnormally cold, spawning will probably be delayed. This means you'll find bass farther back in creek arms or bays than you might have thought.

Before you start practicing, check the present water conditions, including temperature, flow, level and clarity. Monitor these conditions during practice and tournament fishing. Then, should conditions change, you'll have a better idea of what to do. If the water level drops, for instance, the fish will most likely go deeper; if it rises, they'll move shallower.

Pretournament Fishing

Several rods rigged with different baits make it easy to experiment when prefishing

To have a reasonable chance of cashing, you must spend a day or two practice fishing, or "prefishing," as tournament anglers would say. In preparation for major tournaments, some top pros prefish for two weeks or more. You may want to prefish with a friend. This way, you can cover more water in less time, and experiment with more presentations.

Prefishing helps you eliminate unproductive water and zero in on the most productive areas. It also helps you determine which techniques are most likely to work in each situation, and builds up your confidence so you won't panic and prematurely start switching patterns after the tournament starts.

Another prefishing objective: become familiar enough with the body of water that you can navigate confidently and develop a feel for running times. Begin prefishing in an area known to have a high bass population. It's easiest to establish a successful pattern where there are lots of fish. Later, once you find a good pattern, you can try it in out-of-the-way places that aren't fished as heavily.

When trying to establish a pattern, keep close track of details. If you're fishing submerged timber, for example, note whether most of the fish are holding near the ends of the limbs or close to the trunk, and whether they're in the treetops or near the bottom. And try to determine how time of day, water level and weather, especially cloud cover and wind direction, affect the pattern.

Prefishing Tips

KEEP a notebook describing in detail any productive spots that you find when prefishing. Include sketched maps and landmarks, so you can quickly return to the precise spot at tournament time. It's difficult to remember all of these details when you're fishing dozens of spots every day.

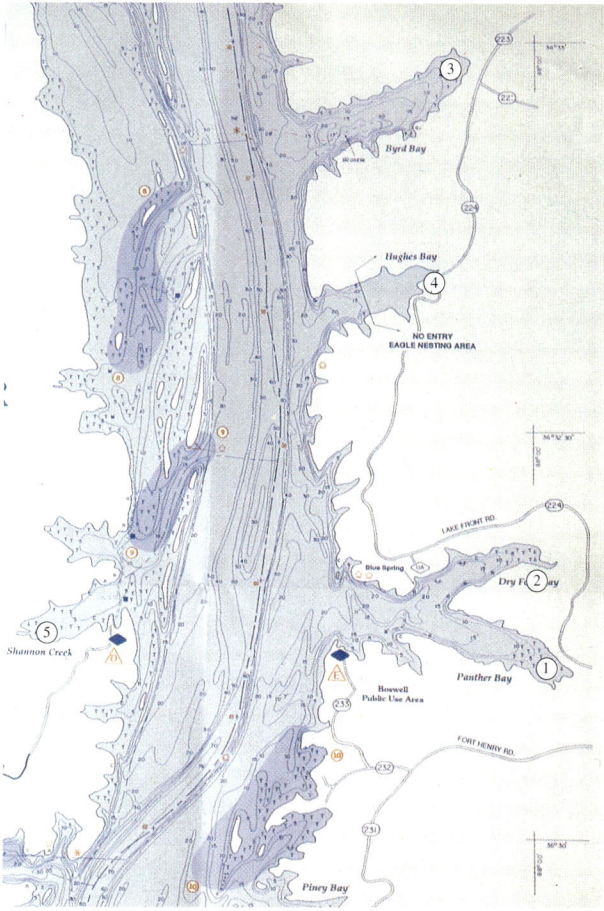

EXPAND locational patterns by looking for other similar areas on a lake map. If, after thoroughly scouting a section of the lake, you found bass only around (1) submerged weeds in a deep creek arm, look for other similar areas, such as (2) and (3). Area (4) lacks weeds and area (5) is too shallow, so they would not be good choices.

To get a better idea of the exact type of structure and cover the fish are using, note the precise spot where you got a strike, then motor over and examine it. You may find a subtle depth change, a stump or a clump of weeds that you may not have noticed from a distance. Use this information to help formulate your locational pattern.

It pays to vary your bait choices and retrieve styles when prefishing. Most tournament anglers carry several rods with different baits tied on each. They experiment with different colors, sizes and types of baits, and different retrieve speeds and tempos, until they find the combination that works best for the location, time of day and weather conditions. When making bait-choice decisions, do a little research to determine what the locals have been using. It may be hard to improve on tried-and-true favorites.

But don't waste time trying to learn a completely new technique. You won't have enough time to perfect it, so even though it's effective for some anglers, you'll do better by sticking with familiar presentations.

When prefishing, try to identify a number of spots that are likely to produce under different wind and weather conditions. Look for some "numbers" spots and other big-fish spots. This way, you'll know right where to go should you need several small fish to stay in contention on a slow day, or one big one to register a knockout blow.

Never "burn" the fish you want to catch in the tournament. You want to get bites so you know where the fish are, and you may want to land a fish or two in each spot so you know how big they are, but you don't want to catch so many fish that you "educate" them. To ensure that you don't catch the fish, bend your hooks closed or cut them off and, instead of setting the hook when you get a strike, just try to jiggle the bait so the fish will drop it.

Tournament Strategies

By the time tournament day arrives, the most difficult part of a tournament fisherman's job is completed. He knows what he has to do – now he must do it.

Your strategy for the day's fishing depends not only on the type of tournament, but also on the overall scope of competition. For instance, you would probably approach a tournament that is part of a total-points annual circuit differently than you would a one-time event. If you're accumulating points, it's important to register a decent weight, even if you don't win, so you should use the numbers philosophy: concentrate on catching as many fish as possible, with the idea that you'll sort out a respectable limit. But in a one-time event, you can go for broke and concentrate on big fish. If you don't catch any, all you've lost is your entry fee.

Another consideration in formulating your strategy is the bass population, itself. If the population is relatively small, the numbers philosophy is best. But if there are lots of bass and most contestants will likely catch a limit, concentrate on big fish. Your strategy will also differ depending on the length of the tournament.

The first thing to do on tournament day is to compare weather and water conditions with those encountered during prefishing. Ideally, conditions will be identical, but this is seldom the case. If conditions are similar, stick with the patterns you found. If not, you'll have to do some adjusting.

Perhaps the most common mistake, particularly among tournament-fishing novices, is to abandon their established patterns too soon. After an hour or so with no fish, they start to panic, so they scrap a proven pattern in favor of an untested one. Had they stuck with the original plan, it probably would have paid off before the day was over.

If the conditions differ from those you faced in practice, use your best judgment to come up with a new pattern. Let's say the weather during prefishing was hot and calm, and you were catching bass on topwaters in shallow weedbeds. But on tournament day, you're faced with blustery, cold-front conditions. Don't abandon your pattern completely; make some minor adjustments first. Try slowing down your retrieve a little. Or, try fishing with a bait that runs a little deeper.

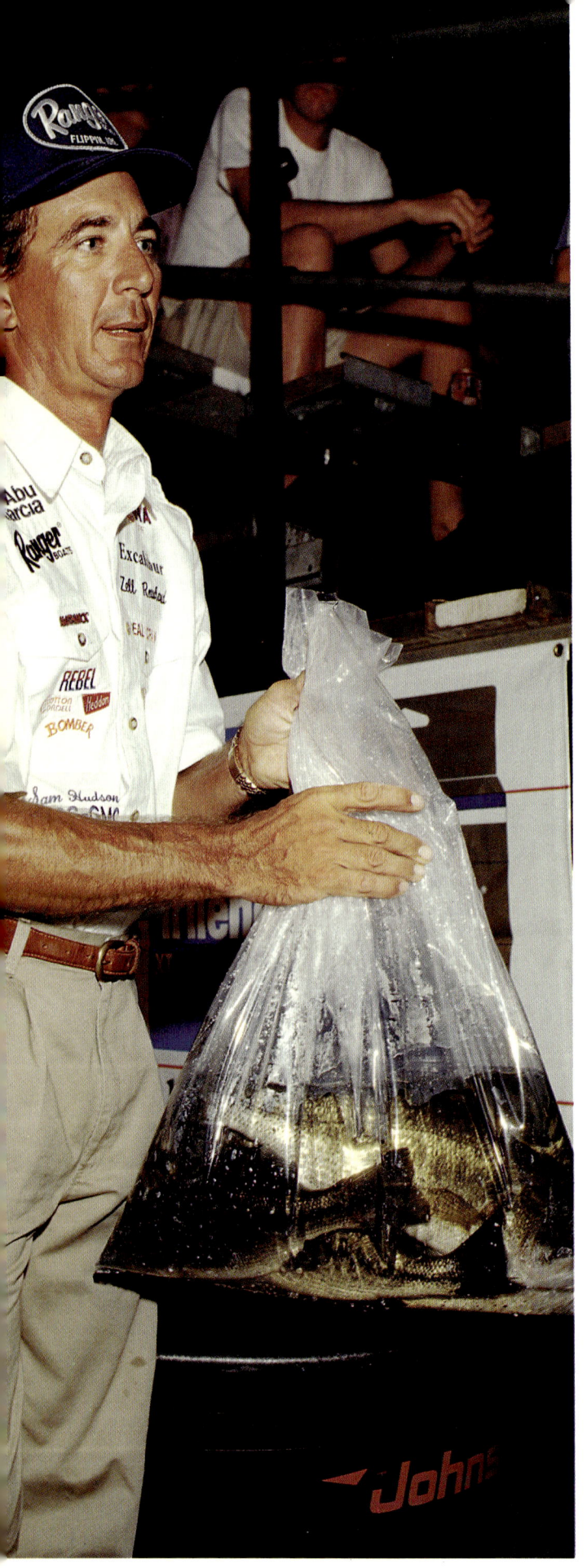

Give your established patterns a chance to work

Pay attention to other tournament boats. If they're moving around a lot, you can bet the bass aren't cooperating. So if you're catching a few fish, but are thinking of moving or trying something different, you may want to reconsider.

The most unnerving situation is to find another tournament boat in your prime spot. Should this happen, observe the other anglers closely to determine exactly what cover and structure they're fishing, and how they're fishing it. If their pattern is different from yours, you may be able to fish right behind them with good success. Even if it's not, it may be possible to milk a few more fish from the spot by working it more slowly and thoroughly.

Following are descriptions of the most common types of bass tournaments, and some specific tips for fishing each type:

BUDDY TOURNAMENTS. In this type of tournament, you team up with a partner of your choice. Joint decisions determine tournament strategy, including where to fish and who will run the boat. The combined weight of a team's catch determines its standing.

Here's how you can improve your success in buddy tournaments:

•Select a partner with whom you're well acquainted; this way, there are no credibility questions, and you'll be less hesitant to suggest new strategies. Avoid switching partners for every tournament. If you stick with the same partner, you'll learn to work as a team.

•Assuming both partners are competent anglers, it pays to do your prefishing separately. This way, you can cover more water and improve your team's chances of finding fish.

•The angler running the boat should plan his casts to leave plenty of good casting targets for his partner. Each angler should watch where the other is casting, to avoid covering the same water.

•If there is a shortage of good casting targets, each angler should use a different presentation, including a different retrieve angle.

•When one angler hooks a fish, the other should immediately cast to the same spot in case there's a school in the area.

•When one angler misses a fish, the other should cast to it immediately. The sooner the fish sees another bait, the more likely it is to strike again.

DRAW TOURNAMENTS. Partners are chosen by a drawing. They must make a joint decision on whose boat to use. Each operates the boat for half the day and makes the decision on where to fish during that time. Fish weights are tallied separately for each contestant. Here are some suggestions for fishing draw tournaments:

•Each angler tends to prefer his own spots, but if your spots are far from those of your partner, you'll waste a lot of time running between them. In this case, it pays to compare fishing spots and make a joint determination on whose are most likely to yield a winning weight.

•Don't exaggerate your prefishing success to convince a partner to fish your spots. His may actually be better, and you'll both pay the price. You'll also lose the opportunity to learn something from your partner, which is one of the reasons for fishing draw tournaments. If you develop a reputation for embellishing your success, partners will not be truthful with you in future tournaments, making accurate assessment of each other's information impossible.

MULTIPLE-DAY TOURNAMENTS. Both buddy tournaments and draw tournaments can be multiple-day events. In draw tournaments, you fish with a different partner each day, and each angler's weight for each day is tallied for a tournament total. The following hints will boost your success in multiple-day tournaments:

•When prefishing, try to locate a few more spots than you would for a single-day event. The extra fishing days mean that spots are pressured more heavily, so you may not be able to catch as many fish from a single spot.

•Try to develop fall-back patterns when prefishing. With the heavy pressure, anglers soon catch the aggressive fish, but you may be able to take a few more fish from a given spot by using a presentation that's a little different. If most anglers are catching the active fish by bulging spinnerbaits over the weedtops, for instance, try a slightly faster retrieve to make the blade break the surface.

•Work the most popular spots, or any small, isolated spots, first. By the second day of the tournament, most of the fish in these spots have been caught or at least spooked. Then, it helps to have a few less obvious spots as a fall-back.

•Assuming you're in a multiple-day draw tournament, don't hesitate to try your partner's pattern on the first day. You may be able to use it in your own spots on subsequent days.

•Should you catch a quick limit of decent fish on the first day, spend the rest of the day scouting for new spots and bigger fish. This way, other fishermen won't know where you caught your fish, and you can use the same strategy the next day without fighting a crowd.

A

Age and Growth of Bass,
  Largemouth bass, 9
  Redeye bass, 15
  Smallmouth bass, 11
  Spotted bass, 12
  Striped bass, 16
Agitators, 109
Alabama Redeye Bass, 15
Alabama Spotted Bass (subspecies), 12
Anadromous Bass, Definition, 6
Apalachicola Redeye Bass, 15
Arroyos, 25, 26

B

Backlash, Reducing, 209
Backwater Lakes, 76, 77, 79, 82, 89
  Bass species in, 77, 81, 84
Balloon Lines, 34, 35
Banks,
  Bass locations, 103, 171
  Fishing techniques, 70, 71, 176
Barometric Pressure,
  And water levels in tidal rivers, 88
Bars in Lakes,
  Bass locations, 144, 182, 183
Bass Biology, 6-17
Bass-Panfish Lakes, 140-149
  Bass species in, 140, 143
  Big Round Lake case study, 142-149
  Fishing techniques, 146-149
  Habitat, 140, 143, 144
Bass-Walleye Lakes, 128-139
  Bass species in, 128
  Fishing techniques, 134-139
  Habitat, 128, 131, 132
  Woman Lake case study, 130-139
Bays, 124
  Bass locations, 112, 126, 128, 131, 137, 144, 146, 177, 233
Beaver Houses and Trenches, 82, 137
Big Round Lake (Wisconsin) Case Study, 142-149
Black Bass, 57
  Definition, 6
Bluff Faces, 58
  Bass locations, 60, 66, 67, 202, 203
  Fishing techniques, 204
Boat Canals, 132, 137, 156
Bobbers, see: Popping Corks; Slip-Bobber Rigs
Boulders, 127, 128
  Bass locations, 70, 113, 114, 134, 224, 225
  Fishing techniques, 116, 226
  See also: Rocky Structure
Brackish Water, 9, 88, 97
Breaklines, 130
  Bass locations, 134, 171, 225
Bridges and Bridge Pilings, 77, 114
  Bass locations, 41, 82, 85, 90, 97
Brush, see: Timber and Brush
Buckbrush, 45, 166
Bulrushes, 143, 154
  Bass locations, 128, 132, 137, 144, 146-148, 156, 159, 160
  Fishing techniques, 148, 149, 159, 161
Buzzbaits,
  Fishing techniques, 82, 93, 94, 105, 147, 160, 171, 208, 214, 215
  For largemouth bass, 43, 66, 67, 82, 93-95, 103, 105, 137, 147, 148, 159, 160, 169, 171, 199, 208, 214, 215
  For spotted bass, 69

C

Cabbage, 124, 132, 143, 146, 225
Calm Weather and Bass Fishing, 34, 44, 63, 64, 71, 122, 134, 147, 160, 171, 175, 182, 227
Canadian Shield Lakes, 118, 120, 122, 224, 225
  See also: Two-Story Lakes
Canals, 91, 153, 155, 159

Carolina-Rigged Soft Plastics, 43, 53, 54, 105, 106, 184
  Draggin' technique, 181-185
Catch-and-Release Fishing, 9, 23, 115, 177
  How to de-gas a largemouth bass, 205
Cattails, 154, 156, 159
Channels in Rivers, 79
  Bass species in, 80, 81
  Connecting or side, 76, 81, 82
  Dredging, 79
  Main, 76-80, 82
Chubs as Bass Bait, 134
Chuggers,
  Fishing techniques, 34, 63-65, 208-211
  For largemouth bass, 28, 43, 66, 67, 82, 83, 94, 208-211
  For smallmouth bass, 31
  For striped bass, 33, 34, 63-65
Chutes in Streams, 113, 116
Clam Beds, 156
Claylines, 127
Clear Water Fishing Techniques, 175-179, 184
Cliff Lake (Ontario) Case Study, 122-127
Cliff Walls, 127
Cloudy Weather, see: Overcast Weather
Cold Fronts, 82, 83, 98, 160, 177, 218
Combination Lakes, see: Two-Story Lakes
Cook, Ken, 231
Coontail, 82, 138, 143, 146, 148
Cooper River (South Carolina) Case study, 89-97
Countdown Technique, 34
Cove Reservoirs, see: Eastern Mountain Reservoirs
Coves, 56
  Bass locations, 40, 68, 177, 183, 202, 203
Crankbaits,
  Fishing techniques, 43, 44, 67, 70, 82, 84, 94, 97, 107, 116, 117, 127, 171, 199
  For largemouth bass, 9, 28, 43, 44, 53, 66, 67, 93-95, 103, 105, 137, 138, 148, 159, 171, 199
  For smallmouth bass, 11, 70, 84, 85, 116, 117, 126, 127, 134
  For spotted bass, 12, 106, 107
  For striped bass, 96, 97
Crawlers (surface plug),
  For largemouth bass, 94
Crayfish,
  As bass bait, 11, 12, 15, 28, 31, 115
  As bass food, 9, 11, 12, 15, 69, 71, 85, 114, 121, 127, 128, 147
  Rigging, 115
Creek Arms, 45, 46, 56, 58
  Bass locations, 36, 40, 43, 60, 61, 63, 64, 66-71, 177, 182, 183
  Fishing techniques, 188
Creek Channels, 43, 51, 53, 67, 71, 218
Creek Chubs as Bait, 70
Crustaceans as Bass Food, 16
  See also: Crayfish
Cut Bait,
  For striped bass, 16, 64, 65
  Making and rigging, 65
Cuts Leading into Rice Fields,
  As bass habitat, 91, 93-95
  Fishing techniques, 93, 95
Cuts Leading into Sloughs,
  As bass habitat, 101, 103, 106, 107
  Fishing techniques, 107
Cypress Trees, Flooded, 48
  Bass locations, 50, 51, 53, 55, 103, 156
  Pitchin' in cypress trees, 55
  Spotting productive cypress trees, 54

D

Dams,
  Bass locations, 33, 34, 41, 60, 64, 80, 81, 90, 96-98, 101, 106, 109

Earthen, 167
Navigation dams, 77
See also: Wing Dams
Deep Reservoirs, 12, 200-203
Descriptions of Bass Species, 9, 10-12, 14-16
Desert Reservoirs, 18-35
  Bass species in, 21, 23
  Elephant Butte Lake case study, 22-35
  Fishing techniques, 26-35
  Habitat, 20-22, 24, 25
Divers, 85
Docks, Posts and Pilings,
  Bass locations, 91, 95, 128, 132, 138, 144, 147, 156
  Fishing techniques, 95, 147
Down Lines, 34, 35
Downriggers, 64
Draggin' Technique, 181-185
Dredging River Channels, 79
Duckweed, 170

E

Eastern Mountain Reservoirs, 56-71
  Bass species in, 57-59
  Lake Cumberland case study, 58-71
  Fishing techniques, 62-71
  Habitat, 56-58, 60, 61
Eddies,
  Bass locations, 77, 82, 85, 97, 103, 106, 109, 113, 115
  Fishing techniques, 97, 116, 117
Eelgrass, 156
Elephant Butte Lake (New Mexico), 5
  Case study, 22-35
Eutrophic Lakes, 140, 142
  Bass species in, 9
  See also: Bass-Panfish Lakes

F

Fencelines in Reservoirs, 41, 43
Finesse Baits and Finesse Fishing,
  For largemouth bass, 28
  For smallmouth bass, 30, 31
  For spotted bass, 69
Fishing Pressure, 21, 111, 128, 153, 155, 163
Flatland Reservoirs, 36-45
  Bass species in, 36, 39-41
  Fishing techniques, 42-45
  Habitat, 36, 38, 40, 41
  Richland-Chambers Reservoir case study, 38-45
Flat Lines, 34, 35
Flats in Lakes, 36
  Bass locations, 25, 34, 43, 50, 53, 132, 144, 218, 225
  Fishing techniques, 71
Flats in Rivers, 82, 85
Flies and Fly-Fishing, see: Divers; Nymphs; Poppers; Sliders; Streamer Flies
Flippin', 26, 28, 66, 82, 103, 196
  Technique for heavy cover, 29
Floating Mats, 66
  Fishing techniques, 66, 67
Florida Bass Lakes, 150-161
  Bass species in, 152, 153, 155
  Fishing techniques, 159-161
  Habitat, 153-156
  Lake Istokpoga case study, 154-161
Florida Largemouth (subspecies), 9, 39, 43, 152, 153, 159
Florida-Rigged Soft Plastics, 159, 161
Folkestad, Mike, 231
Frogs, Rubber, see: Weedless Frogs

G

Gizzard Shad, 16, 23, 39, 59, 78
Glass Bead in Worm Rig, 55, 181
Gravel Bottom, 27, 128, 130, 143
  As bass spawning habitat, 70, 84, 111, 134
  Bass locations, 24

Fishing techniques, 64
Grigsby, Shaw, 175-179, 231
Gulls and Schooling Bass, 6, 160, 177

H

Hard Bottom, 25, 40, 50, 53
  See also: Gravel Bottom; Rocky Bottom
Helicoptering a Spinnerbait, 43, 45, 71, 199
Hellgrammites, 11, 12, 15
Herring,
  Blueback, 89
  Skipjack, 59
Highland Reservoirs, see: Eastern Mountain Reservoirs
Hill-Land Reservoirs, see: Eastern Mountain Reservoirs
Hit-and-Run Technique, 115-117
Holes in Rivers,
  Bass locations, 91, 93, 94, 97
Humps, 58
  Bass locations, 31, 41, 43, 127, 132, 183, 224, 225
  Fishing techniques, 28, 34, 127
Hybrid Bass, 11, 12, 16
Hybrids, 36, 41, 48, 57, 100, 153
  As name for striped bass-white bass hybrid, 16, 109
  See also: Wipers
Hydrilla, 153-155, 182
  Bass locations, 155, 156, 160
  Fishing techniques, 159, 160, 193

I

Ice-Block Lakes, 121, 128, 130, 142
Ice-Scour Lakes, 120
Identifying Bass Species, 9, 10-12, 14-16
Insects as Bass Food, 9, 11, 12, 15, 16, 153
Invertebrates as Bass Food, 128
Islands,
  Bass locations, 50, 82, 124, 224

J

Jig-and-Pig,
  Fishing techniques, 26, 43, 55, 66, 69, 82, 94, 147, 148
  For largemouth bass, 26, 28, 43, 53-55, 66, 67, 82, 83, 85, 94, 95, 103, 105, 138, 147, 148, 160, 169, 171
  For spotted bass, 69, 106
Jigging Spoons,
  Fishing techniques, 28, 43, 44, 63, 67, 94
  For largemouth bass, 28, 43, 44, 66, 67, 94, 95
  For smallmouth bass, 31
  For striped bass, 63, 64
Jigs,
  Countdown technique, 34, 69
  Fishing techniques, 34, 35, 44, 54, 63, 69, 71, 82, 84, 94, 97, 109, 117, 127, 196-205
  For largemouth bass, 28, 43, 44, 53, 54, 82, 137, 169, 196-205
  For smallmouth bass, 11, 31, 70, 71, 84, 85, 115-117, 126-128, 134
  For spotted bass, 12, 69
  For striped bass, 16, 33, 34, 35, 63, 64, 96, 97
  For wipers, 108, 109
  Tandem-jig fishing, 109
  See also: Jig-and-Pig; Vertical Jigging
Jump Fishing, 64
Junctions in Reservoirs, 50

K

Kentucky,
  Lake Cumberland, 58-71
  State record striped bass, 63

King, Stacey, 217-221, 231

L

Lake Bistineau (Louisiana) Case Study, 48-55
Lake Cumberland (Kentucky) Case Study, 58-71
Lake Istokpoga (Florida) Case Study, 154-161
Lake Whittington (Mississippi) Case Study, 164-171
Largemouth Bass, 6, 21, 36, 39, 46, 48, 57, 59, 77, 89, 90, 100, 119, 128, 130, 131, 140, 143, 152, 153
 Biology, 8, 9
 Daily activities, 28, 44, 83, 94, 138, 147, 160, 171
 Fishing techniques, 26-29, 31, 42-45, 53-55, 82, 83, 93-95, 103-105, 137-139, 146-149, 159-161, 169-171, 173-221
 How to de-gas, 205
 Identifying vs. spotted bass, 68
 Lures, baits and rigs, 9, 26, 28, 31, 43-45, 53-55, 82, 83, 93-95, 103, 105, 137-139, 146-149, 159-161, 169-171, 173-221
 Seasonal locations and activities, 24, 25, 28, 40, 41, 50, 51, 53-55, 60, 61, 66, 67, 70, 81, 82-84, 91, 93, 101, 103, 106, 132, 137, 138, 144, 147, 148, 156, 160, 166, 167, 170, 171, 177, 218, 219
 Spawning activities and locations, 9, 24, 26-28, 40, 43, 45, 50, 53, 60, 66, 68, 70, 91, 93, 101, 103, 132, 137, 144, 146, 153, 156, 159, 166, 177, 182, 218
 State record, 189
 World record, 9, 153
Laurentian Shield, 120
Leeches,
 As bass bait, 11, 115-117, 126-128, 134
 As bass food, 9
 Fishing techniques, 117
Length of Bass at Various Ages, see: Typical Length and Weight of Bass
Lillegard, Rick, 223-229
Lily Pads, 82, 103, 105, 106, 154
 Bass locations, 112, 132, 137, 144, 146, 156
 Fishing techniques, 104
Line, see: Rods, Reels and Line Recommendations
Logjams, 113, 114, 116
Louisiana, Lake Bistineau Case Study, 48-55

M

Maidencane, 154, 156
Main-Channel Border in River, 76
Manmade Lakes, 18-71
 See also: Reservoirs; Pits; Ponds
Martin, Pat, 193-199
Menhaden Activity to Locate Striped Bass, 97
Mesotrophic Lakes, 121, 130
 Bass species in, 9, 11
Mesquite, 22, 26, 27
Mice as Bass Food, 9, 169
Mid-Depth Reservoirs, 11
Midwestern Mainstem Rivers, 74-85
 Bass species in, 76-78
 Fishing techniques, 82-85
 Habitat, 76, 77, 80, 81
 Upper Mississippi River case study, 76-85
Milfoil, 24, 28, 143, 182
 Types, 194
 Yo-yoing technique, 193-199
Miller, Ted, 200-205
Minnesota,
 St. Louis River case study, 112-117
 Upper Mississippi River case study, 76-85

Woman Lake case study, 130-139
Minnow Plugs, 217
 Doctoring, 170, 221
 Fishing techniques, 34, 35, 43, 53, 63, 64, 66, 67, 70, 84, 93, 103, 127, 135, 160, 170, 177, 217-221, 227, 228
 For largemouth bass, 43, 53, 66, 67, 93-95, 103, 105, 159, 160, 169, 170, 218
 For smallmouth bass, 70, 84, 85, 126, 127, 134, 135, 218, 226-228
 For spotted bass, 69, 218
 For striped bass, 33, 34, 35, 63, 64, 96
Minnows, 23, 147
 For redeye bass, 15
 For smallmouth bass, 128
 For striped bass, 16
 See also: Shiner Minnows
Mississippi,
 Lake Whittington case study, 164-171
 Pearl River case study, 100-109
Mississippi River, Upper (Minnesota and Wisconsin) Case Study, 76-85
Moon Phase and Fishing, 64
Mountain Reservoirs, see: Eastern Mountain Reservoirs
Mudlines, 61, 67, 69, 127
Multi-Line Trolling, 34, 35, 63, 65

N

Narrows,
 Bass locations, 25, 224
 Fishing techniques, 34
Natural Lakes, 118-161
 Bass-panfish lakes, 140-149
 Bass species in, 9, 11, 15, 12, 118, 121, 128, 140, 143, 152, 153, 155, 165
 Bass-walleye lakes, 128-139
 Eutrophic lakes, 9, 140, 142
 Florida bass lakes, 150-161
 Mesotrophic lakes, 9, 11, 121, 130
 Oligotrophic lakes, 121
 Oxbow lakes, 152, 162-171
 Two-story lakes, 120-127
Neosho Smallmouth (subspecies), 10, 11
New Mexico,
 Elephant Butte Lake case study, 5, 22-35
 State record striped bass, 23, 33
Nightcrawlers,
 Fishing techniques, 117
 For smallmouth bass, 11, 115-117, 126-128, 134
Night Fishing,
 For largemouth bass, 67, 94, 95
 For smallmouth bass, 71
 For spotted bass, 69, 71
 For striped bass, 64, 97
Northern Largemouth (subspecies), 9
Northern Smallmouth (subspecies), 10
Northern Smallmouth Streams, 110-117
 Bass species in, 111-113
 Fishing techniques, 114-117
 Habitat, 111-113
 St. Louis River case study, 112-117
Northern Spotted Bass (subspecies), 12
Nymphs,
 For redeye bass, 15
 For spotted bass, 12

O

Oligotrophic Lakes, 121
Ontario, Cliff Lake Case Study, 122-127
Outlet Channel, 166
Overcast Weather,
 And bass activity, 16, 28, 31, 44, 64, 69, 83, 85, 109, 134, 137, 138, 147, 148, 160, 171
 Fishing techniques, 34, 103, 188

Oxbow Lakes, 152, 162-171
 Bass species in, 165
 Fishing techniques, 168-171
 Habitat, 165-167
 Lake Whittington case study, 164-171
Oxbow Sloughs, 101
Oxygen in Water,
 In manmade lakes, 5, 36, 38, 46, 57, 58
 In natural lakes, 120, 121, 140-142

P

Pearl River (Mississippi) Case Study, 99-109
Peppergrass, 156, 182
Piers,
 Bass locations, 41
 Fishing techniques, 97
Pilings, see: Docks, Posts and Pilings; Bridges and Bridge Pilings
Pitchin', 53
 Technique, 55, 83, 149
Pits, 9
Planing Devices, 35, 63, 65
Plastic Worms,
 Fishing techniques, 43, 55, 67, 71, 84, 94, 107, 147, 184, 196-199
 For largemouth bass, 9, 28, 43, 53, 55, 66, 67, 82, 93-95, 103, 137, 138, 147-149, 160, 169, 171, 184, 196-199
 For smallmouth bass, 31, 70, 71, 84, 85
 For spotted bass, 12, 69, 106, 107
Plugs,
 Fishing techniques, 97
 For largemouth bass, 9, 28
 For striped bass, 16, 33, 96, 97
 See also specific types of plugs
Point Bars in Streams, 113, 117
Points in Manmade Lakes, 36, 59
 Bass locations, 24-26, 31, 40, 43, 50, 60, 61, 67, 69-71, 171, 182, 183, 202, 203, 219, 225
 Fishing techniques, 28, 34, 69, 70, 71, 225
Points in Natural Lakes, 130
 Bass locations, 122, 124, 132, 134, 144, 147, 166, 225
 Fishing techniques, 171, 225
Points in Rivers,
 Bass locations, 84, 101, 106, 107, 112
 Fishing techniques, 107, 117, 127
Ponds, 39
 Bass species in, 9, 11, 15
Pools,
 In reservoirs, 24, 60
 In rivers, 77, 112
Poppers, 85
Popping Corks, 108, 109
Pork Rind, see: Jig-and-Pig
Propbaits,
 Fishing techniques, 28, 126, 148, 160, 208, 209, 212
 For largemouth bass, 28, 43, 147, 148, 160, 169, 208, 209, 212
 For smallmouth bass, 126, 134

R

Rainy Weather,
 And bass activities, 67, 69, 78, 103, 225
 Fishing techniques, 82
Rapids, 112
Redeye Bass, 6
 Biology, 14, 15
 Lures, baits and rigs, 15
Redtail Chub as Bass Bait, 134
Reefs in Manmade Lakes,
 Bass locations, 69, 71
 Fishing techniques, 71
Reefs in Natural Lakes,
 Bass locations, 122, 124, 132, 134
Reels, see: Rods, Reels and Line

Recommendations
Reservoirs, 18-71, 118
 Bass species in, 9, 11, 12, 15, 16, 21, 23, 36, 39-41, 46, 48, 49, 57-59
 Deep, 12, 200-203
 Desert, 18-35
 Eastern Mountain, 5, 56-71
 Flatland, 36-45
 Mid-depth, 11
 Swampland, 5, 18, 46-55
Rice Beds, see: Rice Fields; Wild Rice
Rice Fields, 89
 As bass habitat, 91, 93, 94
 Fishing techniques, 93-95
Richland-Chambers Reservoir (Texas) Case Study, 38-45
Riprap, 60, 77, 80, 82, 84, 97, 166, 171
River Channel, 50, 51, 54, 64, 171, 218, 219
Riverene Lakes, 151, 152
River Lakes, 77, 152
Rivers and Streams, 72-118
 Bass species in, 9, 11, 15, 76-78, 89, 90, 98, 100, 111-113
 Midwestern mainstem rivers, 74-85
 Northern smallmouth streams, 110-117
 Southern largemouth rivers, 98-109
 Tidewater rivers, 86-97
Roadbeds in Reservoirs, 40, 43, 45
Rocky Structure, 24, 59
 Fishing techniques, 69, 97, 116, 117
 Bass locations around, 30, 31, 33, 34, 60, 61, 68, 70, 71, 77, 84, 97, 112-114, 122, 124, 126, 127, 132, 203, 219
 See also: Boulders
Rods, Reels and Line Recommendations,
 Baitcasting, 26, 28, 34, 44, 53, 64, 67, 71, 83, 85, 93, 97, 103, 106, 109, 115, 137, 148, 159, 160, 169, 170, 171, 184, 190, 196, 208, 220, 226, 227
 Flippin', 26, 64, 67, 103, 137, 138, 208, 214
 Fly, 85
 Pitchin', 83
 Spinning, 28, 31, 67, 71, 85, 115, 126, 134, 147, 148, 160, 169, 170, 178
 Surf-casting, 109
Rowland, Zell, 207-215, 231
Rubber Frogs, see: Weedless Frogs
Rubble Bottom, 130

S

Saddles, 219, 224
St. Louis River (Minnesota) Case Study, 112-117
Salt Cedar, 26, 27
Sandgrass, 225
Sandy Bottoms, 128, 130, 143
 As bass spawning habitat, 43, 53, 84, 111, 134, 159, 225
 Bass locations, 82, 85, 94, 101, 106, 107, 111, 225
Schooling Bass,
 And gull behavior, 6
 Largemouth bass, 82, 138
 Smallmouth bass, 127, 134
 Striped bass, 6, 16, 64
 Wipers, 109
Seabed Depression Lakes, 151, 152, 154
Setting the Hook, 67, 104, 126, 138, 179, 184, 191, 208, 209, 220
Shad, 36, 89, 90
 As bass bait, 28, 31, 33, 34, 54, 63-65
 As bass food, 16, 23, 25, 28, 39, 57, 59, 64, 69, 78, 82, 94, 103, 106, 109, 154, 160, 177, 232
 Identifying types, 34
 Rigging, 35, 63, 65
Shell Beds, 156

239

Shelves in Rivers, 97, 106
Shield Lakes, 118, 120, 122, 224, 225
See also: Two-Story Lakes
Shiner Minnows,
As bass food, 121, 122, 131, 154
Catching wild shiners, 159-161
Fishing techniques, 161
For largemouth bass, 9, 159-161
For smallmouth bass, 11, 134
Rigging, 159
Shoal Bass, 15
Shrimp Activity to Locate Striped Bass, 97
Side Planers, 63, 65
Sight-Fishing Technique, 175-179
Sinkhole Lakes, 151
Size Limits on Bass, 59
Slab Spoons, 108, 109
Sliders, 85
Slip-Bobber Rigs, 126, 127, 134
Slip-Sinker Rigs, 134
Slop,
Bass locations, 132, 137
Fishing techniques, 137, 139
Slot Limits, 189
Sloughs, Flooded, in Reservoirs,
Bass locations around, 50, 51, 54
Sloughs in River Systems, 76, 79, 100
Bass locations in, 103, 106
Bass species in, 80, 81, 101
Smallmouth Bass, 6, 21, 23, 57, 59, 76, 113, 118, 119, 121, 122, 128, 130, 131
Biology, 10, 11
Daily activities, 30, 31, 71, 85, 134
Fishing techniques, 30, 31, 70, 71, 84, 84, 115-117, 134, 135, 223-229
Lures, baits and rigs, 11, 30, 31, 70, 71, 84, 85, 115-117, 134, 135, 218, 223-229
Seasonal locations and activities, 24, 31, 60, 61, 66, 70, 71, 80, 81, 84, 85, 112, 113, 124, 126, 127, 132, 134, 137, 218, 224, 225
Spawning activities and locations, 11, 24, 30, 31, 60, 70, 77, 84, 126, 134
World record, 11, 57, 70
Smelt, 224
Snagged Lure, Freeing, 45, 115
Snail Beds, 156
Soft-Plastic Lures,
Fishing techniques, 28, 53, 103-105, 175-185
For largemouth bass, 28, 53, 54, 103-105, 175-185
For spotted bass, 69, 106
See also: Plastic Worms; Soft Stickbaits; Tube Baits; Weedless Frogs
Soft Stickbaits,
Fishing techniques, 53, 69, 71, 178, 187-191
For largemouth bass, 53, 66, 67, 187-191
For smallmouth bass, 70, 71
For spotted bass, 69
Solution Lakes, 151
South Carolina,
Cooper River case study, 72, 89-97
Southern Largemouth Rivers, 98-109
Bass species in, 98, 100
Fishing techniques, 103-109
Habitat, 98, 101
Pearl River case study, 100-109
Spawning Bass, 23, 38, 53, 57, 160, 177
Fishing techniques, 26, 28, 30, 43, 53, 67, 68, 70, 93, 134, 177, 182, 187, 188
Locating, 26, 134, 137
Spawning Habits of Bass,
see references under individual species listings
Spinnerbaits,
Fishing techniques, 26, 28, 43-45, 53, 66-69, 71, 82, 84, 103, 107, 127, 171, 199, 223-229

For largemouth bass, 9, 26, 28, 43, 44, 53, 66, 67, 82, 83, 93, 95, 103, 137, 138, 147, 148, 159, 169, 171, 199
For smallmouth bass, 70, 71, 84, 85, 126, 127, 223-229
For spotted bass, 68, 69, 106, 107
Tipping with pork chunk, 66, 67
Spinners,
Fishing techniques, 116, 117
For redeye bass, 14
For smallmouth bass, 11, 116, 117
For spotted bass, 12
For striped bass, 63
Split-Shot Rig,
Fishing techniques, 117
For largemouth bass, 28
For smallmouth bass, 30, 31, 115-117
Spoons, see: Jigging Spoons; Slab Spoons; Weedless Spoons
Spotted Bass, 6, 49, 57, 59, 100
Biology, 12, 13
Daily activities, 69
Fishing techniques, 68, 69, 71, 106, 107
Identifying vs. largemouth bass, 68
Lures, baits and rigs, 12, 68, 69, 106, 107, 218
Seasonal locations and activities, 50, 60, 61, 66, 68-70, 101, 106, 107, 218, 219
Spawning activities and locations, 60, 68, 70, 106
Spring Holes, 78
Spring Lizards,
For spotted bass, 12
Springs in Natural Lakes, 122, 152, 171
Stable Weather and Bass Fishing, 34, 171
State-Record Bass, 23, 33, 63, 189
Stickbaits,
Fishing techniques, 68, 208, 209, 213, 217-221, 227, 228
For largemouth bass, 137, 169, 208, 209, 213, 217-221
For smallmouth bass, 226-228
For spotted bass, 68, 69
See also: Soft Stickbaits
Stocking, 6, 9, 16, 23, 34, 36, 39, 43, 48, 57, 109
Stock Tanks, Flooded,
As bass habitat, 43
Fishing techniques, 43, 44
Locating, 44
Stormy Weather and Bass Fishing, 34, 98
Stratification of Lakes, 119, 120, 130
See also: Thermocline
Streamer Flies, 11
Streams, Bass Species in, 9, 11, 12, 15, 16
Striped Bass, 6, 21, 23, 36, 48, 57, 58, 59, 89, 100, 153
Biology, 16
Daily activities, 16, 34, 64
Fishing techniques, 33-35, 63-65, 96, 97
Lures, baits and rigs, 16, 33-35, 63-65, 96, 97
Seasonal locations and activities, 24, 25, 33, 34, 60, 63, 64, 90, 91, 97
Spawning activities and locations, 33, 34, 61, 63, 96
State record, 23, 33, 63
Subspecies of Bass, 9-12
Suckers as Bait, 63, 70
Sunfish as Bass Food, 39, 128, 147, 154
Sunny Weather,
And bass activity, 44, 64, 66, 67, 83, 114, 137, 147, 148, 160, 203
Fishing techniques, 103, 175-179, 182, 227
Sunshine Bass, 16, 153
Surface Lures,
Fishing techniques, 28, 30, 34, 35, 207-215
For largemouth bass, 9, 28, 43, 67, 94, 95, 137, 169, 207-215

For redeye bass, 15
For smallmouth bass, 30
For striped bass, 34, 35
See also: Buzzbaits; Chuggers; Crawlers; Propbaits; Stickbaits
Suspended Bass, 27, 31, 67, 69, 71, 223, 225, 232
Swampland Reservoirs, 5, 18, 46-55
Bass species in, 46, 48, 49
Lake Bistineau case study, 48-55
Fishing techniques, 53-55
Habitat, 46, 50, 51

T

Table Quality of Bass, 9, 11, 12, 15, 16
Tailspins,
Fishing techniques, 69, 106
For largemouth bass, 43, 44
For spotted bass, 69, 106
Tailraces, 97, 100, 109
Fishing techniques, 108, 109
Tailwaters,
Bass locations, 41, 81, 98
Temperate Bass, Definition, 6
Texas,
Richland-Chambers Reservoir, 38-45
State record largemouth bass, 189
Texas-Rigged Soft Plastics, 181
Fishing techniques, 28, 43, 94, 184, 196-199
For largemouth bass, 28, 43, 53, 66, 67, 82, 93-95, 105, 137, 138, 147, 148, 169, 184, 196-199
For smallmouth bass, 31, 85
For spotted bass, 106
Thermocline, 23, 34, 39, 49, 59, 121, 122, 131, 142, 143, 155, 165
Threadfin Shad, 16, 23, 39, 59
Tidal Influence, 86-88
Tidewater Rivers, 86-97
Bass species in, 89, 90
Cooper River case study, 89-97
Fishing techniques, 93-97
Habitat, 88-91
Timber and Brush, 22, 182
Bass locations, 24, 25, 28, 36, 40, 41, 43, 45, 50, 51, 57, 58, 61, 66-68, 77, 82, 84, 101, 103, 105-107, 137, 156, 166, 167, 169, 170, 171, 182, 188, 203, 218, 234
Fishing techniques, 26, 28, 29, 43-45, 55, 66, 68, 82, 107, 127, 182, 185, 220
Freeing snagged lure, 45
Types, 26, 27, 45
See also: Cypress Trees, Flooded
Topwater Baits, see: Surface Lures
Trolling,
For striped bass, 34, 35, 63, 64, 97
Multi-line trolling, 35
Trophy Bass,
Types of water for, 21, 36, 43, 84, 159
Tube Baits,
Fishing techniques, 178, 179
For largemouth bass, 28, 178
For smallmouth bass, 31
Two-Story Lakes, 120-127
Bass species in, 121
Cliff Lake case study, 122-127
Fishing techniques, 126, 127
Habitat, 121, 122, 124
Typical Length and Weight of Bass,
Largemouth bass, 9
Redeye bass, 15
Smallmouth bass, 11
Spotted bass, 12
Striped bass, 16

V

Vance, David, 187-191
Vertical Jigging,
For largemouth bass, 28, 43, 44, 94
For smallmouth bass, 31
For striped bass, 63, 64

See also: Jigging Spoons
Vibrating Blades,
Fishing techniques, 94
For largemouth bass, 82, 94
Vibrating Plugs,
Fishing techniques, 94, 160
For largemouth bass, 43, 94, 95, 159, 160, 169
For spotted bass, 106
For wipers, 108, 109

W

Warmwater Discharges, 78
Water Hyacinth, 153-155
Water Level Fluctuations,
In natural lakes, 162, 163, 165, 169, 170
In reservoirs, 20-23, 36, 39, 49, 54, 56, 59
In rivers, 78
Water Temperature Preferences of Bass, 9, 11, 12, 15, 16
Weather, see specific types of weather
Weedless Frogs,
Fishing technique, 104
For largemouth bass, 103-105, 137, 199
Weedless Spoons,
Fishing techniques, 138, 139
For largemouth bass, 137-139, 199
Weeds and Weedbeds, 98, 118, 119, 137, 140, 154, 182
Bass locations, 24, 28, 36, 51, 53, 82, 85, 93, 101, 113, 114, 132, 144, 146-148, 153, 182, 225
Fishing techniques, 82, 93, 94, 95, 138, 139, 147-149, 176, 182, 184, 220, 225, 226
See also specific weeds
Weight of Bass at Various Lengths, see: Typical Length and Weight of Bass
White Bass, 6, 16, 21, 23-25, 36, 46, 57, 59, 76
Seasonal locations and activities, 24, 25, 40, 41, 80, 166
Spawning activities and locations, 24, 40
White Perch, 16, 48, 90, 100, 224
Whiterock, 16
Wichita Spotted Bass (subspecies), 12
Wild Rice,
Bass locations, 132, 137
Fishing techniques, 138, 139
Willows, 166, 167
Windy Weather, 61, 98, 137, 165, 187, 224
And bass activity, 28, 31, 44, 126, 134, 138, 160, 225
And water levels in tidal rivers, 88
Wing Dams, 76, 77, 80, 82, 84, 85
Fishing techniques, 85
Winterkill, 141, 142
Wipers, 16, 48, 100
Fishing techniques, 109
Lures, baits and rigs, 108, 109
Seasonal locations and activities, 101, 109
Wisconsin,
Big Round Lake case study, 142-149
Upper Mississippi River case study, 76-85
Woman Lake (Minnesota) Case Study, 130-139
World Record Bass, 21
Largemouth bass, 9, 153
Redeye bass, 15
Smallmouth bass, 11, 57, 70
Spotted bass, 12
Striped bass, 16
Yelas, Jay, 181-185, 231
Yellow Bass, 6, 48
Yellow Perch as Bass Food, 122, 128, 131, 224
Yo-Yoing Technique, 193-199